AF652384

International Law and the Use of Military

INTERNATIONAL LAW AND USE OF MILITARY

AN OVERVIEW

Major (Retd.) S.K. Sharma

PRASHANT PUBLISHING HOUSE

DELHI-110094

Published by :

Prashant Publishing House

C-34, 28 Foota Road, Gali-3,

West Karwal Nagar, Delhi-110094

Phone : 011-22963970, Mob. : 9810396373

International Law and Use of Military

An Overview

Reserved

First Pubished 2011

ISBN 978-93-80565-18-7

No part of this book may be reprduced or transmitted in any form or by any means, electronic or mechanical, Including photocoying, recording or by any information storage and retrieval system, with-out permission in writing from the Publishers.

PRINTED IN INDIA

Published by Mr. R.K. Jha M/s Prashant Publishing House and Published at H.S. Offset House Press, Delhi.

Preface

International Law is a reflection of power relationships, of interestes, of dominating values and of the structure of international politics. In contrast to national law, international law is not enforced by a central authority with a monopoly of violence. International law is increasingly codified, but there is also customary law deriving from long-standing and agreed practices. Therefore there is more space in international law for conflicting principles and opinions. And it is very common to violate the principles of international law without incurring any reprisals. Others see International Law just as a legitimisation of so-called "just wars", wars legitimised by the UN Charter. Besides these general positions, what role can International Law play in the peace movement's struggle against war? What difference did the International War Crimes Tribunal on former-Yugoslavia make? While it condemns war crimes, does it at the same time justify the military, as the military is the only force capable of arresting war criminals?

During the nineteenth century there was a growing dissatisfaction concerning war. Increasingly war was regarded as too destructive, too disruptive, too devastating, too cruel, too costly and too uneconomic. Peace societies came into being. Pacifists, transnational non-governmental organisations, academics, politicians and even monarchs called for peaceful settlement of disputes between states, by arbitration and international courts for disarmament and the ban of certain weapons. A major event was the famous 1899 Hague Conference. This new thinking was reflected in state practice. Whereas in the 17th and 18th the major powers had fought wars against each other almost incessantly, after 1815 a growing number of states on both sides of the Atlantic managed to avoid war among themselves. Disputes were increasingly settled by arbitration or by international conferences.

The Government has used international law to its advantage in several other cases in the War on Terrorism. In particular, the Government has used the principles of international law at length in its arguments before the United States Supreme Court in *Hamdi v. Rumsfeld.* In its reply brief in *Hamdi*, the Government appealed to general principles of international law in arguing that it had the authority to capture and detain enemy combatants during wartime, at least during the period of conflict, In the same brief, the Government cited Article 105 of the Third Convention and general principles of international law in contending that the laws of war do not grant enemy combatants the right to meet with counsel to contest his or her wartime detention unless formal charges have been filed.

The book deeply highlights the International Law and Military.

—Editor

Contents

1

International Law and Pre-emptive Use of Military Force

Pre-emption, and the pre-emptive use of force in response to an imminent threat, remains a recognized, viable option within the framework of international law. In the Caroline Case of 1837, which provided the foundation for pre-emptive use of force pursuant to customary international law, the then Secretary of State Daniel Webster asserted that necessity and proportionality are imperative to the legitimacy of a pre-emptive strike. While Webster's contentions remain a central tenet of anticipatory actions, the National Security Strategy (the "NSS") of 2006 expanded upon the established framework of NSS 2002, and declared that "[t]o forestall or prevent such hostile acts by our adversaries, the United States will, if necessary, act preemptively in exercising [its] inherent right of self-defense."

Although the Caroline Case and NSS 2006 coexist ipso facto an understanding of necessity, or imminent danger, as an essential element in the legitimate use pre-emptive force, the two drastically diverge regarding the characterization of an imminent threat and the perception of proportionality as requisite aspects of the pre-emptive use of force. Although the current international environment does not permit the United States to afford such threats to materialize, the Administration must remain conscious of established principles of necessity and proportionality. During the Caroline incident, Webster, in correspondence with Lord Ashburton, the British envoy to the

United States, outlined the circumstances under which an anticipatory strike remains legitimate. According to Webster, a nation may only use the pre-emptive use of force if it can confirm a necessity of self-defense, the circumstances of which must remain "instant, overwhelming, [and] leav[e] no choice of means [nor] moment for deliberation." Furthermore, Webster asserted that even if the conditions justify action, the use of force "must be limited by that necessity, and kept clearly within it." Consistent with Webster's political and legal acumen, the pre-emptive introduction of military force remains legitimate if employed in response to an imminent, immediate, and overwhelming threat; provided, however, that such anticipatory self-defense remains in accordance with the principle of proportionality.

Concerning pre-emption, the NSS 2006 maintained a slight resemblance to the precedent expressed in the Caroline Case. The Bush Administration asserted that democracy promotion, in conjunction with international diplomacy and partnerships, remained the principal foreign policy tools of the United States. Conversely, NSS 2006 which characterized the U.S. as being in a war of necessity, effectively marginalized the ideals of deterrence and containment. This marginalization, due, in part, to perceived threats and the need for expeditious actions, purported the grave challenges confronting America. In order to combat modern threats, America "will not resort to force in all cases to preempt emerging threats," yet the U.S. "will, if necessary, act preemptively." In the short term, the Administration retained force as critical to preserving the national security of the United States. Broadly defined, and subject to wide interpretation, the Administration maintained anticipatory strikes as an instrument of foreign policy.

There are limited conditions, specifically the notion of necessity, in which the Caroline Case and NSS 2006 coexist. Both Webster and the NSS 2006 recognize immediate, imminent, and impending attacks as situations which offer no alternatives but the use of force, this fulfilling the requisite legitimizing aspect of necessity. Both recognize force as a last resort, to the extent that the Bush Administration aims to utilize diplomacy and alliances in efforts to dissuade adversaries from attempting to acquire weapons or attacking U.S. interests. The inception of NSS 2006 also affirmed the U.S. "will not rule out the use of force before attacks occur, even if uncertainty remains as to the time and place of an enemy's attack." Therefore, the Bush Administration, which maintains the preferred position in the unmistakable disparity of world military power, reserved anticipatory use of force as a decisive foreign policy device. The U.S.-led invasion of Afghanistan in 2002 proved necessary, although to some extent, anticipatory, as a military response to a previous attack and in accordance with self-defense. Although force in Iraq remains divisive, the U.S. has maintained military reticence regarding current situations in Iran and North Korea, refraining from hastily using force, yet conveying it as an option.

The criterion of proportionality expounded by Webster in the Caroline Case insisted that "act justified by the necessity of self-defense, must be limited by that necessity, and kept clearly within it." Webster implied that a response to a perceived imminent threat must correspond to the threat itself; therefore advocating limited scope in the use of force. Conversely, the Bush Administration aims to, inter alia, deny terrorists safe haven and prevent them from acquiring weapons of mass destruction. Contrary to the principles of Webster, NSS 2006 acknowledged that if there is a need for military action the U.S. will employ required devices, and, "if necessary, respond by overwhelming force." Relative to circumstances, costs associated with the use of military force may prove worth incurring in order to support ubiquitous goals, regardless of ambiguities associated with proportionality. Furthermore, in the current global threat environment, risks remain evident when states act consistently, and exactly proportional.

The Caroline Case effectively instituted a legal distinction and established the principles of necessity and proportionality. In almost complete divergence, the Bush Administration retained the inherent right of self-defense and reserved pre-emptive and anticipatory strikes as an instrument of foreign policy. Though necessity and proportionality remain circumstantially relevant, each must be applied to inherently different contexts within the international milieu. However,

NSS 2006 maintained a margin of flexibility regarding anticipatory self-defense and proportionality, and presented the United States as a hyper power, willing to use pre-emptive and preventive, overwhelming military force, if necessary.

INTERNATIONAL LAW AND PRE-EMPTIVE WAR

A strategy of addressing an emerging threat with a range of options including force was envisioned by the UN Charter. While traditional international law emphasized respect for state sovereignty by placing greater restrictions on the use of force, the literal language of the UN Charter has a more liberal standard when force is used under the auspices of the Security Council. For cases where force is used outside of the Security Council framework, it is not definitively clear whether under the UN Charter a state retains a traditional right of self-defense, including a right of anticipatory self-defense against an imminent threat, or if that right is curtailed to not include anticipatory self-defense. Some commentators argue that the UN Charter itself is no longer a valid source of international law, in which case a right of anticipatory self-defense would exist regardless and traditionally be limited to cases in which there is a threat of imminent attack.

Given the UN Charter's authorization of pre-emptive acts by the Security Council, ultimately the real division over pre-emption is not necessarily over pre-emption itself but over the multilateral framework under which it is carried out, who holds decision-making authority, and the extent to which those arrangements are codified and therefore rendered more stable and predictable. If the original concept of the Security Council was that the ad hoc coalition which won World War II would remain intact to stamp out future Hitlers before they reached a critical level of strength, historical changes such as the Cold War may have altered the course of that plan.

The right and obligation of a governing authority to use force to defend its citizens against an aggressor predates by centuries modern nation-states and modern international law. Christian just war theory, upon which the modern laws of armed conflict are based, recognized such a duty as early as the 4th Century. Since their emergence in the 16th Century, modern nation-states have been believed to hold such a right. While aggression is traditionally considered unlawful, and self-defense lawful, more problematic is the question of whether a first-strike could ever be considered a defensive act rather than an act of aggression. The right of anticipatory self-defense assumes that an aggressor is poised to strike, and that one acts defensively in anticipation of the attack rather than waiting for the attack to occur. Traditionally, it was deemed theoretically possible that even a first-strike could be deemed defensive in nature, and lawful, if it was to forestall an attack that was imminent.

The most widely accepted modern standard for anticipatory self-defense was articulated by U.S. Secretary of State Daniel Webster in diplomatic correspondence with his British counterpart over the *Caroline* incident (often mischaracterized as the *Caroline* "case") and consisted of two prongs. One was that the need to use force in anticipatory self-defense must first rise to the level of being a necessity, and one that is instant, overwhelming, and leaving no choice of means and no moment for deliberation. The other requirement was that the action taken must be proportionate to the threat and not be excessive.

Debate continues over the impact of the UN Charter on this area of international law. The UN Charter has a general prohibition against the use of force, but authorizes the Security Council to use force even in the absence of an act of aggression by the target, and permits unilateral and non-UN multilateral acts of self-defense under certain constraints.

With respect to the Security Council, the literal language of the UN Charter, in Articles 39, 41, and 42, envisions the use of a range of options, such as economic sanctions and varying degrees of force (e.g., blockades as well as all-out war) in response to acts of aggression, breaches of the peace, and threats to the peace. As a result, under the Charter force may be used against even a mere threat when authorized by the Security Council.

For unilateral acts and the multilateral use of force outside of the UN framework, Article 51 of the UN Charter refers to an inherent right of self-defense against armed attack, permitting defensive actions until the Security Council addresses the matter, and requires that such a defensive use of force be reported to the Security Council. The literal language of Article 51 seems to roll back the traditional right of self-defense, requiring that an armed attack have occurred before self-defense can be exercised, and implying that unilateral self-defense is an interim measure until the Security Council addresses the situation. Some commentators argue, however, that by referring to an "inherent" right of self-defense the UN Charter simply retains pre-existing international law regarding self-defense, including anticipatory self-defense. While it is not necessarily clear what role he plays in the matter, it appears that Secretary General Koffi Annan might hold the latter view, referring to states "retain[ing]" the inherent right of self-defense under the Charter.

To the extent the UN Charter can be deemed a relevant source of international law then some right of self-defense remains, which very well may include a right of anticipatory self-defense. At the same time, in international law, if a consistent pattern of state practice demonstrates a departure from preexisting norms, it can be argued that international law has changed. Some commentators suggest that state practice has indicated that with respect to the use of force the UN Charter no longer is a part of international law. If that is the case, then presumably international law would revert to the standard of anticipatory self-defense articulated by Webster.

The bottom line, then, is that with respect to anticipatory force exercised without Security Council authorization, either the UN Charter is essentially defunct with respect to the laws of armed conflict and the Webster standard continues, or the UN Charter is not defunct but retains the Webster standard, or that the Webster standard is displaced by a stricter standard requiring an armed attack to have occurred before one may invoke a right of self-defense. The prevailing view probably is that, one way or another, anticipatory self-defense is permissible but traditionally has required the existence of an imminent threat.

Another aspect of the UN framework, emphasized during the Cuban missile crisis, is that the UN Charter does permit regional security arrangements as long as they are consistent with the purposes and principles of the United Nations. However, the literal language of Article 53 requires that enforcement actions taken under regional arrangements not be initiated without Security Council authorization.

With respect to pre-emption, the National Security Strategy (NSS) issued by U.S. President George W. Bush itself does not necessarily significantly challenge prevailing international law. It rests upon a standard doctrine of anticipatory self-defense, and explores the question of when an attack is imminent. On its face it does not seek to overturn the rule, but to explore how the rule and its underlying purpose could be applied in particular situations not existing in the past.

One could argue that the rule does not actually require an attack to be imminent to act, but rather permits defensive measures to be taken before one passes a point in time when it is too late to prevent catastrophe.

The NSS focuses on several major considerations, one being that the imminence of a terrorist attack is much harder to detect, another being the fact that innocents are often targeted, and the third being the devastating impact of weapons of mass destruction (WMD.) While the text in the NSS relating to pre-emption does not necessarily limit its scope to WMD, it comes in a section dedicated to WMD.

Some commentators have suggested that WMD, and WMD proliferation, might be carved out as a special category under anticipatory self-defense. They argue that the right implied by anticipatory self-defense to act against a threat before it is "too late" may require setting a threshold in the context of WMD at some earlier point in the proliferation process, with that earlier point serving as the equivalent of the imminence of a threat. Such a point, it is argued, could represent the presence of a danger justifying a "defensive" first-strike, perhaps when accompanied by other factors such as a history of aggression, ties to terrorism, or certain criminal activities by the target regime.

Even if an exception were limited to WMD, or rogue state WMD, however, there still would remain the problem of setting a new and potentially destabilizing precedent, with the U.S.

pre-emption policy serving as a basis for other countries initiating or threatening conflicts they might not otherwise have been emboldened to undertake.

Concerns over precedent highlight the fact that international law does in fact mean something, and serves more than simply a cosmetic role providing a rhetorical backdrop for actions taken for entirely different reasons. Whether in a local domestic context or the international arena, law and security go hand-in-hand to the extent that assumptions about reliable rules limit and guide conduct, if only by making more predictable its consequences. Countries do seem to care about what kind of reaction a particular course of conduct will bring. In two major wars, Korea and Gulf War I, the United States in hindsight was accused of having overlooked hints by the aggressors of their intentions, failing to respond strongly enough to the hints. International law can help serve to warn state actors what other states would think of particular courses of action, by clearly articulating norms of conduct and by drawing up more clearly defined parameters for joint action in response to unlawful or otherwise dangerous situations.

The Bush administration therefore faces an important challenge to articulate its own policies clearly and carefully, determine the extent to which the United States is willing to help contribute to the establishment of clear international norms, and explain whether and in what manner an international framework for decision-making will be honoured. Concerns expressed by allies over the shaping of pre-emption do not necessarily evidence an unwillingness to adapt shared understandings of law and security to changing circumstances. Rather, they reflect a fundamental appreciation for the prospect of a stable, effective and sustainable global security system in which the sole superpower ideally provides leadership that is clearly articulated, predictable, reasonable and promotes respect for the law.

The National Security Strategy calls for accurate, honest, and timely threat-assessments and coordination with allies, wisdom reinforced by the Iraq war. One of the biggest lessons from the Iraq conflict might not centre around what to call it (*i.e.*, pre-emption or something else) but rather the weaknesses inherent in relying on potentially flawed intelligence and the difficulties that could be posed in the future if a U.S. administration once again seeks to convince the citizenry and the world community to trust undisclosed information, or disclosed allegations resting on similar intelligence-gathering. Another lesson is that even the United States needs help dealing with a large and complicated problem, whether it is before, during, or after a conflict addressing what the Bush administration deems a grave and gathering threat.

In the past, Bush has been somewhat reserved with respect to his own presentation of a pre-emption doctrine, and his decision to lead a multilateral coalition against Saddam Hussein was presented with a tapestry of arguments among which were references to Security Council resolutions, the ongoing situation since the previous Gulf War, Saddam's ties to terrorists, and humanitarian concerns. Secretary of State Colin Powell also has adopted a multifaceted and internationalist approach, and recently articulated a view of pre-emption that was closely akin to traditional anticipatory self-defense, referring to taking action when "see[ing] ... a danger coming at you ...." Vice President Dick Cheney until recently adopted a more aggressive posture reminiscent of a Cold War ideology — "us good, them bad" — and the United States needing an unfettered capacity to take action anywhere at any time. Publicly, Cheney's focus seems to have shifted away from open support for pre-emption to the engagement of terrorists in an ongoing series of hostilities, the need to appraise the future of the system of global security, and the importance of democracy.

Important questions that must be answered include whether the world is safer with or without a strengthening of international law and carefully crafted international institutions restricting the use of force, and whether the United States is willing to provide the leadership it has demonstrated in the past in these areas.

At the same time, an examination of the global system of sovereign states might not be complete without a consideration of the rightful purpose of sovereignty itself, taken together with the more broad-based views of security expressed by the National Security Strategy, and Bush's decision to draw greater attention to the need to create a safer and more just world by promoting freedom and democracy.

Sovereignty was never appropriately meant to sanctify the frontiers of tyrants and prevent outside intervention against their crimes, but truly *is* meant to serve the cause of peace. The theoretical basis for having nation-states in the first place was the idea that power would be concentrated in the hands of the sovereign, rather than private armies, local warlords, and armed bands, and that sovereigns themselves would be limited with respect to the instances in which they would attack each other, with the overall effect of reducing the incidence of war and violence and thereby protecting innocent lives. This system has been challenged by the nexus of modern technology with the reemergence of warlords and private armies, but it also has been challenged wherever sovereignty rests on oppression rather than democratic legitimacy.

Security and the diverse realities impacting it encompass a growing range of concerns. The National Security Strategy with its consideration of the importance of development and trade relationships, the president's renewed focus on democratization, and an appraisal of the forces of globalization and the connection between terrorism and poverty all point to a new direction in security that is not simply based on force but most definitely is based on prevention. The key, however, will be to not simply be preventive, but to be proactive. To not simply put out fires and react to events, but to invest in human potential and human freedom, to promote respect for human life and the dignity of the human person, and to sign on for the long haul to create a world that is more free, more just, and therefore decidedly more secure.

Addendum

Since the drafting of this article, President George W. Bush delivered his London address of Nov. 19, 2003, in which he refrained from openly rearticulating a policy of pre-emption but did, in his second "pillar," voice the need for free nations to be willing as a last resort to use force to restrain "aggression and evil." While force employed in response to "aggression" could fall into the category of defense against an actual attack, using force to restrain "evil" seems a somewhat more nebulous concept, and Bush did not elaborate as to timing and circumstance. By referring to "free nations" in the plural, Bush did seem to continue a theme of multilateral action.

Efforts at multilateralism would be consistent with his first pillar, the need for international organizations to be effective at meeting today's challenges, with effectiveness measured by results and not just procedure. Bush recognized that global problems such as terrorism do require a global response. He pointed to the need for the United Nations to adequately address threats while also citing an American commitment to NATO, the need for security cooperation between the United States and the European Union, his multilateral approach to North Korea, and the importance of the International Atomic Energy Agency adequately addressing concerns over Iranian nuclear technology.

The question of "where to go from here" would seem to centre around working to build greater effectiveness for international institutions and frameworks for multilateral action, but the third pillar, the president's call for democratization, especially in the Middle East, also is noteworthy. The United States appears to be expressing contrition for past policies of building ties with regimes of less than stellar democratic credentials, and even more importantly to be focusing on policy directions which are not simply pre-emptive or preventive, but actually proactive. Just as at the conclusion of World War II the United States learned from the mistakes of the Treaty of Versailles, it appears that the United States once again is endeavouring to learn from past mistakes by focusing on longer-term goals, addressing the sources of instability and aggression, and aspiring to unite values with practical action by investing in human potential and cultivating the foundations of true peace. As Pope John Paul II cautioned in Coventry in 1982, peace is more than just the absence of war, and must be built thoughtfully and patiently over time. A sincere and farsighted approach to that principle, grounded in freedom, justice, and the rule of law, would appear to be the rightful mission of a United States that assumes a position of global partnership with other free nations.

INTERNATIONAL LAW AND THE UNITED NATIONS: THE USE OF MILITARY FORCE

There are innumerable areas in which the roles of international law and the United Nations intersect in ways that are fundamentally important for our ever more interdependent world, including international trade and communications, environmental protection and the conduct of diplomatic relations. But no issue involving this intersection is of more immediate importance, or more controversial and difficult, than the current status of the international rules governing the use of military force.

As we look out on the world around us, those rules seem to be in serious disarray, their application erratic and their interpretation contested. No universally accepted practice currently governs their use. States are seen as making up the rules as they go along, going to war when they should not be, and not taking military action when they should.

Secretary General Kofi Annan put part of the problem in a nutshell when he said to the General Assembly on 23 September last year, six months after the Coalition invasion of Iraq, if 'States reserve the right to act unilaterally, or in ad hoc coalitions' without waiting for agreement in the Security Council, 'this logic represents a fundamental challenge to the principles on which, however imperfectly, world peace and stability have rested for the last fifty-eight years'.

He put the other part of the problem – states not going to war when they should – equally starkly in his Millennium Report to the General Assembly three years earlier: "...if humanitarian intervention is, indeed, an unacceptable assault on sovereignty, how should we respond to a Rwanda, to a Srebrenica – to gross and systematic violations of human rights that affect every precept of our common humanity?"

In the United Nations Charter of 1945 the use of force was subjected to the rule of law in a much clearer way than had ever previously been attempted, including in the ill-fated League of Nations Covenant, and the law was backed with a system of collective security much more potentially effective than anything that had gone before. The Charter made absolutely clear in Article 2(4) that all UN member states "shall refrain in their international relations from the threat or use of force against the territorial integrity or political independence of any state, or in any other manner inconsistent with the Purposes of the United Nations". It allowed only two exceptions to the prohibition on the use of force in international law: self-defence under Article 51, and military measures authorised by the Security Council in response to "any threat to the peace, breach of the peace or act of aggression".

But it was one thing to create a new legal order, quite another to make it work as intended. The founders of this new order were not naïve, recognising as Adlai Stevenson said at the time, that "(e)verything depends on the active participation, pacific intentions and good faith of the Big Five." And the mutual hostility among the five permanent members themselves which very soon emerged, to be sustained throughout the Cold War years, certainly did threaten to bring the whole edifice down. For forty-four years, until 1989, states repeatedly used military force against others (by one count 200 times and by another 680 times)-a great many of which occasions could not begin to be explained or justified as self-defence under Article 51, although that fig-leaf was regularly relied upon.

But a paralysed Security Council passed very few Chapter VII resolutions, and there was only one large scale collective military action responding to a breach of the peace (Korea in 1950, during the Soviet Union's misjudged period of absence from the Council). The order which prevailed was essentially a new variation on an old balance of power theme.

Through all this the UN security system somehow managed to stay afloat, playing a reasonably significant role at least in defusing and managing conflict. 'Good offices' diplomacy contributed to the peaceful abatement of some 25 per cent of the post 1945 conflicts. And peacekeeping, a role invented by the Secretariat – involving the verification, monitoring, and supervision of ceasefire and broader peace agreements – proved crucial in reducing the risk of a number of further wars, especially in South Asia and the Middle East. But it is hard to argue that the new international legal order promised by the Charter was, for the duration of the Cold War, under anything but stress. All that changed, dramatically, after the Berlin Wall came down. The removal of a major source of ideological and great power conflict liberated the UN to play the global security role its founders intended, as became immediately apparent with the response to Iraq's invasion of Kuwait in 1991. Expectations were reinforced by UN-organised or authorised military deployments in the former Yugoslavia, Somalia, and Haiti. The average number of resolutions passed in a year went from 15 to 60, or from a resolution a month to a resolution a week. Ninety-three percent (247 of 267) of all Chapter VII resolutions of the Council were passed between 1990 and 2002. Before 1989 the Council applied sanctions twice; since then it has imposed sanctions fifteen times.

Not all this activity was either effective or uncontroversial: too often what happened – not least in Somalia in 1993, Rwanda in 1994 and Bosnia in 1995 – was too little too late, misconceived, poorly resourced, poorly executed, or all of the above. And of course in Kosovo in 1999, in what was arguably a very strong case for intervention, a divided Security Council was bypassed completely. But there was reason to believe that step by step, painful and disappointing as so much of the process was, a new and much more responsive international legal order was falling into place.

But now the wheel has turned again, and maybe even more seriously than in the Cold War years. The decision of the U.S., and its coalition allies, to go to war in Iraq in March 2003 in defiance not only of one or more threatened vetoes, but of the clear and overwhelming majority of the members of the Security Council, was a watershed of a wholly different, and more disconcerting kind. Three different kinds of challenges to the international legal order are involved, all of them serious.

First, to the extent that the invasion of Iraq was based on a claim of anticipatory self-defence more far-reaching than any previously asserted, Article 51 has been stretched beyond endurance. Secondly, to the extent that the invasion was based on claims of threats to international peace and security sufficient under Chapter VII to justify Security Council authorization, but with those claims poorly argued and the Council eventually bypassed, the credibility of the whole Charter system has again been frontally challenged. And thirdly, to the extent that the invasion was based on Saddam Hussein's record of tyranny over his own people – but again poorly and inconsistently argued, and with the Council bypassed – we have seen close to being choked at birth what many were hoping was an emerging new norm justifying intervention on the basis of the principle of "responsibility to protect".

Article 51 and Anticipatory Self Defence. It has long been accepted, both as a matter of customary international law predating Article 51 and international practice since, that notwithstanding the language of the article referring only to the right arising "if an armed attack occurs", the right of self-defence extends beyond an actual attack to an imminently threatened one. Provided there is credible evidence of such an imminent threat, and the threatened state has no obvious alternative recourse available, there is no problem – and never has been – with that state, without first seeking Security Council approval, using military force 'preemptively'. If an army is mobilising, its capability to cause damage clear, and its hostile intentions unequivocal, nobody has ever seriously suggested that you have to wait to be fired upon. In this sense, what has been described generically as 'anticipatory self-defence' has always been legal.

The problem arises with another kind of anticipatory self-defence: when the threat of attack is claimed to be real, but there is no credible reason to believe it is imminent. It should be said immediately that the issue here is not with the principle of military action against non-imminent threats as such. It is perfectly possible to imagine real threats which are not imminent – including the nightmare scenario combining rogue states, WMD and terrorists. The problem boils down to whether or not there is credible evidence of the reality of the threat in question (taking into account, as always, both capability and specific intent); whether the military attack response is the only reasonable one in all the circumstances; and – crucially – who makes the decision.

The question is not whether preventive military action can ever be taken: it is entirely within the scope of the Security Council's powers under Chapter VII to authorise force if it is satisfied a case has been made (and the Council and others these days are quite properly giving increased attention, in relation to both WMD proliferation and terrorism, to circumstances in which such cases might be made). The question is whether military action in response to non-imminent threats can ever be taken unilaterally.

This is the question on which the U.S. has led with its chin, and generated a storm of continuing international controversy in the lead up to the 2003 Iraq war, in particular with the release in September 2002 of the National Security Strategy, arguing for a broadening of "concept of imminent threat to the capabilities and objectives of today's adversaries" and stating that "there is a compelling case for taking anticipatory action to defend ourselves, even if uncertainty remains as to the time and place of the enemy's attack".

The biggest problem with extending the scope of unilateral self-defence action under Article 51 in the way contemplated by the Bush administration is that it utterly fails to acknowledge that what is sauce for the goose is sauce for the gander, legitimising the prospect of preventive strikes in any number of volatile regions, starting with the Middle East, South and East Asia. To undermine so comprehensively the norm of non-intervention on which any system of global order must be painstakingly built is to invite a slide into anarchy. We would be living in a world where the unilateral use of force would be the rule, not the exception.

External Threats. When a state poses a threat to other states, or individuals outside its borders, the UN Charter fully empowers the Security Council to take any coercive action at all, including ultimately military action, that it deems "necessary to maintain or restore international peace and security". It doesn't matter whether the threat involves a "threat to the peace, breach of the peace or act of aggression"; whether it is occurring now, or in the imminent future or in the distant future; or whether it is constituted by an act or an omission; or whether it is constituted by the state's own actions or by non-state actors it harbours or supports.

Nor does it matter whether the threat is constituted by an actual or potential act of violence, or simply a challenge to the

Council's authority. If the Security Council decides that a state is not acting in compliance with previous resolutions and for that reason alone, by putting the credibility of the Council's decisions at risk it is posing a 'threat to the peace' – whatever other kind of threat that state may or may not constitute – the Council is fully entitled to make that judgement and act accordingly.

Usually the only question – a huge one politically, but not legally-is how the unquestioned authority of the Council should be exercised, when the Charter offers no detailed criteria, when States see their interests so differently and when some States exercise so much more influence than others. There is growing acceptance that, as the Secretary-General said last September, that there may need to be 'early authorisation of coercive measures to address certain types of threats – for instance, terrorist groups armed with weapons of mass destruction'.

Internal Threats. While the UN Charter is as clear as it possibly could be on the question of external threats, it is much less clear about the right of collective action against a state when the only threat involved is to those within it: the issue of so-called humanitarian intervention. Article 2.7 expressly prohibits intervention "in matters which are essentially within the jurisdiction of any state", but this is in tension with language elsewhere acknowledging individual human rights, and with a mass of law and practice over the last few decades which have set real conceptual limits claims of untrammeled state sovereignty, not least the Genocide Convention.

What is clear is that the Security Council can always authorise Chapter VII military action against a state if it is prepared to declare that the situation, however apparently internal in character, does in fact amount to a 'threat to international peace and security' – as it did for example in Somalia, and eventually Bosnia, in the early 1990s. For all practical purposes, threats to international peace and security are what the Security Council says they are. But more often than not, even in conscience shocking situations like Rwanda in 1994, it has declined to initiate or authorise any enforcement action at all. And that has led to a willingness, in cases where necessity seemed to demand, to bypass the Council, as in

Kosovo in 1999, in ways that – if repeated – can't help but diminish its authority.

The need to actually mean it when we say 'never again' after each Cambodia, or Rwanda, or Srebrenica is in constant tension with desire of sovereign states not to see a diminution of their sovereign authority. The tenacity of that attachment can be seen to this day in the reluctance that has been evident in the Security Council to take on and hold to account Sudan for its contribution to the horrors continuing to unfold.

It was this to try to resolve this tension between the claims of state sovereignty and individual rights that the Canadian Government sponsored the International Commission on Intervention and State Sovereignty (ICISS), which I co-chaired with the Secretary-General's Special Adviser on Africa, Mohamed Sahnoun, and which produced its report, The Responsibility to Protect in December 2001.

The most groundbreaking contribution of the report was the its characterization of the central issue not as the 'right' of anybody to intervene, but rather the responsibility of the international community to act to protect a State's peoples when the State itself abdicated that responsibility, either through ill-will or incapacity. The ICISS Commission spelt it out in the form of two critical principles. The primary responsibility for the protection of a state's own people must lie with the state itself. But where a population is suffering serious harm, as a result of internal war, insurgency, repression or state failure, and the state in question is unwilling or unable to halt or avert it, the principle of non-intervention should lead to a larger principle, that of the international responsibility to protect.

We had no doubt that the proper authority to authorise action in these circumstances was the Security Council, but had to face the problem that the Council has not always acted as it should in the face of conscience shocking violations of humanity. Our bottom line was that the task was not to find alternatives to the Security Council, but to make the Security Council work better. And that led us specifically to formulate a set of criteria for military action, which we argued strongly should be accepted at least informally as guidelines by the

Security Council-and hopefully could ultimately become so embedded in practice that they assumed the status of customary international law.

The 'responsibility to protect' principles were quietly gaining momentum in the academic and political debate, albeit rather submerged by the preoccupations with terrorism and WMD that emerged after 911. But they have been rather thrown off course by the emergence of the argument in relation to last year's invasion of Iraq – as other rationales in terms of bombs and terrorists dropped away – that it was Saddam's murderous tyrannising of his own people that made him a suitable case for humanitarian intervention treatment. The argument was a very strong one a decade and more ago, when Saddam was massacring Kurds in the late 80s and southern Shiites in the early 90s – as the world in both cases looked steadfastly the other way – but it had much less application in recent years, when no such catastrophe was occurring or imminent and, awful as it was, the Iraqi regime's behaviour was not much worse than a score or two of others.

It had all the appearance of a convenient rationalisation rather than genuine motivation, and certainly looked that way to those concerned, for good reasons or bad, about the potential overreach of the humanitarian intervention principle. Was Robert Mugabe to be the next case for military treatment, the ostensible rationale for the enterprise being not his current onslaught on democracy and human rights, but the slaughters in Matabeleland in the 1980s? The net result of all this was that an emerging international norm of real potential utility was once again struggling for acceptance.

FIVE CRITERIA OF LEGITIMACY

So what is the task ahead for those of us who do want to raise our sights, not lower them; who want to reverse the trend toward unilateralism rather than collective action in the use of force; who want to see a new consensus emerge, in the context of internal threats to human security, not only as to when states should not go to war, but when they should; and who, above all, want to recreate the kind of confidence in the role and judgment of the Security Council that will lead to a dramatically reduced inclination to bypass it on the part of those capable of doing so?

What we do need is better process in determining the proper application of the existing rules governing the use of force-particularly in the Security Council, but wherever else such decisions are made as well. Much more attention should be paid – not only in academic discourse but in actual operational decision-making – to the group of principles which have to be satisfied if any decision to use military force is to be not just legal, but legitimate.

The distinction – if it can be operationalised, with criteria of legitimacy simplified, standardised and commonly accepted – is an important one. The effectiveness of the global collective security system, as with any other legal order, depends ultimately not only on the legality of decisions, but the common perception of their legitimacy – their being made on solid evidentiary grounds, for the right reasons, morally as well as legally.

While it is obviously optimal for any military action to be both unquestionably legal under international law and universally accepted as legitimate (as was the case, for example, with the 1991 Gulf War), it is fair to suggest that military action which is technically illegal but widely perceived to be legitimate (as with Kosovo in 1999) does far less damage than action which is generally perceived to be neither legal nor legitimate (Iraq in 2003).

So what are the appropriate criteria of legitimacy which should govern these decisions? The argue for five:

(1) Seriousness of Threat: is the threatened harm to state or human security of a kind, and sufficiently clear and serious, to prima facie justify the use of military force?

(2) Proper Purpose: is it clear that the primary purpose of the proposed military action is to halt or avert the threat in question, whatever other purposes or motives may be involved?

(3) Last Resort: has every non-military option for meeting the threat in question been considered, with reasonable grounds for believing lesser measures will not succeed?

(4) Proportional Means: is the scale, duration and intensity of the proposed military action the minimum necessary to meet the threat in question?

(5) Balance of Consequences: is there a reasonable chance of the military action being successful in meeting the threat in question, with the consequences of action not likely to be worse than the consequences of inaction?

The immediate intellectual origins of these criteria lie in a recommendation of the ICISS Commission in its The Responsibility to Protect report: the context there was the specific one of 'humanitarian intervention' in response to internal threats, but what we described there as 'threshold' and 'prudential' criteria can easily be expressed in the more generalised. The ICISS recommendations owed something, in turn, to the general approach of the Kosovo Commission before it, chaired by Richard Goldstone and Carl Tham in 2000. Even more obviously, their ultimate intellectual origins lie in the whole tradition, and vast literature, of 'just war' theory. But that said, it is very important to emphasise that the criteria here argued for are intended to reflect universal values and not in any way be culture or religion specific. The literature to contradict this: certainly many conversations over recent years with colleagues from different cultural and religious traditions, particularly Islam, have persuaded me that there is absolutely nothing incompatible there with the principles here espoused, and much to support them.

These criteria are simple enough, relevant enough and compelling enough to be employed by any policy makers anywhere – at a national as well as intergovernmental level – in any context when they are deciding whether it's right to fight. But my immediate proposal is that these criteria, or guidelines, however else they are used, be systematically discussed and applied whenever the Security Council is making any determination under Chapter VII as to whether it is appropriate to use military force in response to any 'threat to the peace, breach of the peace or act of aggression' (Art 39). They would apply whether the threat is external or internal; whether the issue is the 'right to react' or the 'responsibility to protect'; or whether the threat is constituted by armies marching, WMD acquisition, terrorism or tribal machetes. The criteria should also be regarded as relevant when the Security Council is considering its response to a claimed act of self-defence under Art 51, or the question of use of force by a regional organisation under Chapter VIII. They also have potential application, should the occasion ever arise, to any 'Uniting for Peace' or similar resolution that might be considered by the General Assembly.

The five criteria be embodied in the Charter or in any formal treaty – that would be much too tall an order to contemplate-only that they be adopted, informally if necessary, and actually applied by the Security Council in its deliberations. If they did win general support they might appropriately at some stage be embodied in a General Assembly declaratory resolution: this, and their regular application in practice, would over time enhance their prospect of being considered rules of customary international law.

It is of course possible to go into much more detail in drafting these criteria, particularly the crucial first one, asking "is the threatened harm to state or human security of a kind, and sufficiently clear and serious, to prima facie justify the use of military force?" For example, in the context of internal threats, the ICISS argued that the 'just cause' threshold should be very narrowly confined, with the bar set high and tight, limited to situations of large scale killing or ethnic cleansing, actual or apprehended.

There have been quite a number of references by the Secretary General and others over recent years to the possible utility of a set of guidelines or criteria of this kind. Prompted initially by the UK in the late 1990s, and later by the ICISS Commission in 2001, there has already been some discussion within the Security Council about the pros and cons of going down this path, at least in the context of humanitarian intervention, in response to internal threats Beyond that, the debate on criteria has not moved much beyond the stage of occasional footnote suggestions and throwaway single lines in speeches stage. It is to be hoped that, that debate can now seriously start, perhaps in the context of the work of the Secretary General's High Level Panel on Threats, Challenges and Change, due to report in December this year. However they might ultimately be drafted, and whatever the form in which they might be adopted, the point of adopting these five criteria of legitimacy (and having them being seen to be applied). Nobody suggests that there is any coin-in-the-slot push button predictability about the kind of answers one will get when one puts the five questions suggesting: opinions will always differ, just as national interests will differ, and it is hardly unknown for interests to influence opinions.

But, as someone who has spent a fair number of years in and around these kinds of deliberations, if not always optimal, at least better outcomes. If the process demands that criteria have to be systematically discussed, it is much more difficult to duck, weave, fudge, dissimulate and just ignore critical issues: colleagues will ask harder questions, and even the press will sometimes start asking the right questions. At the end of the day strong arguments will look stronger and weak arguments weaker, and these appearances do matter.

Putting it succinctly, the point of adopting and applying the five criteria of legitimacy is not to guarantee that the objectively best outcome will always prevail: it is to maximise the possibility of achieving Security Council consensus around when it is appropriate or not to go to war; to maximise international support for whatever the Security Council decides; and to minimise the possibility of individual member states bypassing or ignoring the Security Council.

And if we can achieve any of that, we really will be well on the way to building an international legal order that, despite all the challenges which continue to buffet it, will give us some grounds for optimism that we are not forever condemned to repeat the mistakes of the past.

PRE-EMPTIVE MILITARY ACTION AND THE LEGITIMATE USE OF FORCE

From the "just war" doctrines of the Middle Ages to the Westphalian concept of a sovereign state's "right" to wage war for whatever ends the sovereign judged right to the contorted efforts of 19th Century legal scholars to avoid the problems of the legitimacy of "war" by defining all kinds of military operations as something other than "war" to the futile efforts of the League of Nations and the Kellogg-Briand Pacts to – with various reservations and ambiguities – "outlaw" war to today's discussion of the distinctions between preventive and pre-emptive use of force and the rise of "humanitarian intervention" as a politically correct form of warfare, practical political and military leaders, as well as legal scholars and scholars of international relations, have wrestled with the question of when use of military force is a legitimate instrument of statecraft.

It remains sadly the case that cannon are still the last argument of kings. Not the sincere efforts of leaders and citizens to substitute international institutions and international diplomacy for military power, not the terrible costs of two massive Europe-based world wars, not those of countless smaller internal and international wars throughout the world since 1945, not even the potential consequences of war fought with nuclear, chemical, and biological weapons, as well as the massively increased potential lethality of conventional technology, have fundamentally changed the fact that the threat and use of force are the ultimate instruments of international relations.

Moreover, it is a necessary qualification to the proposition that diplomacy is preferable to force that where vital interests, or at least conflicts over perceived vital interests, are at stake, and where willingness to provide inducements is not unlimited, diplomacy and negotiation are unlikely to succeed unless there is seen to be a real cost to refusal to compromise. The consequences that can be imposed by other means of pressure are puny compared to those of military force. The states (not to mention non-state actors) whose actions are most dangerous and most essential to be constrained are the least likely to be much affected by "international opinion." In such states, the prospects of affecting regime action by appeals to the good sense or innate caution of the citizenry are minimal simply because the regime will have been careful to insulate itself very thoroughly from such public pressures. Even the most powerful international instrument of pressure short of military force – economic sanctions – has a very feeble potential for deflecting such states' actions. Indeed, it is, in some sense too simple even to say that it is an absolute principle that force is a last resort. Certainly, the risks and costs of military force make it both prudent and moral to refrain from its use while there is a reasonable prospect that other means may be effective. But the principle of using force only after exhausting non-military alternatives necessarily implies a willingness to recognize that, at some point, they have been exhausted, and that waiting too long may mean waiting until military options are no longer effective at acceptable costs.

In the limited time and space available, rather than try to cover the whole huge field, it seems appropriate to focus on two specific questions that have come to the fore in the face of fundamental changes in the international security environment since the end of the Cold War:

- When is use of force justified? (Herein of pre-emption)
- Who can legitimately decide on the use of military force? (Herein of unilateralism)

Unilateralism, multilateralism, and international decision-makers. Of the two issues, the second, "unilateralism," is relatively the easier, because the dichotomy between "unilateralism" and "multilateralism" is to a large degree an illusory one.

To be sure, there are today a few in the United States who prefer – or at least affect to prefer – unilateral action as a matter of both principle and expediency. They see American military power as so overwhelming that there is no need for the assistance of others. Equally important, they see American purposes as so noble and the perspectives of other governments as so narrow, even craven, that it is not only possible, but necessary, for the United States to ignore their views. The conclusion these "unilateralists by preference" draw is that involvement of other nations in decision-making about American use of force is unwise in that it risks diluting the clarity of American purposes, while involving other nations in actual operations is pointless because they can add nothing significant to American capabilities and including them merely complicates operations.

Conversely, there is a sharply contrary view that decisions on use of military force must always and only be made on a multilateral basis, and indeed, must be made by international institutions, preferably, and perhaps exclusively, by the United Nations. There are some in the United States – and there appear to be many more in other countries – who insist, or at least affect to insist, that only formal approval by the United Nations can legitimate the use of military force, except perhaps in the case of immediate defense by a certifiably innocent victim against direct military attack across a recognized international border by acknowledged forces of a foreign state.

There is, however, in international law – and more in international practice – widespread acceptance of the concept that, in the end, all decisions on use of military force are unilateral, in the sense of being made by nation states, but those decisions must, for reasons of both prudence and principle, be made in the light of the opinions and interests of others so as to gain their support. The great weight of American opinion takes a view that can fairly be described as "unilateral if necessary, but multilateral if possible – and multilateral should almost always be possible."

To begin with the first element – the reservation of the ultimate right of unilateral action – the current US administration is by no means the first tc espouse the notion that the United States has the right, even the duty, to act alone if the nation's vital interests are at stake, and that, in the end, it is the United States and no one else that makes that decision. The quotation at the top of this paper is indeed from a National Security Strategy document, but it is drawn from that of President Clinton in 1999, not that of President Bush in 2002.

Nor is the idea that decisions on military force are ultimately national decisions confined to superpowers. Indeed, it seems very likely that, in extremis, every country would take that position. Certainly, even those, like the current German government, who are most enthusiastic in theory for multilateral decisions on use of force, insist on reserving the right to make a separate national decision on whether a multilateral approval of military action is sufficiently justified – or sufficiently serves their own nation's goals and principles – to require actually participating in the action. And there are numerous examples of nations that, in general, regard themselves as adherents of a multilateral approach who proven nonetheless ready to use their military forces for their national aims without bothering much about international opinion, as Spain did last summer over the occupation of a disputed Mediterranean island. To point this out is not accuse Germany or Spain or anyone else of hypocrisy or even to call into question the soundness, much less the sincerity, of their general commitment to multilateral decision-making, but only to observe that it has its limits.

But if unilateralism in theory is all but universal, unilateralism in practice is very hard even for a superpower on a matter of any difficulty. First, in most situations, there may not be much of a practical option of truly unilateral action. American military operations are almost always greatly facilitated by having the cooperation and support of others. The US may have overwhelming capability in many, perhaps most, forms of military power, but the direct military contributions of other nations remain highly useful. The military capability gap is real, but it is not infinite, and many allies can make very helpful contributions, in specialized areas like special operations forces, in capabilities where cutting edge technology is not required, and increasingly also where other nations are, albeit on a smaller scale, approaching American capabilities in fields like precision strike or naval forces. Even setting aside direct military contributions, the United States is, in almost all circumstances, heavily dependent on other countries for bases, overflight rights, and access, and usually for even more direct support in the form of intelligence, cooperation in applying economic and political instruments, and, very importantly, in dealing with the aftermath of conflict. Certainly that was the case in Afghanistan. The Bush Administration's National Security Strategy may exaggerate a little when it says, "There is little of lasting consequence that the United States can accomplish without the sustained cooperation of its allies and friends in Europe," but the basic point is correct – and not just about Europe.

And, of course, there are powerful political and psychological dimensions to international support. America, however patriotic even jingoistic and ostensibly disdainful of foreigners our popular culture, is far from unilateral by preference when it comes to military operations. Opinion polls consistently show – in a variety of contexts – that public support for American military operations is far higher where the United States has the support of its allies than where it would be alone. In part, this reaction is no doubt the sensible one that Americans like others to share the costs and risks, but it also appears to reflect a more complex judgment about international affairs: The American public has more confidence that the decisions of our government are right if they are shared and supported by other countries, as evidenced both by their formal positions and statements and by their willingness to send their own military forces to join in.

Moreover, in most situations, it is not that hard for the United States to garner international support. This is in part the consequence of the obvious fact that the United States has a wide variety of levers of influence and persuasion at its disposal. And the United States need not shy from using those levers. Accepting that the use of military force requires – or is at any rate immensely helped by – international support does not require that the United States be neutral about whether that support is forthcoming. Forced to choose between the United States and its adversaries, most countries will, whatever their misgivings, realize that their interests counsel considering the consequences of opposing the United States on an issue so important to it that the use of military force is an issue.

But the proposition that, in the end, the United States can usually count on the support of those countries that matter does not rest simply – on the proposition that frustrating the Americans would have a price. At bottom, those interests of the United States that plausibly could involve the use of American military force are also the interests of much of the rest of the world. An American diplomacy geared to exhausting non-military alternatives as means of meeting fundamental challenges will, if non-military means fail after being seriously applied, in most cases, also convince many other countries that resort to military force is not only justified, but required in their own interest, not just that of the United States.

However, to say that international support for the use of military force is, in most cases, both necessary and obtainable, is not necessarily to say that the only legitimate source of international support is action by the United Nations. The interesting and much-disputed legal issues of how the UN Charter, in particular Article 51 (reserving the inherent right of individual and collective self-defense against armed attack) should be interpreted – and what, to a practicing lawyer is an equally important issue – who has the legitimate authority to interpret it authoritatively are matters more for scholars than practitioners of international relations.

Of course, formal UN support is desirable, both for its own sake, and for its impact on the actions and attitudes of individual countries whose support may be essential. But insofar as the issue is legitimacy, it is hard to make the case that only UN action suffices. In practice, whether "the United Nations" has given its sanction for use of military force means, as a practical matter, whether there is a Security Council resolution that can plausibly be read as authorizing military force.

That, in turn, means whether there is a negative vote by Russia or China. Strictly speaking, of course, the UK or France could also veto, and, in theory, a UN Security Council resolution authorizing the use of military force could fail by reason of not having the affirmative votes of a majority of the Security Council, even if no permanent member voted against it. As a realistic proposition, however, it is indeed hard to imagine a use-of-force situation where a resolution to which none of the "Perm 5" objected enough to use a veto could not get a majority (even if one or more permanent members abstained)-and it is still less plausible that France – not to mention the UK – would exercise a veto in a situation where Russia and/or China would not (always laying aside the – presumably no very unlikely – of a case like Suez in 1956 where the interests of France or the UK were uniquely at issue.)

It follows that to require United Nations approval as an absolute condition of legitimate use of military force is to say that no military action of which Russia or China (or, in principle, France, Britain, or, indeed, the US) strongly disapproves is legitimate, no matter how broadly the action is otherwise supported, or how well justified in other international legal or political terms. To illustrate the point – NATO could legitimately point to various UNSC resolutions as supporting its intervention to reverse Milosevic-led Serbia's expulsion of the ethnic Albanian population of Kosovo in 1999. There was, however, no authorizing action by the Security Council in classic "all necessary means" words, and it is not clear that had one been sought, Russia (or China) would have withheld a veto. That intervention was, nonetheless, broadly regarded as legitimate, whether as a "humanitarian intervention" or as a means of forestalling a spreading conflict in a region of Europe that has bred a host of wars in living memory.

Would a failed attempt to get a formal Security Council authorization really have changed things? For most of the world, the Kosovo intervention was legitimate and would still have been so had a UNSC effort produced a veto. For to say that a UNSCR is essential amounts to saying that – not "the international community" – but Russia, China – and, in principle the other permanent members or alternatively, a majority-blocking group of the non-permanent members – are the absolute custodians of the legitimacy of international force. In these terms, the choice between "unilateral" action and "multilateral" is not between a strictly national decision and a UN Security Council Resolution, but one between efforts to garner as much support from other countries as possible, and an insistence, even a preference, for acting alone. In such efforts, the actions of formal regional institutions like NATO and of informal ad hoc groups like the coalition that fought the first Gulf War (admittedly with UNSCR blessing) and may fight a second one, count for as much as a UN Security Council hamstrung by a veto.

Pre-emption: When does the Right to Self-defense Arise?

The question of "pre-emption" is a much more difficult issue. The concept that "defense" is legitimate, while "offence"– more pejoratively "aggression" – is not, lies deep in all discussions of use of military force. In practice, the distinction has always been hard to draw. Indeed, a good deal of effort has been spent – without notable success or general acceptance in practice – in attempting to abolish the distinction by aspiring to abolish force entirely as a means of settling disputes – by a sort of "no fault" renunciation of force. But the principle of "self-defense" has survived, and is, in fact, formally and explicitly recognized in the UN Charter as an "inherent" right, not one created by the Charter.

Lurking in the concept of "self-defense" is the question of at what point the right arises, of where on the spectrum of prevention, pre-emption, and response, military action is justified. The American government has, especially but not exclusively since the attacks of September 11, 2001, stressed the right of pre-emption in certain circumstances, specifically against terrorists and against rogue states threatening to acquire nuclear and other mass destruction weapons.

So far as the United States striking at terrorists is concerned, the issue is hardly one of pre-emption. Once hostilities have been started by others, it is no longer "pre-emption" for the victim to seek to destroy the source, not just to frustrate specific attacks in the future from the same source. The United States has already been – indeed was years before September 2001 – the victim of attack by the coordinated terrorist groups that are the targets for American attacks today. And, beginning at least with the embassy bombings in 1998, the United States was prepared to use force to destroy Al Qaeda operations and leadership where there was sufficient intelligence of their location, entirely independent of any indication that a specific new attack was being planned. There are, to be sure, many difficult legal, moral, political, and practical issues raised by the "war" on terrorism, and by the American determination to, in the words of President Bush's National Security Strategy, "destroy the threat before it reaches our borders." For example, since terrorists are non-state actors, the sovereignty of other countries is, by definition, involved in American attacks on them. Countries in whose territory terrorists are operating have a responsibility to suppress the operations, and the Administration has declared that it will regard countries that give sanctuary to terrorists as subject to military attack just as much as the terrorists themselves. The sovereignty questions raised by this position – and other issues of legality and legitimacy – are real and sometimes difficult issues, but they are not about pre-emption, but about the conduct of a "war" that does not fit traditional patterns.

The Bush Administration has, however, squarely relied on pre-emption in also enunciating a potentially more far-reaching doctrine of anticipatory action against rogue states that are in the process of acquiring nuclear, chemical, and biological weapons. The NSS says, "We must be prepared to stop rogue states... before they are able to threaten or use weapons of mass destruction against the United States, our allies, or friends." To an important degree, this doctrine is less innovative than either its advocates or its critics profess to believe. Perhaps most important, it is, in its terms, limited to the particular issue of rogue states seeking to acquire WMD; it is not a claim to use force pre-emptively (and unilaterally) whenever the American government judges US interests to be a stake.

Critics, however, argue that the Administration is claiming that self-defense is not limited to "pre-emption" in the sense of forestalling an imminent attack, but "preventive war," in the sense of using military force where the only threat is a vague and uncertain one of possible conflict at some indefinite point in the future. Such "preventive" war, it is argued, is not only in violation of international law, but an unbounded invitation to use of force on mere suspicion of the ambitions or intent of another nation, and indeed an negation of the very concept of international law.

However, far from ignoring international law, the United States government has advanced a sophisticated legal argument for the legitimacy of its position regarding pre-emption against rogue state WMD that is squarely based on international law principles. The argument begins with the proposition that international law unquestionably recognizes a right of self-defense and moreover acknowledges that exercising that right of self-defense does not require absorbing the first blow. As the NSS puts it, under long-recognized international law principles, "nations need not suffer an attack; they can lawfully take action to defend themselves against forces that present an obvious danger of attack."

The classic and widely accepted formulation of that right was stated by Daniel Webster, as American Secretary of State in the 1840's during negotiations about a British cutting out operation in American waters in Lake Ontario against the American ship *Caroline* that was being used to supply rebels in Canada. He wrote the British Minister, Lord Ashburton, that a nation has a right to act first where the "necessity of self-defense is instant, overwhelming, and leaving no choice of means, no moment for deliberation." The Administration argues that Webster's formulation must be "adapted to the capabilities and objectives of our adversaries." The traditional concept of "imminence" assumed a context where the need for mobilization and other preparation meant that there was a realistic prospect of warning of an attack. Stressing that its claim of a right to pre-empt is limited to action "to eliminate a specific threat to the US or our allies and friends," the Administration argues for a standard of "necessity" that recognizes that terrorists and rogue states with WMD would have at their disposal "weapons that can be easily concealed, delivered covertly, and used without warning." Accordingly, it is lawful to "take anticipatory action to defense ourselves, even if uncertainly remains as to the time and place of the enemy's attack."

On balance, the Administration has the better of the legal argument: Webster's formulation – which was adopted in the course of a protest against, rather than a defense of, a pre-emptive operation and therefore takes a restrictive view – speaks of a "necessity of self-defense" that is "instant, overwhelming," etc. Critics argue that only an immediate prospect of specific attack can met that standard. But, in Webster's formulation, it is the "necessity" that must have those characteristics, and such a necessity may exist without an immediate prospect of attack. The right of anticipatory self-defense by definition presupposes a right to act while action is still possible. If waiting for "imminence" means waiting until it is no longer possible to act effectively, the victim is left no alternative to suffering the first blow. So interpreted, the "right" would be illusory. The Administration is accurate when it points out that once a rogue state has achieved a serious WMD capability, effective action to eliminate the capability may well have become impossible. The problem is not so much that WMD be used with little warning – attacks with conventional weapons have all too often achieved tactical surprise – but that surprise use could be decisive and that the capability can be so successfully concealed that pre-emption is operationally impossible even if warning were available. On this basis, a strong case exists that the right of "self-defense" includes a right to move against WMD programs with high potential danger to the United States (and others) while it is still feasible to do so.

The problems with pre-emption, unfortunately, are not lack of legal legitimacy, but operational practicality. A right of pre-emption is one thing; a meaningful capability to pre-empt is quite another. Exercising the right pre-supposes, both logically and practically, that there is some military operation that will achieve the desired result of eliminating the WMD capability that is targeted at an acceptable cost, taking into account the enemy's possible reactions.

The first operational issue with pre-emption is whether the proposed operation will actually eliminate the WMD capability targeted. The problem is not (usually) whether there is a means of executing a pre-emptive attack once targets are identified, but knowing what and where to strike. Precision weapons require precision intelligence, and pre-emption requires that intelligence be comprehensive as well as precise. Too much attention to action movies and too little to the realities of intelligence collection have tended to obscure the difficulty of knowing enough about a nation's WMD programs to have much confidence of eliminating them by pre-emption. Still more difficult operationally is dealing with what the enemy may do in response, even if his WMD capability has been successfully negated.

The contemporary cases of Iraq and North Korea illustrate the operational problem in some of its dimensions: In the Korean case, there is no question about the location of the plutonium-production reactor and the re-processing facility at Yongbyon, and, as former Secretary of Defense William Perry has written, the United States military has the capability to destroy them quickly and without causing release of radioactive materials. Such an attack would block the prospect of North Korea extracting some half-dozen bombs worth of plutonium within the next year. But it would not eliminate the North Korean nuclear program, much less Pyongyang's ability to respond with devastating force. Even with regard to North Korea's nuclear programs, the Yongbyon facilities are only part of North Korea's potential. There has been no claim that the United States knows the location of either the plutonium that was extracted in 1991-92 or of the couple of bombs for which that plutonium may have supplied the fissile material. Nor is there a claim that the United States has the detailed knowledge required for high-confidence targeting of other elements of the North Korean program – notably its incipient uranium-enrichment facilities – much less its extensive chemical weapons capabilities. But the real problem with pre-emption in the North Korean case is that the North Korean capability to respond and escalate does not (so far) rest on its WMD, but on its massive conventional forces – and there is no chance that, that capability could be eliminated pre-emptively, even by a massive effort. Of course, the problem will only grow worse if North Korea is able to expand its nuclear potential, and at some point, if diplomacy fails, it may be the wiser course to act militarily, accepting the limits on American capability to preempt and relying on deterrence and defense to block or blunt a conventional attack in response. But it is the risks of such a course that have made not just South Korea, but the United States as well, so uneager to press the case for military confrontation.

In a sense, the case for dealing with the Iraqi WMD programs by military force now may be said to be the case for not letting Iraq reach the point Korea is at now. Essentially the argument for eliminating Saddam Hussein's WMD by military force if he will not eliminate it himself under UN monitoring is that, despite the real risks, if the capability is not stopped now, it will be too late – and the world and the region will have to deal with a Saddam regime armed with a powerful WMD capability that can neither be pre-empted nor confidently defended against. But it is significant that the military option being considered against Iraq today is pre-emptive only in the strategic, not the operational, sense. The military option is not to strike at the WMD programs directly but to replace the regime, as the only confident means of eliminating its WMD programs. This is not the product of over-ambition, but of operational reality. Intelligence of a granularity and comprehensiveness necessary for an effective pre-emption limited to the WMD programs themselves is no more available in the Iraqi than the Korean case. Indeed, in the Iraqi case there is not even an equivalent to Yongbyon, that is, a single key facility whose destruction is military feasible and would at a stroke deeply set back the WMD efforts. It is this lack of a military option able to eliminate the WMD that makes a campaign to oust the regime the only military option if UN disarmament efforts fail. Happily, Saddam Hussein has less formidable responsive options than does Kim Jong Il because his military is relatively weak and his ability to strike rapidly at high value targets is much less. The American assessment is that none of his potential responses is anything like as significant as the North Korean potential to wreak immense destruction on South Korea, and that the risks entailed by what he can do can be reduced to acceptable levels – and are in any event better run now that faced later when his WMD programs are far more developed. But Iraq has some potentially very destructive responses, and their potential use is a major complication for military planning – and a major source of the reluctance to many to support an invasion.

In short, the contrasting cases of Iraq and North Korea today may be said to illustrate both the conceptual strength of the administration's doctrine of pre-emption against rogue state WMD, and its limitations in practice. There will, unfortunately perhaps, still be plenty of scope for military operations and capabilities aimed at deterrence and for defense if deterrence fails.

2

International Law: A Tool to Delegitimate the Military

Some regard International law as a tool to abolish war or at least-to limit the risk of war.

Others see International Law just as a legitimisation of so-called "just wars", wars legitimised by the UN Charter. Besides these general positions, what role can International Law play in the peace movement's struggle against war? What difference did the International War Crimes Tribunal on former-Yugoslavia make? While it condemns war crimes, does it at the same time justify the military, as the military is the only force capable of arresting war criminals?

International Law is a reflection of power relationships, of interestes, of dominating values and of the structure of international politics. In contrast to national law, international law is not enforced by a central authority with a monopoly of violence. International law is increasingly codified, but there is also customary law deriving from long-standing and agreed practices. Therefore there is more space in international law for conflicting principles and opinions. And it is very common to violate the principles of international law without incurring any reprisals.

Today's international system goes back to the European system of states that was extended over the whole world since the sixteenth century. We can distinguish the classical period of international law and today's international law. One turning point has been the foundation of the League of Nations in 1919.

In today's international law we find side by side the principles of the classical period and new still evolving principles, many of them embodied and articulated in structures, charters and declarations of the United Nations Organisation. A minor turning point are the 1990s. Due to the changes in the power balance, there is now a period of uncertainty, characterised by an intensified discussion about international law, by new interpretations and demands, and by changes in the conduct of international relations.

THE NEW INTERNATIONAL LAW

During the nineteenth century there was a growing dissatisfaction concerning war. Increasingly war was regarded as too destructive, too disruptive, too devastating, too cruel, too costly and too uneconomic. Peace societies came into being. Pacifists, transnational non-governmental organisations, academics, politicians and even monarchs called for peaceful settlement of disputes between states, by arbitration and international courts for disarmament and the ban of certain weapons. A major event was the famous 1899 Hague Conference. This new thinking was reflected in state practice. Whereas in the 17th and 18th the major powers had fought wars against each other almost incessantly, after 1815 a growing number of states on both sides of the Atlantic managed to avoid war among themselves. Disputes were increasingly settled by arbitration or by international conferences.

Ius in Bello

It is necessary to distinguish between ius ad bellum, the right to wage war, and the ius in bello, the rules of conduct in war. During the classical period of international law, certain rules how to conduct wars developed. These rules apply to all parties in a war, aggressors and attacked, without any regard to moral or political jugdments or preferences. The central concern is to avoid unnecessary cruelties and damages, to confine war as much as possible to the combatants and to protect non-combatants, medical personell, the wounded, prisoners of war and civilians.

Another feature of the humanitarian law of war, is the ban of certain weapons, beginning with dum-dum bullets in 1899 to the provisions concerning weapons of mass destruction. Most prominent today is ongoing legal and political debate about nuclear weapons.

A very telling example is the Convention relative to the Treatment of Prisoners of War: officers are accorded preferential treatment even in captivity: e.g. the command structure among prisoners of war is kept intact, officers get better accomodation, are privileged financially and do not have to work physically.

Such provisions reinforce the legitimacy of the military and of military structures. War is seen as a legitimate business where the enemy is to be respected as a business colleague. Obviously, the ius in bello is no tool to delegitimate war or the military. War in itself is not questioned but taken for granted. Unnecessary excesses are to be avoided, violence deemed necessary is legitimated. Some groups of human beings are to be protected as far as possible, but it is perfectly legal to kill, mutilate and imprison so-called combatants whether they have been recruited by force or not.

Ius ad Bellum

The international law concerning the ius ad bellum has changed considerably. The League of Nations made the avoidance of war a prime objective. The Briand-Kellog-Pact of 1928/1929 outlawed any aggressive war. The United Nations Charter of 1945 went further by rejecting any aggressive use violence between states.

The UN Charter recommends the pacific settlement of disputes. But if the recommendations of the Security Council have no effect, if non-military measures have failed, the security council can authorise a war. According to the Charter of the United Nations war, is illegal with the exception of defensive wars and wars sanctioned by the Security Council. The central dilemma of this approach was described by Bart de Ligt in 1937 in a statement on the League of Nations:

"It is true that the League prohibits certain kinds of wars, that is to say, such wars are declared illegitimate by itself. Nevertheless, it allows others, so that at Geneva the distinguish between legal and illegal wars.... So far from liberating mankind form this plague, the League has even introduced new forms of

it. For the ultimate sanction brought into use against a state which has been declared the aggressor, is still war. And so, in the name of all kinds of peace measures, war is sanctioned by the League as a war for Peace."

Human Rights

The UN have turned human rights into an important element of international law. The states are no longer sovereign concerning the treatment of their subjects. Concerning the rights of individual human beings, some international human rights conventions make sure that the military power of states and the ability to wage war is not undermined by human rights.

Concerning the forced recruitment of people for war, international law can make it more difficult to recruit children or conscientious objectors, but forced recruitment in itself is legitimated. The CO provisions in international human rights agreements do not proclaim a human right not to be forced to fight in war; instead they allow some exceptions to the general rule. Thus human rights are subordinated to military interests in international law. The states who want to preserve their power to recruit the population for war, are not the only ones who subordinate human rights to the perceived needs of the military.

HUMANITARIAN INTERVENTION

Within the new international law promoted by the UN, there is a tension between two principles. On the one hand the prime objective is the preservation of peace which inlcudes a ban on intervention in internal affairs of member countries. On the other hand the human rights conventions provide ample reasons to intervene in case of human rights violations.

Hitherto this has not been a major problem since the security council was blocked for decades and the UN charter allows the security council to use military force if "the Security Council deems that the continuance of the dispute is in fact likely to endanger the maintenance of international peace and security." There is no provision for military intervention in case of purely domestic affairs.

Now there is enourmous pressure to change the UN Charter and international law in order to legalise so-called humanitarian military interventions. The pressure emanates most strongly from the NATO countries. They have conducted an illegal aggressive war without a mandate from the Security Council and are interested in having their behaviour legalised by international law. If this was the case, international law would endorse military interventions. Human rights would be more often used than in the recent past in order to justify wars. As could be observed during the Balkan Wars of the 1990s more and more non-governmental and human rights organisations are likely to demand and to support wars in order to further their aims.

One last point: as in national, the wording and meaning of international law are not the only factors to be considered. It is the power to interpret international law that matters most.

INTRODUCTION BY GERNOT LENNERT

How do we handle the tension between human rights and the intention to abolish war? The classical international law had a basic contradiction. If sovereignty is highest principle at the same time the right of one state to wage war, is uphold the sovereignty of others is violated. Each state has sovereignity, but nobody can control the legitimate right of other state to wage war. International law has conflicting principles having different rules for civil and international war. But who decides which one is a civil war and which one international?

Recrutiment to army is not considered as violation of human rights. In countries like Angola, family-members of those refusing to join army, are tortured. So there's a question of how recruitment can be a concern of human rights.

International Criminal Tribunal cannot work if only a few state participate. US do not participate fearing that their soldiers will be sent to court. No American soldier must be tried by a foreign court. At War Crime Tribunal in the Hague a very slow moving system is followed using the documents which are old. Additions from 1977 were not used in the court. U.N. General Assembly decisions are not precedential.

Sanctions are more severe, causing more deaths than biological and chemical weapons which are considered as weapons of mass destruction. Economic sanctions have caused a very high number of deaths in Iraq and Serbia.

Amnesty International is more a legalistic institution than a moralistic one.

International law forbids destruction of power plant. After the first gulf war an agreement was reached that destruction of nuclear power plant is forbidden. But during the second gulf war the U.S General prided himself having bombed nuclear power station near Baghdad. Such agreements were violated in Yougoslavia as well, destroying dams, water tanks, refineries, chemical plants. The powerful will always justify their action.

Is it all Negative?

It is very common to violate the priciples of International Law in any country. But the challenge before us is what strategy can be adopted internationally to use it as an useful tool. Many people feel that the Institute of International Criminal Court is an instrument to stop war, control those who violate human rights. Any law, national or international, is a tool to catch the authority. World Policy is not an acceptable idea to many. But ideas, attitudes, values changing can be part of the world policing. There can be some value in the idea of world peer pressure.

LAWS OF WAR

The law of war is a body of law concerning acceptable justifications to engage in war (*jus ad bellum*) and the limits to acceptable wartime conduct (*jus in bello*). The law of war is considered an aspect of public international law (the law of nations) and is distinguished from other bodies of law, such as the domestic law of a particular belligerent to a conflict, that may also provide legal limits to the conduct or justification of war. Among other issues, modern laws of war address declarations of war, acceptance of surrender and the treatment of prisoners of war, military necessity along with *distinction* and *proportionality*, and the prohibition of certain weapons that may cause unnecessary suffering.

Early Sources and History

Attempts to define and regulate the conduct of individuals, nations, and other agents in war and to mitigate the worst effects of war have a long history. The earliest known instances are found in the Hebrew Bible (Old Testament). For example, Deuteronomy 20:19-20 limits the amount of acceptable collateral and environmental damage:

When thou shalt besiege a city a long time, in making war against it to take it, thou shalt not destroy the trees thereof by forcing an axe against them: for thou mayest eat of them, and thou shalt not cut them down (for the tree of the field is man's life) to employ them in the siege: Only the trees which thou knowest that they be not trees for meat, thou shalt destroy and cut them down; and thou shalt build bulwarks against the city that maketh war with thee, until it be subdued.

Similarly, Deuteronomy 21:10-14 requires that female captives who were forced to marry the victors of a war could not be sold as slaves. In the early 7th century, the first Caliph, Abu Bakr, whilst instructing his Muslim army, laid down the following rules concerning warfare:

These rules were put into practice during the early Muslim conquests of the 7th and 8th centuries. After the expansion of the Caliphate, Islamic legal treatises on international law from the 9th century onwards covered the application of Islamic military jurisprudence to international law, including the law of treaties; the treatment of diplomats, hostages, refugees and prisoners of war in Islam; the right of asylum; conduct on the battlefield; protection of women, children and non-combatant civilians; contracts across the lines of battle; the use of poisonous weapons; and devastation of enemy territory. These laws were put into practice by Muslim armies during the Crusades, most notably by Saladin and Sultan al-Kamil. For example, after al-Kamil defeated the Franks, Oliverus Scholasticus praised the Islamic laws of war, commenting on how al-Kamil supplied the defeated Frankish army with food:

Who could doubt that such goodness, friendship and charity come from God? Men whose parents, sons and daughters, brothers and sisters, had died in agony at our hands, whose lands we took, whom we drove naked from their homes, revived us with their own food when we were dying of hunger and showered us with kindness even when we were in their power.

In medieval Europe, the Roman Catholic Church also began promulgating teachings on just war, reflected to some extent in movements such as the Peace and Truce of God. The impulse to restrict the extent of warfare, and especially protect the lives and property of non-combatants continued with Hugo Grotius and his attempts to write laws of war.

Modern Sources

The modern law of war is derived from two principal sources:

- *Lawmaking treaties* (or *conventions*) — see the section below called "International treaties on the laws of war".
- *Custom*. Not all the law of war derives from or has been incorporated in such treaties, which can refer to the continuing importance of customary law. Such customary international law is established by the general practice of nations together with their acceptance that such practice is required by law.

Positive international humanitarian law consists of treaties (international agreements) which directly affect the laws of war by binding consenting nations and achieving widespread consent—see the section below called "International treaties on the laws of war".

The opposite of positive laws of war is customary laws of war, many of which were explored at the Nuremberg War Trials. These laws define both the *permissive* rights of states as well as *prohibitions* on their conduct when dealing with irregular forces and non-signatories.

Historian Geoffrey Best has called the period from 1856 to 1909 the law of war's "epoch of highest repute." The defining aspect of this epoch was the establishment, by states, of a positive legal or legislative foundation (i.e., written) superseding a regime based primarily on religion, chivalry, and customs. It is during this "modern" era that the international conference became the forum for debate and agreement between states and the "multilateral treaty" served as the positive mechanism for codification. In addition, the Nuremberg War Trial judgment on "The Law Relating to War Crimes and Crimes Against Humanity" held, under the guidelines Nuremberg Principles, that treaties like the Hague Convention of 1907, having been widely accepted by "all civilised nations" for about half a century, were by then part of the customary laws of war and binding on all parties whether the party was a signatory to the specific treaty or not.

Interpretations of international humanitarian law change over time and this also affects the laws of war. For example Carla Del Ponte, the chief prosecutor for the International Criminal Tribunal for the former Yugoslavia pointed out in 2001 that although there is no specific treaty ban on the use of depleted uranium projectiles, there is a developing scientific debate and concern expressed regarding the effect of the use of such projectiles and it is possible that, in future, there may be a consensus view in international legal circles that use of such projectiles violate general principles of the law applicable to use of weapons in armed conflict. This is because in future it may be the consensus view that depleted uranium projectiles breaches one or more of the following treaties: The Universal Declaration of Human Rights; the Charter of the United Nations; the Genocide Convention; the United Nations Convention Against Torture; the Geneva Conventions including Protocol I; the Convention on Conventional Weapons of 1980; the Chemical Weapons Convention; and the Convention on the Physical Protection of Nuclear Material.

Purposes of the Laws

Some of the central principles underlying laws of war are:

- Wars should be limited to achieving the political goals that started the war (e.g., territorial control) and should not include unnecessary destruction;
- Wars should be brought to an end as quickly as possible;
- People and property that do not contribute to the war effort should be protected against unnecessary destruction and hardship;

To this end, laws of war are intended to mitigate the evils of war by:

- Protecting both combatants and noncombatants from unnecessary suffering;
- Safeguarding certain fundamental human rights of persons who fall into the hands of the enemy, particularly prisoners of war, the wounded and sick, and civilians;
- Facilitating the restoration of peace.

Example Substantive Laws of War

To fulfil the purposes noted above, the laws of war place substantive limits on the lawful exercise of a belligerent's power. Generally speaking, the laws require that belligerents refrain from employing violence that is not reasonably necessary for military purposes and that belligerents conduct hostilities with regard for the principles of humanity and chivalry.

However, because the laws of war are based on consensus, the content and interpretation of such laws are extensive, contested, and ever-changing. The following are particular examples of some of the substance of the laws of war, as those laws are interpreted today.

Declaration of War

Some treaties, notably the UN charter (1945) Article 2, and some other articles in the charter, seek to curtail the right of member states to declare war; as does the older Kellogg-Briand Pact of 1928 for those nations who ratified it.

Lawful Conduct of Belligerent Actors

Modern laws of war regarding conduct during war (*jus in bello*), such as the 1949 Geneva Conventions, provide that it is unlawful for belligerents to engage in combat without meeting certain requirements, among them the wearing of a distinctive uniform or other distinctive signs visible at a distance, and the carrying of weapons openly. Impersonating soldiers of the other side by wearing the enemy's uniform is allowed, though fighting in that uniform is unlawful *perfidy*, as is the taking of hostages.

The Red Cross, Red Crescent, & the white Flag

Modern laws of war, such as the 1949 Geneva Conventions, also include prohibitions on attacking doctors, ambulances or hospital ships displaying a Red Cross, a Red Crescent or other emblem related to the International Red Cross and Red Crescent Movement. It is also prohibited to fire at a person or vehicle bearing a white flag, since that indicates an intent to surrender or a desire to communicate.

In either case, persons protected by the Red Cross/Crescent or white flag are expected to maintain neutrality, and may not engage in warlike acts; in fact, engaging in war activities under a protected symbol is itself a violation of the laws of war known as perfidy. Failure to follow these requirements can result in the loss of protected status and make the individual violating the requirements a lawful military target.

Applicability to States and Individuals

The law of war is binding not only upon States as such but also upon individuals and, in particular, the members of their armed forces. Parties are bound by the laws of war to the extent that such compliance does not interfere with achieving legitimate military goals. For example, they are obliged to make every effort to avoid damaging people and property not involved in combat, but they are not guilty of a war crime if a bomb mistakenly hits a residential area.

By the same token, combatants that *intentionally* use protected people or property as shields or camouflage are guilty of violations of laws of war and are responsible for damage to those that should be protected.

Remedies for Violations

During conflict, punishment for violating the laws of war may consist of a specific, deliberate and limited violation of the laws of war in reprisal.

Soldiers who break specific provisions of the laws of war lose the protections and status afforded as prisoners of war, but only after facing a "*competent tribunal*" (GC III Art 5). At that point they become an unlawful combatant but they must still be "*treated with humanity and, in case of trial, shall not be deprived of the rights of fair and regular trial*", because they are still covered by GC IV Art 5. For example in 1976 foreign soldiers fighting for FNLA were captured by the MPLA in the civil war that broke out when Angola gained independence from Portugal in 1975. In the Luanda Trial, after "*a regularly constituted court*" found them guilty of being mercenaries, three Britons and an American were shot by a firing squad on July 10, 1976. Nine others were imprisoned for terms of 16 to 30 years.

Spies and terrorists may be subject to civilian law or military tribunal for their acts and in practice have been subjected to torture and/or execution. The laws of war neither approve nor condemn such acts, which fall outside their scope. However, nations that have signed the *UN Convention Against Torture* have committed themselves not to use torture on anyone for any reason. Citizens and soldiers of nations which have not signed the Fourth Geneva Convention are also not protected by it (Article 4: "*Nationals of a State which is not bound by the Convention are not protected by it*".), whether they are spies or terrorists. Also, citizens and soldiers of nations which have not signed and do not abide by the Third and Fourth Geneva Conventions are not protected by them.

If someone is (or is suspected to be) a citizen or soldier of a nation which has signed or abides by the Fourth Geneva Convention, or is (or is suspected to be) a "prisoner of war" (POW) per the definitions of such "*protected persons*" in the Third Geneva Convention, the following applies: A POW who breaks specific provisions of the laws of war may be penalized, but not penalized worse than the tribunal would penalize its own soldiers for the same offence (and usually a disciplinary, not judicial, punishment if its own soldiers normally wouldn't be brought to trial for a particular offence) and POW's may not be penalized based on rank or gender, nor with corporal punishment, collective punishments for individual acts, lack of daylight, or torture/cruelty. After a conflict has ended, persons who have committed or ordered any breach of the laws of war, especially atrocities, may be held individually accountable for war crimes through process of law. Also, nations which signed the Geneva Conventions are required to search for, then try and punish, anyone who has committed or ordered certain "*grave breaches*" of the laws of war.

History has shown that the laws of war are traditionally more strictly applied to those defeated, as the victorious faction are placed in the role of policing themselves. While it can be argued that the victors may be less strict on their own forces, it can also be argued that the signing of the treaties involved in the laws of war implies a good-faith promise to adhere to them equally. As with many facets of war, the aftermath and subsequent legal proceedings depend heavily on circumstance, and are different for each conflict.

There is an emerging trend in the US to hold private corporations civilly liable for aiding and abetting in war crimes, by knowingly providing substantial assistance in the commission of the crimes. Under international law, the mens rea element is knowledge, not intent that the crimes be carried out. This opens the door not only to hold private security contractors liable, but also other kinds of corporations which employ violent mercenary or terrorist groups as private security forces. Although conflict zones often lack functioning legal systems, and government may even have passed laws immunizing private mercenaries from criminal liability, aiding and abetting a war crime can still be the basis for civil liability in a foreign court with jurisdiction over the defendant corporation.

Role of the United States

While many point correctly to the Lieber Code, which was promulgated by the Union during the American Civil War, as critical in the development of the laws of land warfare, one researcher who analyzed the evolution of these laws concludes that "following the publication of Lieber's code as General Orders 100 in 1863, the United States did not effectively contribute anything to The Hague Laws relating to land warfare as they evolved during this period." This was probably because the United States considered itself a sea power (with corresponding significant participation and contributions to the law of the sea) and did not plan on getting entangled in continental (European) land wars.

International Treaties on the Laws of War

List of declarations, conventions, treaties and judgements and on the laws of war:

- 1856 Paris Declaration Respecting Maritime Law abolished privateering

- 1864 First Geneva Convention "for the Amelioration of the Condition of the Wounded and Sick in Armed Forces in the Field"
- 1868 St. Petersburg Declaration Renouncing the Use, in Time of War, of Explosive projectiles Under 400 grams Weight
- 1874 Project of an International Declaration concerning the Laws and Customs of War (Brussels Declaration). Signed in Brussels 27 August. This agreement never entered into force, but formed part of the basis for the codification of the laws of war at the 1899 Hague Peace Conference.
- 1880 Manual of the Laws and Customs of War at Oxford. At its session in Geneva in 1874 the Institute of International Law appointed a committee to study the *Brussels Declaration* of the same year and to submit to the Institute its opinion and supplementary proposals on the subject. The work of the Institute led to the adoption of the Manual in 1880 and it went on to form part of the basis for the codification of the laws of war at the 1899 Hague Peace Conference.
- 1899 Hague Conventions consisted of four main sections and three additional declarations (the final main section is for some reason identical to the first additional declaration):
    - I-Pacific Settlement of International Disputes
    - II-Laws and Customs of War on Land
    - III-Adaptation to Maritime Warfare of Principles of Geneva Convention of 1864
    - IV-Prohibiting Launching of Projectiles and Explosives from Balloons
    - Declaration I-On the Launching of Projectiles and Explosives from Balloons
    - Declaration II-On the Use of Projectiles the Object of Which is the Diffusion of Asphyxiating or Deleterious Gases
    - Declaration III-On the Use of Bullets Which Expand or Flatten Easily in the Human Body

- 1907 Hague Conventions had thirteen sections, of which twelve were ratified and entered into force and two declarations
  - o I-The Pacific Settlement of International Disputes
  - o II-The Limitation of Employment of Force for Recovery of Contract Debts
  - o III-The Opening of Hostilities
  - o IV-The Laws and Customs of War on Land
  - o V-The Rights and Duties of Neutral Powers and Persons in Case of War on Land
  - o VI-The Status of Enemy Merchant Ships at the Outbreak of Hostilities
  - o VII-The Conversion of Merchant Ships into War-Ships
  - o VIII-The Laying of Automatic Submarine Contact Mines
  - o IX-Bombardment by Naval Forces in Time of War
  - o X-Adaptation to Maritime War of the Principles of the Geneva Convention
  - o XI-Certain Restrictions with Regard to the Exercise of the Right of Capture in Naval War
  - o XII-The Creation of an International Prize Court [Not Ratified]*
  - o XIII-The Rights and Duties of Neutral Powers in Naval War
  - o Declaration I-extending Declaration II from the 1899 Conference to other types of aircraft
  - o Declaration II-on the obligatory arbitration
- 1909 London Declaration concerning the Laws of Naval War largely reiterated existing law, although it showed greater regard to the rights of neutral entities. Never went into effect.
- 1922 The Washington Naval Treaty, also known as the *Five-Power Treaty* (6 February)
- 1923 Hague Draft Rules of Aerial Warfare
- 1925 Geneva protocol for the Prohibition of the Use in

War of Asphyxiating, Poisonous or Other Gases, and of Bacteriological Methods of Warfare

- 1927-1930 Greco-German arbitration tribunal
- 1928 Kellogg-Briand Pact (also known as the *Pact of Paris*)
- 1929 Geneva Convention, Relative to the treatment of prisoners of war
- 1929 Geneva Convention on the amelioration of the condition of the wounded and sick
- 1930 Treaty for the Limitation and Reduction of Naval Armament (London Naval Treaty 22 April)
- 1935 Roerich Pact
- 1936 Second London Naval Treaty (25 March)
- 1938 Amsterdam Draft Convention for the Protection of Civilian Populations Against New Engines of War.
- 1938 League of Nations declaration for the "Protection of Civilian Populations Against Bombing From the Air in Case of War"
- 1945 United Nations Charter (entered into force on October 24, 1945)
- 1946 Judgment of the International Military Tribunal at Nuremberg
- 1947 Nuremberg Principles. formulated under UN General Assembly Resolution 177 21 November 1947
- 1948 United Nations Convention on the Prevention and Punishment of the Crime of Genocide.
- 1949 Geneva Convention I for the Amelioration of the Condition of the Wounded and Sick in Armed Forces in the Field
- 1949 Geneva Convention II for the Amelioration of the Condition of Wounded, Sick and Shipwrecked Members of Armed Forces at Sea
- 1949 Geneva Convention III Relative to the Treatment of Prisoners of War
- 1949 Geneva Convention IV Relative to the Protection of Civilian Persons in Time of War

- 1954 Hague Convention for the Protection of Cultural Property in the Event of Armed Conflict
- 1971 Zagreb Resolution of the Institute of International Law on Conditions of Application of Humanitarian Rules of Armed Conflict to Hostilities in which the United Nations Forces May be Engaged
- 1977 United Nations Convention on the Prohibition of Military or Any Other Hostile Use of Environmental Modification Techniques
- 1977 Geneva Protocol I Additional to the Geneva Conventions of 12 August 1949, and Relating to the Protection of Victims of International Armed Conflicts
- 1977 Geneva Protocol II Additional to the Geneva Conventions of 12 August 1949, and Relating to the Protection of Victims of Non-International Armed Conflicts
- 1978 Red Cross Fundamental Rules of International Humanitarian Law Applicable in Armed Conflicts
- 1980 United Nations Convention on Prohibitions or Restrictions on the Use of Certain Conventional Weapons Which May be Deemed to be Excessively Injurious or to Have Indiscriminate Effects (CCW)
    - o 1980 Protocol I on Non-Detectable Fragments
    - o 1980 Protocol II on Prohibitions or Restrictions on the Use of Mines, Booby-Traps and Other Devices
    - o 1980 Protocol III on Prohibitions or Restrictions on the Use of Incendiary Weapons
    - o 1995 Protocol IV on Blinding Laser Weapons
    - o 1996 Amended Protocol II on Prohibitions or Restrictions on the Use of Mines, Booby-Traps and Other Devices
    - o Protocol on Explosive Remnants of War (Protocol V to the 1980 Convention), 28 November 2003, entered into force on 12 November 2006
- 1994 San Remo Manual on International Law Applicable to Armed Conflicts at Sea.
- 1994 ICRC/UNGA Guidelines for Military Manuals and

Instructions on the Protection of the Environment in Time of Armed Conflict

- 1994 UN Convention on the Safety of United Nations and Associated Personnel
- 1996 The International Court of Justice advisory opinion on the Legality of the Threat or Use of Nuclear Weapons
- 1997 Convention on the Prohibition of the Use, Stockpiling, Production and Transfer of Anti-Personnel Mines and on their Destruction (Ottawa Treaty)
- 1998 Rome Statute of the International Criminal Court entered into force on 1 July 2002.
- 2000 Optional Protocol on the Involvement of Children in Armed Conflict, entered into force on 12 February 2002.

TARGETING AND INTERNATIONAL LAW

During planning, targeting personnel must contend with two external sources of restrictions on weapons and target selection. First, and most basic, are the constraints imposed by inter-national law. Second are other constraints imposed by higher headquarters for military or political rea-sons. This attachment concerns itself solely with the restrictions on weapons and targeting imposed by international law.

General Restrictions on Air Bombardment: The Immunity of Civilians. A4.2.1. Protection of the Civilian Population and Civilian Objects. The civilian population as such, as well as individual civilians, may not be made the object of attack. Acts of violence intended primarily to spread terror among the civilian population are prohibited. Neither may civilian property that is not a military objective be the object of attack.

Non-participation in Hostilities. Civilian immunity carries with a strict obligation on the part of civilians not to take a direct part in hostilities— they must not become combatants. Taking a direct part in hostilities means engaging in acts of war directed toward enemy personnel or material. Civilians who take part in fighting (whether singly or as a member of a group) become combatants and lose their personal immunity.

Requirement to Distinguish. The requirement to distinguish between combatants and civilians and between military objectives and civilian objects imposes obligations on all the parties to a conflict. This is true whatever the legal status of the territory on or over which combat occurs. For example, civilians may not be used in an attempt to render an area immune from military operations. Also, civilians may not be used to shield a defensive position, to hide military objectives, or to screen an attack. Neither may they be forced to leave their homes or shelters in order to disrupt the movement of an adversary.

Military Objectives. Military attacks must be directed only against military objectives. Military objectives are those objects which by their nature, location, purpose, or use make an effective contribution to military action and whose total or partial destruction, capture, or neutralization in the circumstances offers a definite military advantage.

Many objects are clearly military objectives — for example, the enemy's military encampments or armament (such as military aircraft, tanks, antiaircraft emplacements, and troops in the field). Factories, workshops, and plants that directly support the needs of the enemy's armed forces are also generally conceded to be legitimate military objectives.

Controversy exists over whether, and under what circumstances, other objects such as civilian transportation and communications systems, dams, and dikes can properly be classified as military objectives. Modern transportation and communications systems are deemed military objectives because they are used heavily for military purposes in intense conflicts.

However, the inherent nature of an object is not controlling. Even a traditionally civilian object (such as a civilian house) can be a military objective when it is occupied and used by military forces during an armed engagement. The key factor is whether the object makes an effective contribution to the adversary's military action, so that its capture, destruction, or neutralization offers a definite military advantage in the circumstances ruling at the time.

Precautions in Attack. Only a military objective is a

lawful object of attack. Therefore, constant care must be taken when conducting military operations to spare nonmilitary objects and persons, and positive steps must be taken to avoid or minimize any civilian casualties or damage. The principle of pro-portionality must always be followed, which prohibits an attack when the expected collateral civilian casualties or damage to civilian objects is excessive or disproportionate to the military advantage anticipated by the attack.

Types of Precautions. The extent of danger to the civilian population varies with the type of military objective attacked, the type of terrain, the type of weapons used, the kind of weather, and whether civilians are nearby. It also depends on the combatant's ability and mastery of bombardment techniques, the level of the conflict, and the type of resistance encountered during the attack. Therefore the following steps must be taken:

Identification of Military Objectives. Initially, those who plan or decide upon an attack must do everything feasible under the specific circumstances at the time to ensure military objectives, and not civilians or civilian objects, are in fact being attacked. Sound target intelligence enhances military effectiveness by showing that the risks undertaken are militarily worthwhile.

Incidental Civilian Casualties Must Be Minimized. Attacks are not prohibited against military objectives even though they may cause incidental injury or damage to civilians. In spite of precautions, such incidental casualties are inevitable during armed conflict.

- This incidental injury or damage must not outweigh the expected direct military advantage. That is, the potential military advantage must be balanced against the probable degree of incidental injury or damage to civilians. If an attack is carried out efficiently, using the principle of economy of force, against a military installation, it would not be likely to violate this rule.
- On the other hand, if the attack were directed against objects used mainly by the civilian population in an urban area (even though they might also be military objectives), its military benefits would have to be carefully weighed against the risks to civilians.

- Required precautionary measures are reinforced by traditional military doctrines, such as economy of force, concentration of effort, target selection for maximization of military advantage, avoidance of excessive collateral damage, accuracy of targeting, and conservation of resources.

Cancellation or Suspense of Attacks in Case of Mistake. Target intelligence may be found to be faulty before an attack is started or completed. If it is apparent that a given target is not a military objective, or that the target is under the special protection of international law, the attack must be cancelled or suspended. An example of such special protection would be a hospital protected under the 1949 Geneva Conventions.

Warning Requirement. Under the Hague Regulations, a warning must be given prior to bombardment, when circumstances permit, to permit the civilian population an opportunity to avoid injury. The "Hague Rules", written at the Hague Peace Conference of 1907, deal largely with how to fight an enemy who is in the field, and is still fighting, while the Geneva deal chiefly with the respect due our enemy, who is no longer able to fight, as well as treatment of civilians and civilian objects. If civilians are unlikely to be affected by the attack, the warnings need not be given. A general warning may satisfy this requirement, because a specific alert could jeopardize the attack force or the mission.

Prohibition of Attack on Undefended Areas. Under the Hague Regulations, towns, villages, dwellings, or buildings that are undefended may not be attacked or bombarded. An undefended place is any inhabited place near, or in, a zone where opposing armed forces are in contact, and which is open for occupation by an adverse party without resistance.

Separation of Military Activities

International law generally gives civilians "immunity" from attack during armed conflict. However, the parties to a conflict must also take all the precautions practical to protect their own civilian population, individual civilians, and civilian objects. For example, they should remove civilians from military objectives and avoid locating military objectives in or near densely populated areas.

Under the 1949 Geneva Conventions, safety zones or demilitarized zones may be created between the parties of the conflict. Although the creation of such zones is unlikely if past experience is any indication, if created they would be an effective measure to enhance protection of a state's own civilian population.

Under these rules, persons who are combatants are required to wear uniforms, and facilities such as hospitals should be clearly marked. Similarly, international law also requires belligerents to locate military objectives away from hospitals and not to use civilians to shield military objectives from attack.

Result of Failure to Separate Military Activities. A state's failure to segregate and separate its own military activities and to avoid placing military objectives in or near a populated area may greatly weaken protection of its civilian population. Such protection is also compromised when civilians take a direct part in hostilities or are used unlawfully in an attempt to shield attacks against military objectives.

Special Protection. In additional to the general rules for protecting civilians and civilian populations, there are specific rules for protecting certain persons and facilities. Under the 1949 Geneva Conventions, the following persons and objects must be protected from attack:

Wounded and Sick, Medical Units and Hospitals, and Medical Means of Transport.

- Hospitals and other fixed or mobile medical establishments.
- Medical personnel and chaplains.
- Medical transport.
- Medical aircraft, when flying at agreed times on agreed routes.
- Hospital ships and, to the extent possible, sick bays of warships.
- Wounded, sick and shipwrecked persons must not knowingly be attacked, fired upon, or unnecessarily

prevented from discharging their proper function. However, the incidental injury of personnel or damage to objects that are at, or near, a military target which is being attacked by fire, gives no just cause for complaint.

Religious, Cultural, and Charitable Buildings and Monuments. Because they are not used for military purposes, buildings devoted to religion, art or charitable purposes, as well as historical monuments, may not be made the object of air bombardment. However, combatants have a duty to identify such places with distinctive and visible signs. When such buildings are used for military purposes, they may qualify as military objectives and may be attacked. Lawful military objectives are not immune from attack because they are located near such buildings, but all possible precautions must be taken to spare the protected buildings.

Prisoner of War (PW) Camps. Prisoners of war may not be the object of attack. They may not be kept in a combat zone or used to render an area immune from military operations. When military considerations allow it, prisoner of war camps are identified by the letters "PW" or "PG" placed so they are clearly visible from the air. The use of PW camp markings for any other purpose is prohibited.

Weapons: The Distinction Between an Unlawful Weapon and Unlawful Use of a Weapon. International law may prohibit completely the use of a specific weapon or may prohibit a specific use. A weapon is illegal per se if international law has forbidden its use in all circumstances. Poison as a gas, as a coating on munitions, or as a contaminant of water is an example of such an illegal weapon. However, any weapon may be used unlawfully; for example, firing a rifle at civilians or at combatants who have surrendered.

GENERAL PRINCIPLES APPLICABLE TO WEAPONS

Unnecessary Suffering. It is forbidden to employ any method or weapon of warfare which causes superfluous injury or unnecessary suffering. This firmly established rule, incorporated into the Hague Regulations, is a concrete expression of the general principles of proportionality and humanity. All weapons cause suffering. Whether particular weapons or methods of warfare cause unnecessary suffering (and hence are unlawful per se) is best determined by the practice of states. The critical factor is whether the weapon has been designed, or is used, so that it will cause suffering or aggravation of wounds as a separate element in the attack, and not the degree of suffering itself.

Treaties banning specific weapons, such as gas and toxin weapons, also give specific content to this principle. The rule against unnecessary suffering also prohibits the infliction of suffering for its own sake, or for mere indulgence in cruelty. International law has condemned the use of expanding bullets against combatants and determined that it is illegal per se to use:

- Projectiles filled with glass or other materials inherently difficult to detect medically
- Any substance on projectiles that tends unnecessarily to inflame the wound they cause
- Irregularly shaped bullets. It is illegal to score the surface, or file off the ends of the hard cases, of bullets, so that they will expand upon contact and thus aggravate the wound they cause

Indiscriminate Weapons. The law of armed conflict also prohibits the use of any weapon that cannot be directed at a military target. However, a weapon is not unlawful simply because its use may cause incidental civilian casualties. An indiscriminate weapon is one that cannot be controlled, through design or function. Some weapons are considered indiscriminate because, although they can be directed at a military objective, they may have otherwise uncontrollable effects that cause disproportionate civilian injuries or damage. Biological weapons are an example. 150

BIOLOGICAL AND CHEMICAL WEAPONS

Biological Weapons. International law prohibits the use of biological weapons or methods of warfare. These weapons are also prohibited by the 1972 Convention of the Prohibition of the Development, Production, and Stockpiling of Bacteriological (Biological) and Toxin Weapons and on their

Destruction. The US, along with many other states, is party to this treaty.

Chemical Weapons. The 1993 Convention on the Prohibition of the Development, Production, Stockpiling, and Use of Chemical Weapons And on Their Destruction (Chemical Weapons Convention), entered into force on 29 April 1997 and bans the use of chemical weapons as a method of warfare. The Chemical Weapons Convention corrects a shortfall in the 1925 Geneva Protocol for the Prohibition of the Use in War of Asphyxiating, Poisonous or Other Gases and of Bacteriological Methods of Warfare, which prohibits the use of chemical weapons in combat, but not their development, production, stockpiling or transfer.

Herbicides and Riot Control Agents. US policy on herbicides and riot control agents in war is set forth in an Executive Order: The United States renounces, as a matter of national policy, first use of herbicides in war except use, under regulations applicable to their domestic use, for control of vegetation within US bases and installations or around their immediate defensive perimeters and first use of riot control agents in war except in defensive military modes to save lives, such as:

- Use of riot control agents in riot situations in areas under direct and distinct US military control, to include controlling rioting prisoners of war.
- Use of riot control agents in situations in which civilians are used to mask or screen attacks and civilian casualties can be reduced or avoided.
- Use of riot control agents in rescue missions in remotely isolated areas, of downed aircrews and passengers, and escaping prisoners.
- Use of riot control agents in rear echelon areas outside the zone of immediate combat to protect convoys from civil disturbances, terrorists, and paramilitary organizations. The Secretary of Defense shall take all necessary measures to ensure that the use of riot control agents and chemical herbicides in war by US Armed Forces is prohibited unless such use has Presidential approval in advance. Executive Order Number 11850,

> 8 April 1975. The Chemical Weapons Convention bans the use of riot control agents as a method of warfare. However, the use of riot control agents permitted under Executive Order 11850 has been deemed consistent with the Chemical Weapons Convention since the listed uses are not considered 'as a method of warfare. '

Poison. Article 23(a) of the Hague Regulations forbids states to employ poison or poisoned weapons. The prohibition against poison is based on its uncontrolled character, on the fact that it is inevitably disabling or fatal, and on the traditional belief that it is treacherous to use poison.

Nuclear Weapons. The US does not regard the use of explosive nuclear weapons, whether by air, sea, or land forces, as a violation of existing international law. Nuclear weapons can be directed against military objectives as can conventional weapons. However, the authority of United States forces to employ nuclear weapons resides solely with the President. Moreover, the United States is a party to numerous treaties that regulate the use of nuclear devices. Some examples are the Additional Protocol II to the Treaty for the Prohibition of Nuclear Weapons in Latin America, the Outer Space Treaty, and a treaty prohibiting nuclear weapons on the seabed.

CONVENTIONAL WEAPONS AND WEAPONS SYSTEMS

Aircraft, Rockets, and Guided Missiles. The use of aircraft, rockets, and guided missiles by land, sea, or air forces against combatants and other lawful military objectives is clearly permissible.

Fragmentation Weapons. The use of explosives and fragmentation particles, such as those contained in projectiles, mines, bombs, rockets, missiles, and hand grenades, is not prohibited under the law of armed conflict. Cluster bomb units, a more recent development in warfare, are only a refinement or special type of fragmentation munition.

Incendiary Weapons. Incendiary weapons, such as incendiary ammunition, flame throwers, napalm, and other incendiary agents, have widespread uses in armed conflict. They are clearly regarded as lawful in situations requiring their use. Any controversy over their use arises from a concern for the medical problem in treating burn injuries and from arbitrary attempts to analogize their use to the use of prohibited means of chemical warfare. The potential danger of spreading fire has also raised concerns about civilian protection. Their use should be avoided in urban areas, to the extent that other weapons are available and are equally effective.

Delayed Action Weapons. Airdropped mines and other delayed action weapons are legal. However, mines are unlawfully used when they are attached as booby traps to any object that is protected under international law, such as to wounded and sick personnel, dead bodies, or medical facilities. Also objectionable are portable booby traps, such as fountain pens, watches, and trinkets, that would expose any civilians who might be attracted to the object, to an injury. Mines must not be used to prevent the rescue of wounded and sick persons, or to deny civilians protection. Under the Hague Convention VIII, there are specific treaty restrictions on the use of mines in sea warfare.

3

International Law and Armed Conflict

BACKGROUND

The law regulating the use of force at sea has long been due for a re-evaluation in the light of developments in methods and means of warfare at sea and the fact that major changes have taken place in other branches of international law of direct relevance to this issue. This need was reflected in Resolution VII of the 25th International Conference of the Red Cross, which noted that "some areas of international humanitarian law relating to sea warfare are in need of reaffirmation and clarification on the basis of existing fundamental principles of international humanitarian law" and therefore appealed to "governments to co-ordinate their efforts in appropriate fora in order to review the necessity and the possibility of updating the relevant texts of international humanitarian law relating to sea warfare".

Although the law relating to land warfare has been reaffirmed in recent treaties, in particular the two Protocols of 1977 additional to the Geneva Conventions of 1949, this has not been the case as regards the law of armed conflict at sea. The Second Geneva Convention of 1949 deals only with the protection of the wounded, sick and shipwrecked at sea, with some adjustments in Additional Protocol I of 1977, in particular the extension to shipwrecked civilians of the protection laid down in the Second Geneva Convention. However, these treaties do not address the law regulating the conduct of hostilities at sea. Almost all of the treaties on this subject date from 1907, when the Second International Peace Conference at The Hague adopted eight Conventions on the law of naval warfare. One of these has since been overtaken by the Second Geneva Convention and another, on the creation of an international prize court, never entered into force. A third, which regulated bombardment of land targets by naval forces, has in practice been overridden by the rules regulating attacks in Protocol I of 1977. However, these rules in Protocol I apply only to naval attacks that directly affect civilians on land, and therefore do not cover attacks by naval forces on objects, in particular vessels and aircraft, at sea. The 1907 treaties themselves did not represent a complete codification of the law of war at sea, but dealt with certain subjects, namely, the status of enemy merchant ships and their conversion into warships, the laying of automatic contact mines and the immunity of certain vessels from capture. An attempt to draft a more complete treaty took place in London in 1909, but the final Declaration did not enter into force. A non-binding code was drafted by the *Institut de droit international* and adopted in Oxford in 1913. Together, the 1909 London Declaration and the 1913 Oxford Manual give a good idea of pre-First World War customary law.

Events in the First World War showed that the Hague treaties and traditional customary law had begun to be overtaken by developments in methods and means of warfare. The use of submarines, in particular, which were unable to follow procedures required of surface ships, resulted in the torpedoing of merchant vessels in ways which were in violation of the accepted law of the time. Efforts were made, in particular by Great Britain in the 1920s, to outlaw submarines altogether but as this proposal was not accepted a treaty was adopted in 1936 specifying that submarines must abide by the same rules as warships. However, this attempt at regulating new methods of warfare did not solve the problem, which was exacerbated by the subsequent widespread use of aircraft, seamines and long-range missiles. This led to many arbitrary sinkings in the Second World War, including many hospital ships and Red Cross vessels carrying relief supplies.

The customary law that developed prior to the First World War had made an appropriate balance between military and humanitarian needs that suited naval practices and the sailing ships of the nineteenth century. As it is not possible to return to those times, the law needs to be adjusted so that the same balance can be respected with rules that are appropriate for modern conditions. Another major factor is that there have been important developments in other areas of international law such as the United Nations Charter, the law of the sea, air law and environmental law since the Second World War which must be taken into account in any restatement of the law applicable to armed conflicts at sea. The development of the law of armed conflict on land is also of importance, in that all armed conflicts involve operations in which the land, air and sea forces work in close cooperation and it would therefore not be appropriate to have totally different standards. Furthermore, all aspects of armed conflict should be in conformity with the basic principles of international humanitarian law, wherever the theatre of operations might be. However, at the same time it is recognized that there are certain specificities of naval operations that need to be taken into account, in particular the fact that neutral interests are involved at sea to an infinitely greater extent than is the case with land operations.

All these factors have led to a troubling degree of uncertainty as to the content of contemporary international law applicable to armed conflicts at sea. Although operations at sea are not at all as frequent as those on land, several recent conflicts have shown the need for greater certainty in the law applicable to naval warfare. The Falklands/Malvinas conflict brought the first major naval operation since the Second World War, and although it fortunately did not result in any serious problems as regards the safety of civilian or neutral shipping, it did raise significant questions with regard to the use of exclusion zones. Another problem which came to light was the negative effect on the efficiency of hospital ships of the rule in the Second Geneva Convention which prohibits hospital ships from using a secret code. The war between Iran and Iraq, on the other hand, saw extensive attacks on neutral civilian shipping as well as the use of exclusion zones by the belligerents. The downing of the Iranian airbus by the *Vincennes* forcefully brought to light the practical difficulties involved in the correct identification of civilian objects by belligerent naval forces and the unclear relationship between the work of civilian air traffic authorities and the perceived needs of belligerent forces in the area. The second Gulf war involved extensive naval activity when the Coalition forces established a blockade, without formally designating it as such. Of particular interest were the methods used to enforce the blockade and the exceptions to it that were allowed for humanitarian reasons. The extent to which the United Nations Security Council was bound by the rules of international humanitarian law was also an important issue. Finally, it should be mentioned that the laying of seamines has created some difficulty. Such mines were laid in the Iran/Iraq war and some were removed by neutral States. In June 1995, a vessel chartered by the International Committee of the Red Cross to provide relief supplies to civilians in Sri Lanka was severely damaged and sank when it hit a seamine. The government of Sweden has on several occasions proposed a new treaty to the international community on the use of naval mines, first of all in 1989 at the United Nations Disarmament Commission, then in 1991 before the First Committee of the UN General Assembly and now as an additional Protocol to the 1980 Convention on Certain Conventional Weapons. Unfortunately, there is some doubt as to whether this latest initiative will be successful as the Review Conference of the 1980 Convention, which will meet in September-October 1995, will concentrate on landmines and, to a lesser degree, laser weapons.

In recent years some States have prepared naval manuals or further developed and updated military manuals which include sections on the law of naval warfare. The most notable recent naval manual is the United States Commander's Handbook on the Law of Naval Operations (NWP 9A) and its annotated supplement. The new German manual, Humanitarian Law in Armed Conflicts ZDv 15/2, published in 1992, has an important section on armed conflict at sea and a new manual, a large section of which will cover naval operations, is currently being prepared by the United Kingdom.

Although recent conflicts have not involved the very extensive sinking of civilian and other non-combatant shipping that occurred in the Second World War, it still needs to be clearly established that indiscriminate naval operations are unlawful and for this purpose detailed international regulations are necessary.

DEVELOPMENT OF THE SAN REMO MANUAL AND ITS INTENDED PURPOSE

The San Remo Manual was drafted over a period of six years and adopted in June 1994. It is accompanied by a full commentary, entitled the "Explanation". The participants in the groups of experts that prepared the Manual were a mixture of governmental personnel and academics attending in their personal capacity from twenty-four countries.

A series of annual meetings, beginning in San Remo in 1987, were convened by the San Remo International Institute of International Law in cooperation with a number of other institutions, including the International Committee of the Red Cross and several National Societies. The second meeting, which was held in Madrid in 1988 in cooperation with the Spanish Red Cross, established a Plan of Action to draw up a statement of contemporary international law applicable to armed conflicts at sea. Subsequent meetings were held in Bochum, Toulon, Bergen, Ottawa, Geneva and, finally, Livorno. The first four of these meetings were organized in cooperation with the National Societies of Germany, France, Norway and Canada respectively. The ICRC played a major role throughout. Apart from coorganizing the meeting held in Geneva, it offered its advice to the Institute throughout the process, coordinated the drafting work and helped contribute to the administrative and secretarial work. The ICRC also convened three meetings of the rapporteurs, whose reports were the basis of discussion in the annual meetings, in order to organize the drafting of the "Explanation".

The Manual is not a binding document. In view of the extent of uncertainty in the law, the experts decided that it was premature to embark on diplomatic negotiations to draft a treaty on the subject. The work therefore concentrated on finding areas of agreement as to the present content of customary law, which were far more numerous than initially appeared possible. As a second step the experts discussed controversial issues with a view to reaching an agreed compromise on innovative proposals by way of progressive development. However, although the Manual was to contain provisions of this latter type, most of them were always meant to be an expression of what the participants believed to be present law. Thus in many respects the San Remo Manual was intentionally designed to be a modern equivalent of the Oxford Manual of 1913. The experts believed that the drafting of such a document would help clarify the law, thus removing the impression that there was such a degree of disagreement as to render its uniform development in customary law or eventual codification impossible. The experts particularly noted, when embarking on this project, that the result would be very helpful for dissemination purposes and would encourage the drafting of more national manuals.

In 1990, the experts decided that it was important to publish, at the same time as the Manual, a commentary which would indicate the sources of the rules found in the Manual, relate the discussion concerning the more controversial provisions and explain why certain decisions were made. The commentary would also be an indication of which provisions were generally accepted as being declaratory of customary law and which were in the nature of proposals for the progressive development of the law. The intention was that the Manual be read together with this commentary (later named the "Explanation").

CONTENT OF THE SAN REMO MANUAL

The experts' intentions were achieved as regards the content of the Manual and Explanation, and indeed the success of the meetings was such that more issues were dealt with, for example the environment, than was initially planned.

The Manual consists of 183 paragraphs arranged in six parts. Part I, entitled "General Provisions", covers the scope of application of the rules, the effect of the United Nations Charter, the areas of sea in which military operations may take place and definitions of terms used.

Part II, "Regions of Operations", specifies the rules applicable to belligerents and neutrals in different areas of the sea: namely, internal waters, the territorial sea and archipelagic waters; international straits and archipelagic sea lanes; the exclusive economic zone and continental shelf; and, finally, the high seas and seabed beyond national jurisdiction.

Part III, "Basic Rules and Target Discrimination", is by far the longest part and begins by specifying the fundamental tenets of international humanitarian law, which are normally associated with the law applicable to land warfare, but which participants believed are also applicable to warfare at sea. After enunciating the rule that the right of the parties to choose methods or means of warfare is not unlimited, this section repeats the basic rules of the principle of distinction, including the prohibition of indiscriminate attacks, the rule prohibiting the use of weapons that cause unnecessary suffering or superfluous injury, the prohibition of the denial of quarter, and the need to pay due regard to the natural environment.

The rest of Part III contains sections on precautions in attack, enemy vessels and aircraft exempt from attack, enemy or neutral vessels or aircraft that may be subject to attack, and special precautions regarding civil aircraft.

Part IV is entitled "Methods and Means of Warfare at Sea" and contains rules on the use of certain weapons (missiles and other projectiles, torpedoes and mines), the rules applicable to blockades and "zones", and a section on deception, ruses of war and perfidy.

Part V, "Measures Short of Attack Interception, Visit, Search, Diversion and Capture", contains seven sections covering the following subjects: determination of the enemy character of vessels and aircraft; visit, search and diversion of merchant vessels; interception, visit, search and diversion of civil aircraft; and capture of enemy or neutral vessels, civil aircraft and goods.

Part VI, "Protected Persons, Medical Transports and Medical Aircraft", does not attempt to repeat the detailed provisions in the Second Geneva Convention and Additional Protocol I on these categories, but instead specifies that these detailed rules remain applicable and goes on to indicate certain additional rules largely based on recent developments.

Although certain sections of the Manual are not of direct relevance to the rules of international humanitarian law as such, in particular those sections dealing with the effect of the United Nations Charter and regions of naval operations, they were nevertheless felt by the participants to be a necessary component of this Manual, as they help to provide a framework of legal certainty which in turn helps to secure the correct implementation of the rules of international humanitarian law. In particular, the Manual specifies that the rules apply to all parties, irrespective of which party was responsible for the outbreak of the conflict, and that they also apply to operations authorized or undertaken by the United Nations.

However, the most important contribution of the Manual is the reaffirmation and updating of international humanitarian law, taking into account the four Geneva Conventions of 1949 and Additional Protocol I of 1977.

The most important innovation compared with the traditional pre-1914 law was the introduction of a clear formulation of the principle of distinction as formulated in Protocol I. Although in traditional law the only ships that could be attacked on sight were belligerent warships and auxiliaries, various military measures could be taken against both belligerent and neutral shipping that assisted the enemy's war effort, for example by carrying military materials or helping the enemy's intelligence. Such measures were usually limited to the capture of the merchant vessels concerned, and destruction of the vessels was allowed only in certain specific instances and subject to certain conditions, in particular that provision be made for the safety of the passengers and crew. As mentioned above, the introduction this century of new means of warfare, in particular submarines and aircraft, has led to difficulty in the implementation of the traditional law and to attacks on merchant shipping in both World Wars. In order to cope with this, and on the basis of recent State practice and Additional Protocol I, the experts decided to introduce the concept of the military objective. The purpose was to limit attacks to warships (a category which includes submarines), auxiliaries and merchant vessels that directly help the military action of the enemy, while retaining the option of using traditional measures short of attack to other defined vessels. The Manual repeats the definition of military objective found in Article 52 of Additional Protocol I, and it was felt that this would accommodate military needs and at the same time benefit from the gains made by international humanitarian law since the Second World War. However, in addition to this general definition, and unlike Additional Protocol I, the Manual contains examples of activities that would normally cause vessels engaged in them to become military objectives, and this list is meant to provide some concrete guidance. The relevant paragraph reads as follows:

The following activities may render merchant vessels military objectives:

(a) engaging in belligerent acts on behalf of the enemy, e.g., laying mines, minesweeping, cutting undersea cables and pipelines, engaging in visit and search of neutral merchant vessels or attacking other merchant vessels;

(b) acting as an auxiliary to an enemy's armed forces, e.g., carrying troops or replenishing warships;

(c) being incorporated into or assisting the enemy's intelligence gathering system, e.g., engaging in reconnaissance, early warning, surveillance, or command, control and communications missions;

(d) sailing under convoy of enemy warships or military aircraft;

(e) refusing an order to stop or actively resisting visit, search or capture;

(f) being armed to an extent that they could inflict damage to a warship; this excludes light individual weapons for the defence of personnel, e.g., against pirates, and purely deflective systems such as chaff; or

(g) otherwise making an effective contribution to military action, e.g., carrying military materials.

There is also a paragraph relating to the possible attack of neutral vessels, but which, not surprisingly, is narrower and stricter. In addition, the Manual lists vessels that are specifically exempt from capture, on the basis of either treaty law or customary law:

The following classes of enemy vessels are exempt from attack:

(a) hospital ships;

(b) small craft used for coastal rescue operations and other medical transports;

(c) vessels granted safe conduct by agreement between the belligerent parties including:

(i) cartel vessels, e.g., vessels designated for and engaged in the transport of prisoners of war;

(ii) vessels engaged in humanitarian missions, including vessels carrying supplies indispensable to the survival of the civilian population, and vessels engaged in relief actions and rescue operations;

(d) vessels engaged in transporting cultural property under special protection;

(e) passenger vessels when engaged only in carrying civilian passengers;

(f) vessels charged with religious, non-military scientific or philanthropic missions; vessels collecting scientific data of likely military applications are not protected;

(g) small coastal fishing vessels and small boats engaged in local coastal trade, but they are subject to the regulations of a belligerent naval commander operating in the area and to inspection;

(h) vessels designated or adapted exclusively for responding to pollution incidents in the marine environment;

(i) vessels which have surrendered;

(j) life rafts and lifeboats.

The Manual contains a section on precautions to be taken before launching an attack, similar to those found in Article 57 of Protocol I, which is intended to help avoid unlawful attacks.

However, the Manual does not deal only with vessels. The experts recognized that aircraft play an important part in naval operations and that any realistic manual would have to take this fully into account. Therefore there are similar provisions, *mutatis mutandis*, on aircraft that may be attacked and those which are exempt from attack. There is also a section on special precautions in relation to civil aviation in order to try to avoid making attacks on innocent civilian aircraft. For this purpose, the experts made reference to international civil aviation rules promulgated by the ICAO. In general these provisions in the San Remo Manual are a pragmatic attempt to marry military necessities, international humanitarian law and civil aviation rules.

The use of different sea areas, although not strictly within the scope of international humanitarian law, was also an important innovation which needed to take into account the contemporary law of the sea, in particular as contained in the 1982 Law of the Sea Convention. Here again, it was not always so easy to combine military necessities whilst respecting as far as possible the provisions of that Convention. Controversial areas were rules relating to the protection of the environment, freedom of navigation and the special rights of exploration and exploitation in the exclusive economic zones of neutral States, and particularly the lawfulness or otherwise of the creation of zones (normally referred to as exclusion zones) which adversely affect the right of navigation of neutral shipping. Despite this, it may be seen as an important achievement that the Manual specifies that if such zones are created international humanitarian law must be nevertheless respected in its entirety.

Of great importance is the fact that the Manual includes rules relating to the protection of protected persons similar to those in both the Geneva Conventions of 1949 and Additional Protocol I of 1977. Since the last comprehensive international instrument on the law of naval warfare dates back to 1913, this inclusion was necessary. The Manual does not repeat the entire content of the Second Geneva Convention and Protocol I, which would be unnecessary, but makes a specific reference to the fact that provisions on the protection of protected persons are to be found in those instruments. It does, however, contain a section on the status and treatment of all persons recovered at sea. In particular it specifies that civilians captured at sea are protected by the Fourth Geneva Convention; this is an improvement on the traditional law, which indicates only that they are subject to the discipline of the captor. Apart from specific provisions on the treatment of the wounded, sick and shipwrecked found in the Second Geneva Convention and Additional Protocol I, much of the law in existing treaties and other authorities on the status and treatment of persons captured at sea is fragmentary and incomplete. Therefore in addition to clarifying accepted rules of customary law, some of the rules in the Manual are in the nature of progressive development. The same section of the Manual contains some specific rules relating to the protection of medical ships and aircraft found in Protocol I and encourages the use of the means of identification introduced by Annex I of that Protocol.

Finally, specific mention must be made of the fact that the Manual lays down that starvation blockades are unlawful and requires the blockading power to allow relief shipments if a secondary effect of the blockade is that civilians are short of food or other essential supplies. This is a definite departure from traditional law and reflects the new rules prohibiting the starvation of the civilian population and stipulating the provision of relief supplies which were introduced in Protocol I in 1977 and are now generally seen as having become an established part of international customary law.

As the San Remo Manual is the only comprehensive international instrument that has been drafted on the law of naval warfare since 1913, it is likely to have an important impact. It has already influenced the provisions relating to naval warfare in the German manual and it is quite likely that future manuals will also be so influenced. In this way the San Remo Manual should help consolidate contemporary international customary law, promote its coherent development and thereby provide a much firmer foundation for possible future treaty developments than could otherwise have been the case. The Manual and accompanying Explanation will also be very useful for dissemination purposes, which should in turn promote a better respect for the law.

HISTORICAL BACKGROUND OF JUST WAR THEORY

One of the perennial realities of human existence is war. From the earliest recorded events of human history all the way through to modern times, human communities have engaged in armed conflict as a method of dispute resolution. While war has been a constant part of the human experience, there has also been a tendency within virtually all human civilizations to limit the extent of war and the methods by which warfare may be conducted. In Western civilization, this limitation on warfare has taken shape as an effort to limit both the determination of when war is appropriate and the means used in battle.

Within the Western moral, legal, and political arena, the connected questions of when war is appropriate and what means are acceptable in warfare has been the subject of a great deal of examination. The basic theory which has arisen within Western culture to evaluate the legitimacy of military action is called just war theory. The just war theory has received widespread acceptance both within Western culture and in the international community as a means by which a war may be determined to be justified or not. Just war theory, which has both religious and secular proponents, is perhaps the most universally recognized moral theory by which the use of force may be evaluated.

This article will attempt to determine whether the decision by the United States government to launch air strikes against Iraqi military forces in September, 1996 is justified under just war theory. This article will first present a general overview of just war theory, including its background, main sources, and generally recognized principles. This article will then present a brief factual overview of the U.S. action, and will analyze that action in light of the criteria of just war theory, demonstrating that the recent U.S. military strikes against Iraq do not meet the criteria of just war theory as commonly understood.

A GENERAL OVERVIEW OF JUST WAR THEORY

Just war theory has a varied and diverse background. The just war tradition includes the contributions of philosophers and theologians dating back to Roman times. As James Tuner

Johnson has pointed out, Just war is an historical tradition formed by experience and reflection, including much that is neither specifically theological (or even religious), nor philosophical. It has been strongly influenced by international law, the traditions of chivalry, and soldierly practices derived from the experience of many battles.

Just war theory as a method of evaluating military actions has been recognized historically by thinkers as varied as Cicero, St. Augustine, St. Thomas Aquinas, Grotius, and Daniel Webster. It is a theory which has been used by Christians and non-Christians alike to determine whether or not the decision to go to war and the means used to prosecute that war are just. It is crucial to keep this varied and complex pedigree of the just war tradition in mind when dealing with just war theory, otherwise it becomes possible to restrict the "breadth and diversity of the tradition," which could in turn lead to a serious misapplication of the theory in a particular circumstance. Understanding, then, that the theory of just war is one in which many sources mingle over the course of centuries, it is helpful to make a brief overview of those sources before delving into the main task of explaining and applying just war theory to the particular problem raised in this article, namely, whether the recent use of force by the United States against Iraq is justified under the theory.

The Religious Sources of Just War Theory

Many of the key thinkers who have expounded on just war theory through the centuries have identified themselves with the Christian faith, both in its Catholic and Protestant varieties. Just war theory has also gained a general acceptance among Christian theologians, philosophers, and jurists as a method of passing judgment on the morality or immorality of a particular conflict. The general Christian conception of just war theory forms the core of secular just war theory and as such has had a tremendous influence on the secular conception of the just war.

Early Christian approaches to war were largely pacifistic in nature, due to a focus in the early Church to the notion that Christians were distinct from the rest of society. However, with the growing Christianization of the Roman Empire, and the increasing political and social influence of the Christian Church, Christian theologians during the fourth and fifth centuries began to develop justifications for the use of force which would eventually take shape over time as just war theory.

The first major Christian theologian to address himself to the task of determining the circumstances under which war is legitimate was St. Augustine of Hippo. Augustine held that "[t]he natural order, which is suited to the peace of moral things, requires that the authority and deliberation for undertaking war be under the control of a leader." For Augustine, war is a permissible part of the life of a nation, and the power of prosecuting a war was part of the natural powers of a monarch, ordained to uphold peace. War, far from being something which Christians should shun, is part of the life of a nation, ordained by natural law, a law which according to the New Testament is ordained by God.

Augustine's conception of the just war did not create a carte blanche for bloodshed. In formulating his ideas on war, St. Augustine was careful to state the purposes for which war may be fought, and the procedural means which must be satisfied in order for a war to be just. "[F]or it makes a great difference," he wrote, "by which causes and under which authorities men undertake the wars that must be waged." For Augustine, for a war to be just, it must be fought for the right reasons, and it must be waged under rightful authority.

Augustine held that the only reason which justified war was the desire for peace. "Peace is not sought in order to provide war, but war is waged in order to attain peace." Augustine criticizes other motives for war, such as "[t]he desire for harming, the cruelty of revenge, the restless and implacable mind, the savageness of revolting, the lust for dominating, and similar things," and refers to them as things which are "justly blamed in wars." In fighting a war, the goal must be to do that which is necessary to obtain peace; "[l]et necessity slay the warring foe, not your will." Augustine also includes under the subject of necessity the just treatment of prisoners and conquered peoples, making it clear that mercy should be shown to the vanquished, particularly if they are no longer a threat to peace. Besides right intention, St. Augustine also held that it was necessary for a war to be waged under lawful authority. The purpose of the war-making powers of the state is to ensure peace, which in turn helps to foster the common-good of those in society. Augustine recognized that it was necessary for the authority and decision to undertake war to be made by a recognized leader. In addition, the soldiers who serve under the leader must serve the peace and common-good of society. Warfare which is declared by unlawful authority therefore fails to meet this criteria, as does warfare which is not directed toward peace and the common good.

The second major Christian thinker to deal with the issue of war is St. Thomas Aquinas (1225-1274). Aquinas based himself upon St. Augustine's view of war, elaborating on the teachings of the bishop of Hippo. In explicating his theory regarding the justness of a war, Aquinas focused on defining the right to make war and the importance of the intent which stands behind the decision to go to war. In his attempt to formulate a simple rule which would give guidance on these issues, Aquinas argued that a war is justified when three basic, necessary conditions were met: 1. the war was prosecuted by a lawful authority with the power to wage war; 2. the war was undertaken with just cause; and 3. the war was undertaken with the right intention, that is, "to achieve some good or to avoid some evil." Together with St. Augustine, Aquinas' views on the justification of war form the basic core of just war theory, and it is from their concepts that the theory of just war is adapted and expanded by later thinkers.

Secular Sources of Just War Theory

The secular sources for just war theory span a considerable length of time. They include such philosophers as the ancient Roman Cicero and the Dutch Protestant Hugo Grotius. In addition, modern decrees on justifiable warfare, such as the commission to the Nuremberg War Crimes Tribunal, and the United Nations Charter also act to flush out the modern conception of just war theory.

Cicero, the great Roman orator, jurist, and philosopher was one of the first to deal with the questions of justifiable war.

Cicero held that the use of force was justifiable only when the war was declared by an appropriate governmental authority acting within specific limits. For Cicero, the ability to wage war rested with the state, and the state alone, and could be lawfully waged only "after an official demand for satisfaction has been submitted or warning has been given and a formal declaration made." In addition, Cicero also proposed the existence of a universal norm for human behaviour which transcended the laws of individual nations and governed their relations with each other. Cicero's belief in this universal norm was grounded in his view that there was a humani generis societas, a "society of mankind [sic] rather than of states." This view of a universal standard of behaviour for nation-states which exists outside of promulgated law would have a profound impact on later just war theorists, particularly on Hugo Grotius.

Grotius was a 16th century Dutch Protestant who is sometimes referred to as the father of international law. Grotius, who lived in the aftermath of the brutal Thirty-Years War in Europe, wrote extensively on the right of nations to use force in self-defense in his book Jure Belli ac Pacis ("On the Rights of War and Peace"), which was published in 1625. It was largely Grotius who secularized just war theory, making the theory more acceptable for the age of the Enlightenment. For Grotius, a war is just if three basic criteria were met: 1) the danger faced by the nation is immediate; 2) the force used is necessary to adequately defend the nation's interests; and 3) the use of force is proportionate to the threatened danger.

Grotius grounded his agreement with Cicero's notion of the need for a declaration of war in the natural law, and also argued that the purpose of just war theory is to provide "succor and protection for the sick and wounded in war, combatants and civilians alike." A result of this view is the notion that just war theory exists externally of any recognized legal system, that it is a part of the "law of nations" which is followed by all civilized nations. For Grotius, it is not necessary to prove just war theory by consulting with any of the established laws of the nations of Europe, or their customs. Rather, those laws are known through the universal medium of the natural law, a law which transcends nations and their own particular legal codes, a law which is binding on all human societies in their interactions with each other.

After Grotius, just war theory underwent relatively few modifications until the nineteenth century. During the first century of it's existence, the United States' government came to acknowledge the legitimacy of just war theory. In 1842, the U.S. Secretary of State, Daniel Webster, acknowledged the legitimacy of the customary norms employed by Grotius to define the just war. This recognition occurred as a result of attempts to resolve the so-called "Caroline Incident."

The Caroline Incident occurred when the British attempted to prevent supplies from reaching Canadian rebels. In their attempts to restrict the flow of material to the rebels, the British burned the U.S. ship Caroline and killed several U.S. citizens. When the United States protested, the British government responded that its actions were justified as a matter of self-defense. Webster responded by stating that the only way for the British claim to self-defense to stand was if it met the traditional elements of just self-defense. Webster outlined those elements as consisting of necessity of self-defense, and the reasonable and not excessive use of force. In essence, this definition of just self-defense mirrors that proposed by Grotius.

During the remainder of the 19th and early 20th centuries, just war theory underwent modest development. There were treaties, such as the Hague Conventions, which codified just war theory, but there was little major development in just war theory. That changed with the end of the Second World War. As a result of World War II, two basic documents were issued which resulted in increased recognition of just war theory in the international arena. The first document is the charter for the Nuremberg war crimes trials, and the second is the United Nations Charter. The Nuremberg Charter encapsulated the reigning notion of just war theory as represented by both St. Thomas Aquinas and Grotius. The Nuremberg Tribunal established that just war theory, as Grotius understood it, is universally binding customary law.

The United Nations Charter also has contributed to just war theory by recognizing the inherent right of each sovereign nation to self-defense. Article 51 of the U.N. Charter affirms the right of each nation to self-defense, until the Security Council can take action in order to restore and stabilize international peace and security. Article 51 states two key points in regard to international relations and the rightful use of force in international disputes: 1) the regulation of the use of force; and 2) collective security. The U.N. Charter effectively outlaws the use of military force as a method of resolving international conflicts between nation-states. At the same time, the charter recognizes the inherent right of each nation to defend itself from an attack from an exterior foe which is by its very nature unlawful. This right of a nation to engage in defensive military actions has also been upheld by the International Court of Justice in its ruling in the case of Nicaragua v. United States of America. In that case, Nicaragua brought action against the United States for its support of insurgency forces attempting to overthrow the Sandinista government in Nicaragua. The International Court of Justice in its ruling held that the right of a nation to engage in self-defense, as customarily understood, was incorporated into Article 51 of the U.N. Charter. As the Court stated, "[i]n the language of Article 51 of the United Nations Charter, the inherent right (or droit naturel) which a State possesses in the event of an armed attack, covers both collective and individual self-defense."

GENERALLY RECOGNIZED PRINCIPLES OF JUST WAR THEORY

As the proceeding section has demonstrated, just war theory, despite its diverse sources and historical development, has several commonly recognized elements. These elements are traditionally divided into two basic categories which deal with the two basic fundamental issues regarding the legitimacy of war. The first issue, sometimes referred to in Latin as the jus ad bellum (literally, "that which is right or just to engage in resort to war"), concerns when it is appropriate to resort to war as a method of conflict resolution. The second issue, jus in bello (literally, "that which is right or just within war") deals with what methods of warfare are permissible within the context of a war which meets the criteria of the jus ad bellum. Since this article is interested only in evaluating the validity of the decision made by the U.S. government to launch air strikes against Iraq, it will limit its discussion on just war theory to the jus ad bellum.

The core elements of the jus ad bellum consist of those principles which were originally recognized by the medieval commentators on just war theory as being most central to the whole doctrine of just war. As elucidated by St. Thomas Aquinas, the core principles consist of the following three elements: 1) just cause; 2) competent authority; and 3) right intention.

Just cause is classically understood to refer to self-defense. The use of military force is justified when it is used to repel an unjust aggressor and to retake that which the unjust aggressor has taken. It is generally acknowledged that a nation may use force to protect a neighboring state from attack from an outside hostile power. Thus, defense of self, or defense of another, are legitimate reasons for a nation-state to resort to military force.

The second element of jus ad bellum is that the war must be declared by competent authority. As recognized by theorists like Cicero and Aquinas, for a war to be just, the decision to go to war must be lawfully made. If an illegal or non-legal authority within an nation made the decision to go to war, such a decision would be unjust, for it would violate the basic principles of how a given society is governed.

Finally, the war must be fought with right intention, meaning that the motives for the war must not be to inflict undue suffering on the enemy state; the defending nation must use only that amount of force which is necessary for it to achieve its just cause. The motives of those engaged in making the decision to go to war must not be tinged with vengeance or a desire for retribution. Rather, the decision to go to war must be essentially protective; the goal of war is to obtain a just and durable peace. Such a peace is unlikely if the war is waged out of hateful or vengeful motives, with a desire not solely for self-protection but the total destruction of the enemy. If in it's actions, the defending state's use of force exceeds what is necessary for the success of its just cause, the defending state's right intention is problematic. Seen this way, right intention serves to reinforce the requirement that the state which seeks to justly use force be acting in a truly defensive capacity, rather than engaging in military adventurism on the pretext of self-defense.

APPLICATION OF JUST WAR THEORY TO U.S. ACTIONS

On September 3, 1996 the United States military began air strikes against Iraqi military positions in both northern and southern Iraq. The air strikes were in retaliation for official Iraqi government support for the Kurdistan Democratic Party (K.D.P.), a Kurdish faction which had, with Iraqi assistance, taken control of the northern city of Irbil. The K.D.P, one of two Kurdish factions which at that time were vying for control of the northern Kurdish safe haven, had swept its U.S.-backed Kurdish rival, the Patriotic Union of Kurdistan (P.U.K.) out of the city.

The U.S. military retaliation lasted for two days. On September 11 and 12, Iraqi forces launched anti-aircraft missiles at U.S. warplanes patrolling the southern "no-fly zone" near the border with Kuwait. This action prompted U.S. Secretary of Defense William Perry to state that "the responses we will make...will be disproportionate with the provocations which are made against us." The U.S. justified its actions by citing to a 1991 U.N. resolution which demanded that Iraq cease oppressing the Kurds.

The threat of retaliation on the part of the United States led the Iraqi government to agree to cease targeting U.S. and other allied patrol aircraft in the southern no-fly zone. This led to a de-escalation of the tensions in the region. On September 25, the United States announced that it no longer supported the Kurdish safe haven in northern Iraq, and that it had plans to relocate pro-U.S. Kurds to the United States. When questioned by the House of Representatives International Relations Committee about the policy shift, Robert Pelletreau, the senior Clinton Administration advisor on Iraq, stated that the Clinton Administration never had a policy of defending the Kurdish safe haven from Iraqi repression.

Analysis of U.S. Action

Under the generally recognized principles of just war theory, the actions taken by the United States cannot meet the requirements of the jus ad bellum. The requirements of the jus ad bellum under just war theory are essentially three-fold: just cause; competent authority; and right intention. The decision by the United States to launch air strikes against Iraq in September 1996 do not meet the requirements of the just cause prong, nor is it likely to meet the requirement for right intention.

The issue under the first requirement is whether the United States acted with just cause in using military force to punish the Iraqi government for its intervention in the conflict between Kurdish factions in northern Iraq. Just cause has generally been understood to mean self-defense. If self-defense is narrowly construed in this case, the United States obviously does not meet the just cause requirement because the original provocation by the Iraqis (the intervention in the northern Kurdish safe haven) was not directed against any American territory or citizens. However, just war theory has usually recognized the principle of defense of another, where one state may come to the aid of another state which is being unjustly attacked by a third state. If this understanding of self-defense as including defense of another is used, an argument can be made that the United States' actions are justified as an effort to defend the Kurds in the safe haven. Since the United States sought to retaliate against Iraqi actions against the Patriotic Union of Kurdistan, an argument could be made that the U.S. military strikes were carried out in an effort to defend the P.U.K.

A more serious problem with the United States' use of military force in this situation concerns the nature of the Iraqi military action which provoked the U.S. action. Unlike the Iraqi invasion of Kuwait, the Iraqi military's support of the K.D.P. occurred within the recognized borders of Iraq. There was no international act of aggression by the Iraqis because the Iraqi military operations did not cross international boundaries. The dispute between the Kurdish factions in the north was a dispute that took place within the recognized borders of Iraq, borders which are recognized under international law and the United Nations Charter. The military actions undertaken by Iraqi forces were undertaken within the boundaries of Iraq. As such, there are only two states involved in this conflict: the United States and Iraq. There simply is no

Kurdish state for the United States to be able to defend. It is widely accepted under international law that there is no right for a nation to intervene on behalf of a revolutionary group in another nation. For this reason, the claim that the U.S. use of force was legitimate in order to defend the Kurds is problematic.

A central problem with the U.S. action is that it seems unlikely that the U.S. use of force was intended to defend the Kurds. The original U.S. justification for the attack, namely Iraqi aggression in the north, becomes problematic when seen in the light of the policy statement made before Congress by the senior Clinton Administration advisor on Iraq.

The fact that most U.S. military action took place in the southern Iraqi no-fly zone set up by the United Nations at the close of the Gulf War also makes the original justification for the attack hard to accept. Within a month of the military intervention, which was undertaken ostensibly to increase the security of the northern Kurdish safe haven, the United States announced plans to completely abandon its policy supporting the integrity of the northern Kurdish zone. Further, the U.S. attacks were disproportionately targeted at the south, away from the Kurdish zone, in an effort to "materially [reduce Iraq's] ability to mount a threat" to the Gulf states. This only makes sense if the actual U.S. intent in this use of force was not to protect the Kurds, but Kuwait.

It is probable that the United States is unable to meet the requirements of the just cause criteria of the just war theory. It is unlikely that the United States acted in defense of the Kurds in the north. Even if the U.S.'s actions were based on a desire to defend the Kurds, the attacks were launched against a sovereign nation which was not engaged in acts of international aggression.

For these reasons, the United States' action fails to meet the just cause criteria of the just war theory; thus failing to meet the overall requirements for its military action against Iraq to be justifiable under the theory. Despite the failure of the United States to meet the just cause criteria of just war theory, it is still useful to examine the U.S. actions in regard to the other criteria of just war theory in order to see how those criteria apply in this case. The second requirement for just war under the criteria of jus ad bellum is that the war be prosecuted by competent authority. Were the U.S. military strikes undertaken under the color of legitimate, legal authority? It would appear that the U.S. did act within the constraints of this requirement. The President of the United States, under the American Constitution, has the lawful authority, as commander-in-chief, to use military force, so long as Congress is notified. The constitutional and legal requirements of this action were met, so the U.S. action was carried out by competent authority.

Finally, the last requirement is that the military action be carried out with right intention. Right intention requires that the action be carried out without the motivation of inflicting gratuitous suffering out of a desire to punish the aggressor nation-state. The U.S. strikes were precise and carefully targeted against military targets. In this regard, it can safely be said that the United States did not inflict gratuitous suffering on either the Iraqi people or the Iraqi military. However, there is an issue as to whether the U.S. action was designed to punish Iraq for its use of force in support of the K.D.P. If the attacks were designed as a punishment for Iraq, then right intention would not be met. The U.S. strikes were targeted not only at Iraqi forces in the Kurdish safe haven; most of the attacks were launched against military positions south of Baghdad. This behaviour would indicate that the purpose of the attacks was not to rectify a particular situation, but to punish Iraq. Such a punitive intent colors the whole of the U.S. action, and makes it difficult to see how the U.S.'s use of force could meet the criteria of right intention.

LAW OF ARMED CONFLICT AND THE RULES OF WAR

LOAC Defined

The LOAC arises from a desire among civilized nations to prevent unnecessary suffering and destruction while not impeding the effective waging of war. A part of public international law, LOAC regulates the conduct of armed hostilities. It also aims to protect civilians, prisoners of war, the wounded, sick, and shipwrecked. LOAC applies to international armed conflicts and in the conduct of military operations and related activities in armed conflict, however such conflicts are characterized.

LOAC Policy

DoDD 5100.77, *DoD Law of War Program*, requires each military department to design a program that ensures LOAC observance, prevents LOAC violations, ensures prompt reporting of alleged LOAC violations, appropriately trains all forces in LOAC, and completes a legal review of new weapons. Although some of the services often refer to LOAC as the law of war (LOW), within this this article LOAC and LOW are the same. LOAC training is a treaty obligation of the United States under provisions of the 1949 Geneva Conventions. The training should be of a general nature; however, certain groups such as aircrews, special forces, special operations, infantry, medical personnel, and security forces, etc., receive additional, specialized training that addresses the unique issues they may encounter.

INTERNATIONAL AND DOMESTIC LAW

LOAC comes from both customary international law and treaties. Customary international law, based on practice that nations have come to accept as legally required, establishes the traditional rules that govern the conduct of military operations in armed conflict. Article VI of the US Constitution states that treaty obligations of the United States are the "supreme law of the land," and the US Supreme Court has held that international law, to include custom, are part of US law. This means that treaties and agreements the United States enters into enjoy equal status as laws passed by Congress and signed by the President. Therefore, all persons subject to US law must observe the United States' LOAC obligations. In particular, military personnel must consider LOAC to plan and execute operations and must obey LOAC in combat. Those who violate LOAC may be held criminally liable for war crimes and court-martialed under the Uniform Code of Military Justice (UCMJ).

Principles

Three important LOAC principles govern armed conflict—military necessity, distinction, and proportionality.

Military Necessity. Military necessity requires combat forces to engage in only those acts necessary to accomplish a legitimate military objective. Attacks shall be limited strictly to military objectives. In applying military necessity to targeting, the rule generally means the United States Military may target those facilities, equipment, and forces which, if destroyed, would lead as quickly as possible to the enemy's partial or complete submission.

As an example of compliance with the principle of military necessity during Operation Desert Storm, consider our targeting and destruction of Iraqi SCUD missile batteries and of Iraqi army and air forces. These actions quickly achieved air superiority and hastened the Iraqi military's defeat.

Military necessity also applies to weapons review. AFI 51-402, Weapons Review, requires the Air Force to perform a legal review of all weapons and weapons systems intended to meet a military requirement. These reviews ensure the United States complies with its international obligations, especially those relating to the LOAC, and it helps military planners ensure military personnel do not use weapons or weapons systems that violate international law. Illegal arms for combat include poison weapons and expanding hollow point bullets in armed conflict. Even lawful weapons may require some restrictions on their use in particular circumstances to increase compliance with the LOAC.

Distinction. Distinction means discriminating between lawful combatant targets and noncombatant targets such as civilians, civilian property, POWs, and wounded personnel who are out of combat. The central idea of distinction is to only engage valid military targets. An indiscriminate attack is one that strikes military objectives and civilians or civilian objects without distinction. Distinction requires defenders to separate military objects from civilian objects to the maximum extent feasible. Therefore, it would be inappropriate to locate a hospital or POW camp next to an ammunition factory.

Proportionality. Proportionality prohibits the use of any kind or degree of force that exceeds that needed to accomplish the military objective. Proportionality compares the military advantage gained to the harm inflicted while gaining this advantage. Proportionality requires a balancing test between the concrete and direct military advantage anticipated by attacking a legitimate military target and the expected incidental civilian injury or damage. Under this balancing test, excessive incidental losses are prohibited. Proportionality seeks to prevent an attack in situations where civilian casualties would clearly outweigh military gains. This principle encourages combat forces to minimize collateral damage—the incidental, unintended destruction that occurs as a result of a lawful attack against a legitimate military target.

The Geneva Conventions of 1949

Some of the most important LOAC rules come from the Geneva Conventions of 1949. The Geneva Conventions consist of four separate international treaties. These treaties aim to protect combatants and noncombatants from unnecessary suffering who may become wounded, sick, shipwrecked, or POWs during hostilities. They also seek to protect civilians and private property. The four treaties govern the treatment of wounded and sick forces, POWs, and civilians during war or armed conflict.

Combatants

The Geneva Conventions distinguish between lawful combatants, noncombatants, and unlawful combatants.

Lawful Combatants. A lawful combatant is an individual authorized by governmental authority or the LOAC to engage in hostilities. A lawful combatant may be a member of a regular armed force or an irregular force. In either case, the lawful combatant must be commanded by a person responsible for subordinates; have fixed distinctive emblems recognizable at a distance, such as uniforms; carry arms openly; and conduct his or her combat operations according to the LOAC. The LOAC applies to lawful combatants who engage in the hostilities of armed conflict and provides combatant immunity for their lawful warlike acts during conflict, except for LOAC violations.

Noncombatants. These individuals are not authorized by governmental authority or the LOAC to engage in hostilities. In fact, they do not engage in hostilities. This category includes civilians accompanying the Armed Forces; combatants who are out of combat, such as POWs and the wounded, and certain military personnel who are members of the Armed Forces not authorized to engage in combatant activities, such as medical personnel and chaplains. Noncombatants may not be made the object of direct attack. They may, however, suffer injury or death incident to a direct attack on a military objective without such an attack violating the LOAC, if such attack is on a lawful target by lawful means.

Unlawful Combatants. Unlawful combatants are individuals who directly participate in hostilities without being authorized by governmental authority or under international law to do so. For example, bandits who rob and plunder and civilians who attack a downed airman are unlawful combatants. Unlawful combatants who engage in hostilities violate LOAC and become lawful targets. They may be killed or wounded and, if captured, may be tried as war criminals for their LOAC violations.

Undetermined Status. Should doubt exist as to whether an individual is a lawful combatant, noncombatant, or an unlawful combatant, such person shall be extended the protections of the Geneva Prisoner of War Convention until status is determined. The capturing nation must convene a competent tribunal to determine the detained person's status.

Military Targets

The LOAC governs the conduct of aerial warfare. The principle of military necessity limits aerial attacks to lawful military targets. Military targets are those that by their own nature, location, purpose, or use make an effective contribution to an enemy's military capability and whose total or partial destruction, capture, or neutralization in the circumstances existing at the time of an attack enhance legitimate military objectives.

Targeting Personnel. The LOAC protects civilian populations. Military attacks against cities, towns, or villages not justified by military necessity are forbidden. Attacking noncombatants (generally referred to as civilians) for the sole purpose of terrorizing them is also prohibited. Although civilians may not be made the object of a direct attack, the LOAC recognizes that a military target need not be spared because its destruction may cause collateral damage that results in the unintended death or injury to civilians or damage to their property.

Commanders and their planners must take into consideration the extent of unintended indirect civilian destruction and probable casualties that will result from a direct attack on a military objective and, to the extent consistent with military necessity, seek to avoid or minimize civilian casualties and destruction. Anticipated civilian losses must be proportionate to the military advantages sought. Judge advocate, intelligence, and operations personnel play a critical role in determining the propriety of a target and the choice of weapon to be used under the particular circumstances known to the commander when planning an attack.

Targeting Objects. The LOAC specifically describes objects that shall not be the targets of a direct attack. Reflecting the rule that military operations must be directed at military objectives, objects normally dedicated to peaceful purposes enjoy a general immunity from direct attack. Specific protection applies to medical units or establishments; transports of wounded and sick personnel; military and civilian hospital ships; safety zones established under the Geneva Conventions; and religious, cultural, and charitable buildings, monuments, and POW camps. However, if these objects are used for military purposes, they lose their immunity. If these protected objects are located near lawful military objectives (which LOAC prohibits), they may suffer collateral damage when the nearby military objectives are lawfully engaged.

Aircraft and Combat

Enemy Military Aircraft and Aircrew. Enemy military aircraft may be attacked and destroyed wherever found, unless in neutral airspace. An attack on enemy military aircraft must be discontinued if the aircraft is clearly disabled and has lost its means of combat. Airmen who parachute from a disabled aircraft and offer no resistance may not be attacked. Airmen who resist in descent or are downed behind their own lines and who continue to fight may be subject to attack. The rules of engagement (ROE) for a particular operation often provide additional guidance consistent with LOAC obligations for attacking enemy aircraft.

Enemy Civilian Aircraft. An enemy's public and private nonmilitary aircraft are generally not subject to attack because the LOAC protects noncombatants from direct attack. Since WWII, nations have increasingly recognized the necessity to avoid attacking civil aircraft. Under exceptional conditions, however, civil aircraft may be lawfully attacked. If the civil aircraft initiates an attack, it may be considered an immediate military threat and attacked. An immediate military threat justifying an attack may also exist when reasonable suspicion exists of a hostile intent, as when such aircraft approaches a military base at high speed or enters enemy territory without permission and disregards signals or warnings to land or proceed to a designated place.

Enemy Military Medical Aircraft. Enemy military medical aircraft is generally not subject to attack under the LOAC. However, at least six instances may lead to a lawful attack. Enemy military medical aircraft could be lawfully attacked and destroyed if it:

- Initiates an attack.
- Is not exclusively employed as a medical aircraft.
- Does not bear a clearly marked Red Cross, Red Crescent, or other recognized symbol and is not otherwise known to be an exclusively medical aircraft.
- Does not fly at heights, at times, and on routes specifically agreed to by the parties to the conflict and is not otherwise known to be an exclusively medical aircraft.
- Flies over enemy territory or enemy-occupied territory (unless otherwise agreed upon by the parties).
- Approaches its enemy's territory or a combat zone and disregards a summons to land.

Enforcing LOAC Rules

Military members who violate the LOAC are subject to criminal prosecution and punishment. Criminal prosecutions may take place in a national or international forum. In theory, US Armed Forces could be prosecuted by courts-martial under the UCMJ or through an international military tribunal, such as those used in Nuremberg and Tokyo after WWII or in Yugoslavia and Rwanda.

The defense, "I was only following orders," has generally not been accepted by national or international tribunals as a defense in war crime trials. An individual airman/soldier/sailor/marine remains responsible for his or her actions and is expected to comply with the LOAC.

Reprisal. Prosecuting a LOAC violation may not be possible or practical if the enemy who violates the LOAC remains engaged in armed conflict. However, there is no statute of limitations on a war crime. Moreover, the LOAC permits combatants to engage in acts of reprisal to enforce an enemy force's compliance with LOAC rules. Reprisals are acts in response to LOAC violations. The act of reprisal would be otherwise forbidden if it was not for the prior unlawful act of the enemy. A lawful act of reprisal cannot be the basis for a counter-reprisal. Reprisals are always prohibited if directed against POWs; wounded, sick, or shipwrecked persons at sea; civilian persons and their property; or religious or cultural property. To be lawful, a reprisal must:

- Timely respond to grave and manifestly (clearly) unlawful acts.
- Be for the purpose of compelling the adversary to observe the LOAC and not for revenge, spite, or punishment.
- Give reasonable notice that reprisals will be taken.
- Have had other reasonable means attempted to secure compliance.
- Be directed against the personnel or property of an adversary.
- Be proportional to the original violation.
- Be publicized.
- Be authorized by national authorities at the highest political level. Only the President of the United States, as Commander in Chief, may authorize US forces to take such an action.

ROE (Rules of Engagement)

Competent commanders, typically geographic combatant commanders, after JCS review and approval, issue ROE. ROE describe the circumstances and limitations under which forces will begin or continue to engage in combat. Normally, execution orders (EXORD), operations plans (OPLAN), and operations orders (OPORD) contain ROE. ROE ensure use of force in an operation occurs in accordance with national policy goals, mission requirements, and the rule of law. In general, ROE present a more detailed application of LOAC principles tailored to the political and military nature of a mission. ROE set forth the parameters of an airman's right to self-defense. All airmen have a duty and a legal obligation to understand, remember, and apply mission ROE. During military operations, LOAC and specifically tailored ROE provide guidance on the use of force. The standing rules of engagement (SROE) of the CJCS give commanders direction on the use of force in self-defense against a hostile act or hostile intent. The SROE do not limit an airman's inherent right to use all means necessary and appropriate for personal or unit self-defense. Some basic considerations based on the SROE follow:

- The use of force in self-defense must be necessary and limited to the amount needed to eliminate the threat and control the situation.
- Deadly force should only be used in response to a hostile act or a demonstration of hostile intent. Deadly force is defined as force that causes or has a substantial risk of causing death or serious bodily harm.
- Failure to comply with ROE may be punishable under the UCMJ.
- ROE questions and concerns should be promptly elevated up the chain of command for resolution.

4

International Law and Distinctive Nature

There is no agreed definition of international law and it is easier to describe the role of international law and the tasks it performs than to rely on a dictionary definition. The international legal regime (that is, the system of international law) may be described as 'consisting of a body of laws, rules and legal principles (sometimes not easy to isolate or identify as one or the other) that are based on custom, treaties or legislation and define, control, constrain or affect the rights and duties of states in their relations with each other'. Unfortunately almost every meaningful statement in that description may be queried or require modification as this course will illustrate. It is, however, a working model. Among the things it fails to take account of is the dynamic quality of international law which has led – and is leading – to changes in both the subjects of international law and its content. Although states are still central to the international law regime there is no doubt that for some purposes at least, some international organisations such as the United Nations, the International Labour Organization and the World Bank are now subjects of international law. And individuals too have been granted subject status for some purposes.

It was traditionally thought that because international law governed the relations between states it did not affect their domestic arrangements. Because each state was said to be sovereign, this suggested that internally a state could behave as it wished. If this was ever true in practice, it certainly requires modification now. In particular, the development of human rights law places obligations upon state governments to conform to international norms in their domestic governance.

Sometimes international law is criticised for the lack of sanctions it is able to apply in the event of non-compliance or breach of obligation. Dixon, in your readings, answers this criticism by explaining that sanctions are not a necessary element of a legal regime. Some writers, of whom Cassese is one, regard the development of international law as rather disappointing. Many would prefer to see it as a stage on the way to world governance in which the role of law would be much more like that in a domestic legal regime. Such goals, however, also have their own severe critics. These regret the way in which international law has come to constrain states in their internal conduct and sense a conspiracy to remove power from democratic states to a central and largely unaccountable body.

The differences between international law and domestic law It is indisputable that there are significant and crucial distinctions between international law and domestic law. In international law there is of course no supreme legislature which can promulgate binding international laws. There is no international law-making body and no equivalent of a domestic legislature.

The international legal regime is overwhelmingly, but not exclusively, one which requires the consent of those whom it would govern. International law can, by and large, be created only by consent – it can rarely coerce those state subjects who would not be bound. It is this that leads Cassese in your readings to suggest that the international law regime is best understood as a horizontal system of organisation rather than vertical. By this he means that whereas in domestic law, laws are passed down to the subjects from the law making body, in international law it is the parties themselves who make the law for themselves. Cassese regards this as unsatisfactory but it might be better seen as the necessary result of international law being concerned primarily with rules directed to sovereign states.

Similarly there is no international court before which states in breach of international law may consistently be forced to appear. There is an International Court of Justice but this concerns itself only with disputes between parties who have standing before the Court (and only states do have standing if the Court is to make an authoritative ruling rather than giving an advisory opinion). The Court has no role in punishing states in breach of their international law obligations. Its role is to resolve disputes between states, and without use of sanctions. And although some states have accepted the compulsory jurisdiction of the International Court of Justice this will only be effective in disputes between states where all parties to the dispute have accepted that compulsory jurisdiction. A minority of states do so. More frequently the Court will have jurisdiction only where the parties to the dispute consent to the jurisdiction of the Court for a particular dispute. Thus here too the emphasis remains upon consent.

This emphasis on consent rests upon two crucial, but not natural, facts. The first is that each state is said to be sovereign in its own territory. This does not mean that the rulers of any state can rule with utter impunity. Humanitarian law in particular has been accepted (generally, if not in particular cases) as constraining states in their internal governance. Nevertheless there is universal acceptance that while subject to some qualifications, sovereignty gives total control of domestic jurisdiction. This remains true even though a state may willingly accept limits upon its sovereignty, as have for instance the states of the European Union.

The second fact is that there is universal acceptance of the sovereign equality of states – that is, each is equal in its sovereignty. Needless to say, and this does have implications for the arguments presented in this course, the sovereignty is formal and legal in its equality rather than actual. The relative power of states does not alter this aspect of equality. Just as under the rule of law, each individual has formal equality before the law, so in international law each state is equal. This acceptance of sovereignty and sovereign equality makes clear just why it is generally unrealistic to expect a greater level of coercion and sanction in international law than presently exists.

THE CHANGING NATURE OF INTERNATIONAL LAW

The reading you have completed from Cassese suggests that it is useful to recognise four major stages in the development of international law. His history will reinforce the argument that it is largely to be found in the history of Europe. This is certainly true of the first two stages and partly true of the third.

What emerged as international law in the first period up to 1914 was almost exclusively rules governing the relations between states. Overwhelmingly this was inter-state regulation and individuals scarcely figured at all. Of course, in so far as states have always been inanimate entities, the reality was that international law governed the relationships between state governments (composed of people but in their official capacity). It has been suggested that this period should be seen as one in which international law was primarily descriptive in that it described how states generally conducted affairs with other states, but was hardly normative – it did not seek to direct states as to their conduct, but merely recognised practice. In particular there was little or no restraint upon the threat or use of force by states powerful enough to do as they wished. Such international rules as there were reflected the interests of those same states.

Following the First World War, with the creation of the League of Nations and the Permanent Court of International Justice (PCIJ) (the forerunner of the International Court of Justice), perspectives on world organisation changed significantly. The creation of the League of Nations recognised for the first time the importance of a structure that could take part in the governing of relations between nations. One of its central goals was to limit the right of states to resort to war to a number of stated causes, and it also provided for cooling off periods before resort to war. The PCIJ was available for the adjudication of disputes.

These changes could not be described as dramatic in their effect. And of course the League of Nations failed to preserve peace. Its efforts were hindered by the decision of the USA to remain outside of the League and by the non-participation of the Soviet Union. The Bolshevik revolution in Russia in 1917 also challenged such economic and political consensus as existed in Europe. The League did not challenge the European colonial empires and some argued that French and British influence in the League was excessive. Nevertheless the War had concentrated minds to the extent that it became fashionable to emphasise the desirability of peace. In 1928 the Paris Pact on the Banning of War was signed, though its effects were hardly satisfactory. The judicial structure of the PCIJ survived although it achieved less than its advocates had anticipated. One aspect of the League's functioning remains historically important. Under its auspices many Minority Treaties were negotiated. These were more important as precursors of human rights protection in international law than as successes in their own terms. Peace treaties negotiated at the end of the War insisted that certain nation states with significant ethnic minorities accepted, in return for recognition, agreements to protect the rights of these minority populations. The responsibility for guaranteeing and supervising these treaties was allocated to the League, which developed a (rather ineffective) 'minority petition procedure' which has been described as the procedure that initiated trans-national claims making. You should remember a final point. Although the Minority Treaties were implicitly about human rights, they were concerned not with the rights of individuals but with those of groups or collectivities. Developments in Cassese's third period are continuing in their significance. The end of the Second World War led to:

- the creation of the United Nations
- the Nuremberg trials which asserted that individuals had responsibilities in international law
- the development of concepts of self-determination and an era of decolonisation with ex-colonies at last able to contribute to international law creation.

The principal goal of the UN was to be the preservation of peace, stimulated, as your reading observes, by the potential of nuclear weapons to annihilate humanity. Also of great and continuing international law significance was the drafting and signing of the Universal Declaration of Human Rights — not least for its assertion of individual human rights. Most of these developments will be discussed in subsequent chapters because they all remain of importance in the present role of international law.

Much the same may be said of Cassese's final period, from the end of the Cold War to the present, although the significance of the changes wrought by the end of the USSR is still by no means clear. What is clear, however, is that the end of the Cold War dramatically changed the balance of power between states. Because of the frequent use of the veto in the Security Council between 1948 and 1990, actions by the UN aimed at preserving or creating peace had been very limited. Many thought that the demise of the USSR would enable the UN to become much more powerful and active. The first Gulf War, aimed at restoring the sovereignty of Kuwait, seemed to suggest that this might be the case.

INTERNATIONAL LAW AND COMMON SENSE

One issue that is important to think about at the beginning of this course is the assertion that is sometimes made that the international law way of understanding the world is actually very 'Eurocentric'. What is asserted is that although the method of international law looks very reasonable and obvious to those trained in the common law or civil law tradition, in fact it is important to be able to see it as something contingent rather than necessary. This means that we have to be able to appreciate that international law is not common sense but a particular way of attempting to deal with international relations and problems.

The foundations of current international law were laid in an era which predates the creation of the majority of nation states. Equally clearly the antecedents of international law are overwhelmingly European (within which, for this purpose, we should include the United States) and the system was one which evolved in a time of European hegemony, most overtly expressed through colonialism. Because of this it can be persuasively argued that the international legal regime is crucially European in its method and in its ideology. What is meant by this is that an argument may be made (and probably should be made) to the effect that international law reflects one particular way of perceiving the world, in which even the most fundamental premises underlying the system – such as those of the nature of sovereignty, and even the acceptance of the principle of *pacta sunt servanda* (roughly translated as 'treaties must be observed' but with rather wider implications) – are arguably imbued with Western perceptions

Before discussing the significance of this further, a broader but related point must be made. It is not insignificant that most (British in particular) international law textbooks seem implicitly to reject the assumption that international law is intimately and necessarily interrelated with contemporary international events. The inference to be drawn from the content of some of the most eminent texts is not only that law is separate and distinct from political relationships and international relations, but because of this, a study of international law can be a very pure one indeed. (Rather like pure mathematics which remains a sensible subject even though its applications may be entirely absent.) To the extent that the political world does impinge upon such texts, it tends to be a historical rather than contemporary world, and it is a history which is usually decontextualised and 'objective'. History, if necessary, is treated as an uncontested series of facts. Very often if the greatest international events appear at all, they appear only in the form of desiccated legal decisions or opinions.

The majority of such texts also have a remarkably standard set of contents, with the main differences to be found in the depth of analysis and variety of emphasis. Such orthodoxy should breed suspicion, particularly if it is accepted that any study of international law must be concerned with the politics that underlie it, the power relations that it may disguise, and the ideology that the law way of thinking conceals. In turn it should be clear that the ideological assumptions which underpin international law are not only to be found in the content of international law but equally in the very process and procedure of the law.

To illustrate this proposition it is useful to consider one exception to the generalisation about British international law textbooks. This is Antonio Cassese's *International law in a divided world* which, although written while the Soviet Union was yet extant (in 1986), remains pertinent. (Significantly perhaps, it is written by an Italian scholar who is also the author of one of your textbooks.) In this book written 20 years ago, Cassese does address the lack of universal acceptance of international law method. His argument with regard to the so-called 'developing' countries and the 'socialist states' (obviously inappropriately labelled but nevertheless significantly different from the liberal capitalist states of the West at the time when he was writing) is that there are crucial differences in perceptions in, or of, international law. At this point I mention only his assessment of the ideological perception of the governments of certain African states. Obviously, given the very different cultural traditions of these states and their inhabitants, with emphasis upon lineage and clan, a different perception of international law is not unlikely. Cassese suggests that for such states international law cannot be seen as an abstract problem solver (as it often appears in textbooks and international texts); rather 'to them international law is relevant to the extent that it protects them from undue influence by powerful states and is instrumental in bringing about social change with more equitable conditions stimulating economic development'.

Whether or not we are comfortable with such enormous generalisations is less important than the consequences that are drawn from the statement. Cassese argues that it is because of this generalisation that we can see many developing states very much preferring to 'elaborate general principles as opposed to detailed and precise legal rules', and he uses a telling quotation from an Egyptian international lawyer which requires comment: ...in dealing especially with the Western countries, anything which could be formulated in the very precise terms of an operational rule was considered nonsense [by developing countries] while Third World representatives in general attached great weight to general principles which sometimes could not be refined into operational rules. If we look at the same thing from a different point of view I would say that in most cases the attitude of the Third World was defined by the total effect of a proposed solution, the Western powers put too much emphasis on the mechanistic elements [of law] while for Third

World countries if by going through all the motions and respecting all the procedural rules you end up with an unjust solution, this would be bad law. And if you have a general directive, even if you cannot reduce it to very precise procedural rules, it is still good law, though it may be imperfect in terms of application.

In some ways that quotation summarises a fundamental distinction in perceptions of international law in particular (but also, to some extent, of municipal law). It is of the essence of the law way (meaning the 'rule of law way') of dealing with the world, that the rules precede the facts to which they are to be applied. Indeed it is this that makes the writing of 'pure international law textbooks' apparently sensible. It is also of the essence of both contract law and treaty law that in general, rules are laid down providing for future possibilities. To most of us this seems, no doubt, obvious and sensible but the quotation should highlight the potential shortcomings of the structuring of rules to ensure justiciable disputes (disputes in a form that allows law to be applied). If the application of rules or treaty provisions, or even contracts, leads to results which one party is very unwilling to accept, particularly arising from situations unforeseen or unexpected at the time of the rule or contract formulation, then those who do not identify with the Western view of international law might well consider it dysfunctional. The preoccupation of international lawyers with the need to structure problems in a way which makes them justiciable is of central importance. Indeed, from the perspective of Western international lawyers, treaties, rules or resolutions which do not allow the formulation of problems in this way are often accorded significantly less respect. (A point to which we will return.)

Crucially (and this proposition underlies much of the argument of this course), only if the 'rule of law' approach to international law is seen as a particular way of organising the world, rather than as common sense, can we begin to appreciate the significance of international law in the international community as a whole. What has been suggested to be singular about the international law way of encompassing the world is both:

- 'rule magic', by which I mean that situations in the future are governed by rules which, when made, had either not contemplated the facts of all future cases or, when they were made, they were made without the participation of a party now said to be subject to them
- and, the method by which social facts are translated (or selected) as legally relevant.

What always distinguishes legal disputes from other disputes will be the structuring of the issues whereby many of the facts which parties (or at least one party) to the dispute might think important are irrelevant for the purposes of legal resolution. What is the significance of this? Firstly it should be made clear that in translating social and political situations into the legal world, one effect is often to apparently de-politicise a dispute. Legal questions have an appearance of legal objectivity and political neutrality. It is the law which is being questioned and considered and this seems very different from political dispute.

Why should International Law be Defined as Law?

Most international lawyers would claim that what distinguishes international law from international relations and brings it within the definition of law is that it is a 'distinctive mode of discourse' – that is, the law way of discussing international issues is distinctive because of the rules, procedure and process which it brings to bear upon questions. Indeed even the formulation of the questions in a dispute will be affected by the input of international law knowledge. Secondly, every state does accept the existence of international law as something distinct from ordinary international intercourse. Dealing with the second point first, this acceptance of the reality of international law by states is important in the refutation of those who suggest that international law is not really law. In domestic law it can be argued that the fact that laws are often broken and wrongdoers often escape punishment is of only marginal importance to the existence of law. Much more significant is that most citizens have actually internalised the values of criminal law even if they do not agree with them. Domestic wrongdoers very seldom attempt to deny the authenticity of the law, rather they try to justify their transgression.

This is just as true in international law. When Saddam Hussein ordered the invasion of Kuwait in 1990 he did not announce that he intended to flout or, worse still, ignore international law. Rather he attempted, perhaps not terribly convincingly, to defend his actions as being consistent with international law. Thus he not only suggested that the invasion was legitimate self defence but he also referred to historic Iraqi claims over the territory of Kuwait. When the United States invaded Grenada in 1983 it too, albeit belatedly and a little half-heartedly, attempted to justify the invasion legally. The fact that the 'justification' withstood little scrutiny is less important for our argument than the fact that the United States felt bound to make it. Very much the same was true of the US invasion of Panama to capture General Noriega. Even the claim by China that both Tibet and Taiwan are integral components of the Chinese territory is couched in terms calculated to appeal to international law. More recently the intervention by NATO in the territory of the former Republic of Yugoslavia was defended as being consistent with international law; while it is argued (at least by Israel and the United States) that Israel's activities in Palestine are not necessarily a breach. Most recently of course has been the bitter legal debate concerning the intervention of the US 'coalition' in Iraq. Quite remarkably the debate over the legality of the intervention has been absolutely central to the debate over intervention itself. There are those, both teachers of international law and politicians, who argued forcefully that the matter should have been finally resolved by its persuasively argued illegitimacy. This debate was very important in the 2005 general election in the UK.

As to the first point, the distinctiveness of international law derives in part from its sources and origin. International law and laws essentially came into existence either through treaties (which obviously require the consent of those who are to be bound by them) or through custom, and usually, but not always, custom which has been long established. Of course not all custom is held to be international law, rather only that which has been regarded by states as legally binding custom. Thus custom becomes international law only when the states observing the custom do so in the belief that the custom is indeed a part of international law. The fact that there is no law-creating legislature really, it can be argued, simply reflects the reality of sovereignty. As Shabtai Rosenne observes in a book published in 19841, 'International law is a law of co-ordination, not, as is the case of most internal law, a law of subordination. By law of co-ordination we mean to say that it is created and applied by its own subjects, primarily the independent states (directly or indirectly), for their own common purposes.'

But let us return to the argument that the law way of dealing with international issues is a distinct way (that is to say that legal discourse is distinguishable from the language of general international relations). In domestic terms it can be argued that what distinguishes most clearly the law way from the social way of resolving disputes is that law always requires a translation of social facts in to legal facts. This is no less true of international law. But the argument also suggests that this necessary translation is both law's greatest strength and paradoxically its greatest weakness. It is a strength in that when a dispute is put in legal terms with legal issues, it becomes legally resolvable in that there will be (almost invariably) a legal solution to the legal problem. It may also be a weakness because the resolution, while it will resolve the legal issue, may not resolve the social (untranslated) problem. The law way of resolving disputes works 'best' when all the parties to the dispute accept the legalisation of the dispute.

Very much the same applies in international law, which is a central factor in explaining the reasons why only a minority of states accept the compulsory jurisdiction of the International Court of Justice. There is little point in having a dispute legally resolved if the underlying political problems remain. Unless the parties to the dispute, together with the constituencies they represent, accept that the legal outcome resolves the problem, the resolution itself may in fact simply lead to further disputes. In due course when we consider at some length the role, effect and politics of the International Court of Justice, this argument will be made by reference to selected cases which have come before it. Suffice to say at this point, that while any number of cases could be selected to illustrate the proposition, a crucial feature of the translation from social to legal dispute will always be concerned with the initial selection of legally relevant facts. Almost invariably the selection of these facts not only structures the legal issues and thus the questions for judgment, but involves at the least a modification of the political arguments.

INTERNATIONAL LAW

One of the earliest of these rules was the immunity of ambassadors and envoys. The rule gives state A assurance that when it sends its ambassador into state B, the ambassador will not be personally harassed or injured. But state A must pay a price for this confidence: it must itself refrain from injuring or harassing B's ambassador. Behind every rule of international law is a similar cost-benefit component. The idea of cost-benefit in turn suggests two even more fundamental principles of international law—the principle of equality and the principle of reciprocity. Under the principle of equality, state A has the same rights and obligations under international law as state B. Thus, A may be an island state of one square mile and B may be a superpower; they have equal rights, duties, and obligations under international law. Under the principle of reciprocity, state A is put on notice that if it harms B's ambassador, state B may retaliate by harming, or at least arresting and holding hostage, A's own ambassador.

Rules of international law have arisen because states have perceived their national interest to be served by a set of rules, norms, and principles that are grounded in equality and reciprocity. Even though the international legal system has no legislature, no chief executive, and no court of universal jurisdiction, its rules are obeyed as much as, if not more than, the rules of law within any given state. International law is not more frequently violated than, for example, ordinary criminal law. Moreover, as the rules of international law increase in coverage and density over time, the overarching principle of reciprocity ensures that the rules will be treated as a package. Thus, if state A violates a particular rule of international law because it has decided that its self-interest requires the violation, state A may find that other states will retaliate by violating other rules that state A wants to preserve. In 1979, when Iran resorted to the historically unprecedented action of arresting fifty United States diplomats and consular officers, the United States retaliated by invading Iran's bank accounts and freezing $13 billion of Iranian assets. This invasion of a state's property was clearly a transgression of international law on its face, but it was justified as a "countermeasure" to force Iran to release the prisoners. Iran had no rational economic choice but to cave in. It returned the prisoners unharmed to the United States, and the United States unfroze the assets. The selection by a victimized state of a different rule of international law for its countermeasure is a variation of game theory's tit-for-tat strategy, which might be called "tit-for-a-different-tat." It is a fundamental principle that operates to reinforce the authority of the entire package of international rules.

In early times, when the rules of international law were few, resort to war was a more likely form of retaliation than it is today. As the rules of international law grew more dense with the passage of time, as more nations appeared on the scene, and as communication among states and people became easier, many more possibilities for tit-for-a-different-tat countermeasures have arisen. A victimized state today can select a countermeasure that is proportionate to the initial violation. A significant result is the lessening of the tendency of tit-for-tat retaliation to escalate. There is less need to resort to the ultimate countermeasure—war itself.

If a controversy arises between two states, where do we find the applicable rules? First we see if the states have entered into a treaty that governs the dispute. If so, the treaty rules prevail in all cases except where the treaty itself may be illegal (for example, treaties concerning the transport of human slaves); illegal treaties are banned by the customary international law of *jus cogens*. If the treaty is ambiguous, the parties look to the customary international law of treaty interpretation, codified in the Vienna Convention on the Law of Treaties (1969).

If the controversy is not covered by a treaty, then the parties look to customary international law. This pervasive body of law, which may be viewed as the default rules of international law, is similar to common law, except that it developed through the practice of states and not primarily through judicial decisions. As states engaged in practices over a period of time, those practices became regarded as constituting norms, deviation from which was deemed unjustified or illegal. These norms were almost invariably in the long-term interests of the majority of states, or they would not have evolved and persisted.

After treaties and custom, rules of international law may be found in various subsidiary sources. "General principles of law," reflecting the laws of most states, have been used as sources of procedural rules for international courts and tribunals.

The decisions of national courts on questions of international law are not, strictly speaking, determinations of international law itself, but rather constitute authoritative expressions of the practice of the state in which the court sits. This practice, in turn, contributes to the formation of customary international law. "Equity" has sometimes been championed as a source of international law, but the decision of the International Court of Justice in the *Continental Shelf Cases* put an end to that contention. A still-surviving subsidiary source of international law is the writing of international law scholars. It is felt that a person who devotes his life to the study of international law has achieved a measure of respect for the principles of reciprocity and equality that give some degree of authoritative weight to his conclusions about the content of various rules and norms.

Domain

The domain of present-day international law is vast. It includes:

The Oceans

Seventy-one percent of the earth's surface is *water*. International rules, codified in the United Nations Convention on the Law of the Sea (1994), prescribe the breadth of the territorial sea (12 miles) and the extent of the exclusive economic zone (200 miles), the determination of the continental shelf, fisheries and conservation regimes, preservation of endangered acquatic species, mineral exploitation of the seabed, identification of vessels, freedom of navigation and commerce, and many other areas.

Polar Regions

The Arctic Circle is a water mass, subject to oceanic rules. Antarctica is a continent divided into sectors in which some nations have established predominant claims, subject to general principles of international law respecting environmental management and mining activities.

Airspace

The subjacent state has sovereignty over its airspace, but extensive treaty regimes have carved out principles of identification, duress, over-flight, and liability for accidents.

Outer Space

Once considered open territory, all space above the airspace and all extraterrestrial objects are now regarded as the "common heritage of mankind." The United States, for instance, does not own the Moon, even though it was the first to land a spaceship there.

Artificial Satellites

Increasingly, the stratosphere is being populated with artificial communications and reconnaissance satellites. International law has developed rapidly in this area. The satellites belong to the nations that send them up; other nations have no right to shoot them down. If they fall to earth, the nation owning them has strict liability to pay for all damages.

Global Environment

If state A builds a factory near its border with state B, and the factory emits pollutants that drift over state B, A is liable for damages. Any nation that degrades the global environment (for example, by spillage from an oil tanker) is responsible under international environmental law to clean up the damage. Still controversial is the developing international law of state responsibility for preserving the environment in light of the desire of many nations for rapid economic growth. States so far have only been able to agree on a principle of "sustainable development," a nice-sounding but elusive concept.

Global Market

The transboundary movement of goods, services, and investment is governed by "private international law"—a complex interacting series of contractual arrangements. Yet the line between private and public international law is fuzzy; when there is a resort to default rules, they are the rules of public international law. For example, when governments engage in business transactions, are they shielded by sovereign immunity? Increasingly, the answer of public international law is "no." What about concession agreements—contracts between a government and a foreign corporation? The concession agreements themselves typically spell out their conflict-of-law rules, but if the rules are ambiguous or incomplete, then public international law steps in. Recently, antitrust rules have become a subject of international legal regulation. A state may want to regulate anticompetitive activities of subsidiary corporations abroad, yet this intrusive "legislative reach" is bounded by an international rule of reasonableness.

Global Communication

Some nations and religious groups want to regulate the content of international information disseminated over the airwaves and through the worldwide Internet. Content restrictions include advocacy of war or revolution, criticism of government officials or policies, regulation of advertising claims, and suppression of real or fictional depictions of pornography. International law in this area is developing rapidly. Its tendency is in the direction of freedom of information, with some clear exceptions such as child pornography.

International Crimes

The basic rules of international criminal law were developed in the great codification conventions of The Hague in 1899 and 1907 and Geneva in 1949. The Nuremberg and Far East Tribunals after World War II applied these rules to individuals. Nearly five decades later, these precedents have become salient again. The International Criminal Tribunal for Former Yugoslavia, established in The Hague, has been active in prosecuting and trying military and civilian leaders responsible for atrocities committed in Bosnia, Serbia, Croatia, and Kosovo.

The public respect accorded this tribunal augurs well for the establishment of an International Criminal Court of universal jurisdiction. The jurisdiction of these special international tribunals over crimes including genocide, murder of civilians, deportation, persecution, rape, pillage, torture, and enslavement is not exclusive. National courts also can exercise jurisdiction over persons who have allegedly committed crimes against humanity or war crimes.

Terrorism and Hijacking

Both terrorism and hijacking are international crimes. But with the terrorist attacks on the World Trade Centre in New York City on September 11, 2001, the United States and many of its allies have declared a "war on terrorism," a concept that expands the notion of "war" to include nonstate actors. The classic international law rules regarding belligerency and neutrality need to be revived in dealing with global terrorism. Under the old rules, a state loses its neutrality if it furnishes material support to one of the belligerents. These rules may now be applied to states that harbor terrorists, making such states a legitimate target in the war against terrorism.

Humanitarian Intervention

States may use military force for the limited purpose of preventing large-scale atrocities in other states. The American interventions in Granada (1983), in Panama (1989), and with NATO's assistance in Kosovo (1999), in varying degrees exemplify this rule. In order to be legitimate under international law, military intervention must satisfy the following minimal criteria: (1) the goal must be to prevent a significant human-rights abuse; (2) the means employed must be proportionate to this goal (in other words, the cure cannot be worse than the disease); (3) all means short of military intervention must have been tried first; (4) U.N. and multilateral support must at least be solicited; (5) it cannot be part of the goal of the intervenor to seek territorial aggrandizement for itself; (6) it cannot be part of the goal of the intervenor to seek a permanent change in the political independence of the target territory; (7) the intervenor must withdraw its forces as soon as the humanitarian goal is accomplished.

Human Rights

This is the most controversial extension of public international law. Under the classic concept, only states had standing under international law; people were invisible. But since the Holocaust of World War II, the Nuremberg trials, and Eleanor Roosevelt's superb drafting of a General Assembly resolution entitled "The Universal Declaration of Human Rights" (1948), people are demanding direct access to public international law. Prior to 1945, a state could do anything it wanted to its citizens within its own territory, including murdering them, without any international accountability. Today, genocide, torture, enslavement, and other crimes, possibly extending to persecution and deportation, are illegal under customary international law even if they occur entirely within the territorial boundaries of a state and involve the state's own nationals. The law of human rights has a long way to go, but it is conceptually the biggest breakthrough in the 5,000-year history of international law. In effect, it is changing "international law" into "interpersonal law." One of the major sources of controversy concerns the hierarchy of human rights: are personal liberties more important than food and shelter? Are fair judicial procedures more important than the right to a job or the right to vacations with pay? Should capital punishment be banned? What about capital punishment of juveniles? Should abortions be legalized throughout the world? Should women have equal legal rights as men in countries that wish to preserve their cultural and religious values that hold that women to be subservient to men? It is no wonder that law students are increasingly demanding courses in international human rights.

Group Rights

Among the claims asserted by various groups are the right to self-determination, autonomy, secession, native community practices, native language, and freedom of religious exercise. In the past, these claims were considered to be within the exclusive jurisdiction of the state containing a particular group. But today these claims are becoming internationalized as the result of multilateral conventions and the growing popular conviction that attacks on groups are a form of cultural genocide.

Nationality

The most important link between a person and a state is nationality or citizenship. International law imposes the requirement of a "genuine link" for nationality to be effective. This concept applies particularly to the nationality of vessels, and rules out "flags of convenience" where there is no genuine link between the ship and its state of incorporation.

The State

Finally, and most fundamentally, international law defines the state itself. It sets forth the basic principle that a government that is in effective control over a defined territory, and owes allegiance to no other government, is a state. The form of government is immaterial; it can be a democracy, a dictatorship, or totalitarian. Once a state is recognized as such, it immediately obtains the benefits, and incurs the obligations, of all the rules, norms, and principles of international law in all the categories enumerated above. It is also bound by the international law of state succession. If government X of state A is overthrown by a revolutionary force, and a new government Y is installed, all the treaties and obligations entered into by the former government X remain binding because they were incurred on behalf of state A itself. Thus a revolutionary government cannot get rid of the state's previous treaties, as the Soviet Union partially attempted (but never succeeded) after the Revolution of 1917. States may no longer increase their size by aggression and conquest, as they used to centuries ago. Since the Kellogg-Briand Pact of 1928, acquisition of territory by force is illegal. Saddam Hussein learned this when he conquered Kuwait; the international community joined together in the Persian Gulf War to divest him forcibly of his conquest. But states may add to their territory by the consent of other states. An example is the purchase of Alaska from Russia in the nineteenth century.

INTERNATIONAL LAW IN NATIONAL COURTS

In some countries, such as Germany under article 25 of its Constitution, international law has the same standing in the courts as national law. In the United States, the relationship between international law and national law is more complex. Any treaty in which the United States is a party constitutes the supreme law of the land under article VI of the Constitution. Whether an individual may bring a lawsuit under a treaty depends on whether *or not* the treaty is "self-executing." A treaty that requires further legislation by Congress *for its implementation* is not self-executing.

Various statutes have expanded the international rights of American citizens in national courts. A person may sue a foreign country for expropriating his property without compensation; a person who is tortured abroad may, with certain restrictions, bring suit in an American court. The former "sovereign immunity" of foreign countries in American courts has been restricted by the Sovereign Immunities Act of 1976, which provides a "commercial exception" to immunity. Finally, federal courts increasingly recognize international customary law as comprising part of federal common law. But despite these advances, the United States seems to be moving slowly toward incorporating international law as part of its national law.

INTERNATIONAL LAW-DEFINITION

International law deals with the relationships between states, or between persons or entities in different states. It subdivides into "public international law", and "private international law". When used without an adjective, "international law" generally refers to "public international law", and this article concentrates on that meaning.

Traditionally, international law had states as its sole subjects. With the proliferation over the last century of international organizations, they have been recognized as its subjects as well.

More recent developments in international human rights law, international humanitarian law and international trade law have led to individuals and corporations being increasingly seen as subjects of international law as well, something which goes against the traditional legal orthodoxy. Since international law increasingly governs much more than merely relations between sovereign states, it may be better defined as law decided and enforced at the international, as opposed to national level.

Sources of International Law

International law knows three primary sources: international treaties, custom, and general principles of law (cf. Art. 38 of the Statute of the International Court of Justice). International treaty law is comprised of obligations states expressly and voluntarily accept between themselves in treaties. Customary international law is derived from the consistent practice of States accompanied by *opinio juris*, i.e. the conviction of States that the consistent practice is required by a legal obligation. Judgments of international tribunals as well as scholarly works have traditionally been looked to as persuasive sources for custom in addition to direct evidence of state behaviour. Attempts to codify customary international law picked up momentum after the Second World War with the formation of the International Law Commission (ILC). Codified customary law is made the binding interpretation of the underlying custom by agreement through treaty. For states not party to such treaties, the work of the ILC may still be accepted as custom applying to those states. General principles of law are those commonly recognized by the major legal systems of the world. Certain norms of international law achieve the binding force of peremptory norms (*jus cogens*) as to include all states with no permissible derrogations. Legal principles common to major legal systems may also be invoked to supplement international law when necessary.

Interpretation of International Law

Where there are disputes about the exact meaning and application of national laws, it is the responsibility of the courts to decide what the law means. In international law as a whole, there are no courts which have the authority to do this. It is generally the responsibility of states to interpret the law for themselves. Unsurprisingly, this means that there is rarely agreement in cases of dispute.

States with disputes relating to international law may decide to settle their dispute through the legal process with mutual consent (consent can be given in advance through treaty provisions). The dispute settlement may occur through arbitration, where the arbitrators are selected by the disputing parties, or in the International Court of Justice (ICJ). Decisions made through arbitration may be binding or non-binding depending on the nature of the arbitration agreement, whereas decisions resulting from contentious cases argued before the ICJ are always binding on the involved states. The ICJ may also be called upon to give 'advisory opinions' by organs of the United Nations, which are not binding, but often carry force because of the strength of the legal arguments made within those opinions.

Enforcement by States

Apart from a state's natural inclination to uphold certain norms, the force of international law has always come from the pressure that states put upon one another to behave consistently and to honor their obligations. As with any system of law, many violations of international law obligations are overlooked. If addressed, it is almost always purely through diplomacy and the consequences upon an offending state's reputation. Though violations may be common in fact, states try to avoid the appearance of having disregarded international obligations.

States may also unilaterally adopt sanctions against one another such as the severance of economic or diplomatic ties, or through reciprocal action. In some cases, domestic courts may render judgment against a foreign state (the realm of private international law) for an injury, though this is a complicated area of law where international law intersects with domestic law.

States have the right to employ force in self-defense against an offending state that has used force to attack its territory or political independence. States may also use force in collective self-defense, where force is used against another state. The state that force is used against must authorize the participation of third-states in its self-defense. This right is recognized in the United Nations Charter.

ENFORCEMENT BY INTERNATIONAL BODIES

Violations of the UN Charter may be raised by the aggrieved state in the General Assembly or brought to the attention of the Security Council. Enforcement measures may include resolutions censoring the offending state, economic sanctions, or even military action if the violation involves the use of force or threatens international peace or security.

Though states (or increasingly, international organizations) are usually the only ones with standing to address a violation of international law, some treaties, such as the International Covenant on Civil and Political Rights have an optional protocol that allows individuals who have had their rights violated by member states to petition the international Human Rights Committee.

History

Through the ages a code developed for the relations and conduct between nations. Even when nations were at war, envoys were often considered immune to violence.

The first formal attempts in this direction, which over time have developed into the current international law, stem from the era of the Renaissance in Europe.

In the Middle Ages it had been considered the obligation of the Church to mediate in international disputes. During Council of Constance (1414)-Pawel Wlodkowic-rector of Jagiellonian University (Cracow,Poland), theologist, lawyer and diplomat presented the theory that all, including pagan, nations have right to self-govern and to live in peace and possess their land. In the 16th and 17th centuries the Church gradually lost its direct influence in international affairs, as Catholic and Protestant powers emerged and struggled for dominance and survival. At the beginning of the 17th century, several generalizations could be made about the political situation:

1. Self-governing, autonomous states existed.
2. Almost all of them were governed by monarchies.
    i. England and Polish-Lithuanian Commonwealth had a constitutional monarchy.
    ii. Not all monarchs were hereditary: the Holy Roman Emperor and the ruler of Polish-Lithuanian Commonwealth were elected.
    iii. Switzerland, the Netherlands, and many Italian city-states were republics.

3. After the Thirty Years' War, there was relative stability in Europe for 130 years (until the 1789 French Revolution).
4. Land, wealth, trading rights, and monopolizing the new lands were the topics of war.

Some people assert that international law developed to deal with the new states arising, others claim that the lack of influence of the Pope and the Catholic church gave rise to the need for new generally-accepted codes.

The Dominican professor Francisco de Vitoria (in Latin *Franciscus de Victoria*) of theology at the University of Salamanca lectured on the rights of the natives. He did so while Spain was at the height of its power, after the violent Spanish conquest of Peru in 1536. Charles V, Holy Roman Emperor, protested against the friar, but in 1542 new laws put the natives under protection of the Spanish crown. Vitoria is generally recognized as the founder of modern international law.

The French monk Emeric Cruce (1590-1648) came up with the idea of having representatives of all countries meeting in one place to discuss their conflicts so as to avoid war and create more peace. He suggested this in his *The New Cyneas* (1623), choosing Venice to be the selected city for all of the representatives to meet, and suggested that the Pope should preside over the meeting. Of course, during the Thirty Years' War (1618-1648), this was not acceptable to the Protestant nations. He also said that armies should be abolished and called for a world court. Though his call to abolish armies was not taken seriously, Emeric Cruce does deserve his place in history through his foresight that international organizations are crucial to solve international disputes.

Hugo Grotius (or Huig de Groot) (1583-1645) was a Dutch humanist and jurist considered central to the development of international law. He became a lawyer when he was 15 years old and got sentenced to life in prison after going against Maurice of Nassau, son of William of Orange in a trial, but he escaped and fled to Paris. In France, he developed his ideas on international law with his *Mare Liberum* (Latin for "Free seas"), in which he challenged the claims and attempts of England, Spain, and Portugal to rule portions of the oceans and seas. He gained new international fame in 1625 with his book *De Jure Belli ac Pacis* (The Law of War and Peace), as it became the first definitive text on international law. It was published only two years after *The New Cyneas*.

Much of Grotius's content drew from the Bible and from classical history (just war theory of Augustine_of_Hippo). In his work he did not condemn war as only a political tool, considering cases in which war is appropriate. He further developed the just war theory. A *just war* fits certain criteria:

1. It can be to repel an invasion.
2. It can be to punish an insult to God.
3. There has to be a just cause (one of the two mentioned above).
4. It has to be declared by the proper authorities.
5. It must possess moral intention.
6. It must have a chance of success.
7. It must abstain from brutal practices.
8. Its end result must be proportional to the means used.

The statesmen of the time believed no nation could escape war, so they prepared for it.

King Henry IV's Chief Minister, the Duke of Sully, proposed the founding of an alliance of the European nations that was to meet to arbitrate issues and wage war not between themselves but collectively on the Ottoman Turks, and he called it the Grand Design, but was never established.

After World War I, the nations of the world decided to form an international body. U.S. President Woodrow Wilson came up with the idea of a "League of Nations". However, due to political wrangling in the U.S. Congress, the United States did not join the League of Nations, which was one of the causes of its demise.

5

International Law and Aftermath of Operation Iraqi Freedom

Although contentious debate is not uncommon at legal conferences, what was striking about the discourse during this multilateral conference was that the divide over the legality of United States' actions generally reflected two approaches to international law. Specifically, those critical of Operation Iraqi Freedom or humanitarian intervention tended to focus on the war's alleged incompatibility with the U.N. Charter, customary law, or International Court of Justice (ICJ) precedent, thereby limiting their analysis to "internal" sources of law—those that can be traced to a manifestation of state consent. In contrast, those more supportive of Operation Iraqi Freedom or humanitarian intervention tended to employ a more normative approach. They thereby allowed, in addition to traditional manifestations of sovereign consent, "external" references to enter into their legal calculus, whether directly or by way of interpreting traditional sources of sovereign consent. Providing some of these external reference points for the assembled attorneys were Dr. Martin L. Cook and Professor Michael Novak's presentations on Ethics, Just War and Just Peace. The conference, in short, was a prototypical example of what one academic, Professor David J. Bederman, astutely observed as today's "debate" in international law:

[T]he issue is whether law for the international community is exclusively the product of consent by the participants in the system (however manifested) or also of enduring truths that somehow reflect the fundamental values of that community. Put another way, are all rules in a legal community internally generated by means and institutions chosen by the participants, or is there also a metaphysic of first principles that governs the system?

The purpose of this article is to examine these two approaches through the illustrative use of the articles in this symposium issue, to highlight how this debate is fueled by increasingly normative judgments by States and NGOs, and to suggest a third approach to international law to better foster the rule of law, one consisting of recognizing the key values held on both sides of the debate.

TWO APPROACHES TO INTERNATIONAL LAW

Moreover, although seemingly mutually exclusive, positivism and natural law may not be as doctrinally incompatible as they appear at first glance. Nevertheless, as a general description, these two designations do signal a legal perspective or mindset that many times results in disparate analysis and conclusions regarding the lawfulness of international actions, and these terms are used in this chapter to illustrate the divide.

Positivism

Those favoring the view that international rules are "internally" generated by a legal community's participants are essentially espousing a positivist approach to international law, founded on the binding force of expressed or implied state consent. Rejecting any nexus between laws and morality, positivism injects sovereign lawmaking legitimacy into legal tradition. The first international legal positivist might have been John Austin, whose nineteenth century attack on the existence of international law as "law" and his focus on the "fact" of obedience to a superior sovereign did away with what one legal expert, Professor Philip Bobbitt, described as "two of the core ideas that had shaped international law from its inception at the time of the birth of the modern state: natural law and the theory of the just war." Thus, to a positivist, although "law might well be derived from moral precepts, such precepts become law only when commanded by a sovereign." Positivists, faced with an international system consisting of independent sovereigns unanswerable to a higher authority, understandably emphasize tangible treaties and state customs as "the supreme sources of international norms."

Currently, these formal sources of international law are described in many sources, among them the Restatement (Third) of the Foreign Relations Law of the United States, official U.S. government sources, and Article 38 of the Statute of the ICJ, which identifies sources of law as follows: treaties, customs as evidence of general practice, principles of law recognized by civilized nations, and as subsidiary sources, judicial decisions and the writings of jurists.

Natural Law

In contrast to self-generating legal positivists, international legal practitioners and academics taking the other side of the debate, those that allow for the existence of a metaphysics of first principles in international law, can be characterized as naturalists, taking a natural law approach to international law.

Natural law can be defined as a "system of deductive reasoning from which the natural rights of men and sovereign nations may be discovered," with its binding force resulting from "its adherence to reason." Natural law in this sense serves both as "'a guide to individual conduct' and... 'as a standard for the laws enacted by the state.'" Contrary to the positivist perspective, naturalists note that "[n]atural law is common to all nations because it exists everywhere through natural instinct, not because of any enactment." Historically, international law was first formulated by proponents of natural law theory, who provided the foundation of international law principles such as the peaceful resolution of disputes, self-defense, and the right of humanitarian intervention. Although many, in the words of one writer, have attempted to describe the natural law approach as "relegated to the yellowed annals of legal history," recent history, and the ongoing debate in international law that underlay the conference in Garmisch, indicates that it is the doctrine that "just will not die."

A Crucial Aside

As noted earlier, positivism and natural law have variants within themselves, are not recent approaches to the international law, or law in general, and have spawned other approaches to law. Although seemingly mutually exclusive, positivism and natural law at some level may not be as doctrinally incompatible as they appear at first glance.

Positivism and Natural Law As Approaches to the Nature of Law

As the confirmation debate over the Supreme Court nominations of Robert Bork and Justice Clarence Thomas illustrated, the debate between natural law and positivism is not a sterile modern equivalent of the medieval dispute over the number of angels that can dance on the head of a pin. On the contrary, these approaches are embedded in many States' domestic law concepts. From the debate between Thrasymachus and Socrates over the nature of justice, continuing through the Roman era, and up to the present, those who believe in a natural law have clashed with positivists who deny that law is integrally laden with morals or values apart from personal preferences and choice. Current approaches to law roughly reflect this division. The New Haven, Neo-Realism, and Perspective schools, because they look toward something outside of the fact of the law itself to validate international law, have been described as developing from naturalism, while the Legal Process, Nominalism, and Consensualism schools have been characterized as developing from a positivist focus on the fact of a rule as law, irrespective of the content.

The Mutuality of Natural Law and Positivism

Naturalism and positivism, as described above, are based on disparate conceptions of the legitimizing factors of international law. Nevertheless, despite the historical longevity of this debate, the separation of naturalism and positivism as mutually exclusive options in international theory developed only in the nineteenth century, and gained increased vitality in the twentieth century. This division, according to at least one commentator, has been an unfortunate distraction in the development of a coherent and full theory of international law, one alien to past international legal theoreticians. Both naturalism and positivism can encompass elements of their opposing theory, and studying this relationship could contribute to a fuller, more robust approach to international law. Thus, with regard to positivist theory, some argue that when the nature of international consensus is assessed, the continuing role of naturalist analyses becomes apparent. Others have asserted modern positivism recognizes that the law is not independent of its context, and some authors have commented that because secondary rules (those that determine the conditions under which particular acts give rise to legal obligations) are not validated by state consent, a State cannot meaningfully consent to the international legal system. With regard to naturalism, some commentators have injected an element of positivist consent into this theory by arguing that natural law "evolves through time as a dialogue among legal theorists, philosophers, and others," and that, any given point in time, the "natural" within the legal order "will be that era's best approximation of natural justice." Similarly, one author has opined that domestic natural law legal theory eventually collapses into positivism, with the judge's decision (reached utilizing a naturalist approach) becoming legally binding and serving as the sovereign in place of the legislature, an observation that can be applied to state international actions. Accordingly, any description of the these two approaches to international law should be tempered with the knowledge that, ultimately, the best doctrine in international law that is not an "either-or approach," but rather a holistic approach, one that bridges the gap between the apparently dueling conceptions of international law that are becoming increasingly apparent in the actions and discourse of the international international community.

THE CONFERENCE: ADVANCING THE DEBATE

During the conference, speakers and participants approached the topic of "The Rule of Law in Conflict and Post-Conflict Situations" from perspectives that reflected either an adherence to a naturalist or positivist template, or sometimes a combination of both. Using the articles in this symposium, this section illustrates how these various approaches may be manifested during this type of debate.

Kosovo

The U.S.-led military action in Kosovo, where the North Atlantic Treaty Organization (NATO) bombing campaign stopped Slobodan Milosovic's murderous campaign against civilian Albanian Kosovars and ultimately lead to his indictment and trial before the UN's International Criminal Court for the Former Yugoslavia, provided recent history's first dramatic example of the gap between positivist and naturalist conceptions of international jus ad bellum law. As such, this humanitarian intervention captured the attention of the conference participants, and formed the backdrop for Professor A.P.V. Rogers's article, Humanitarian Intervention and International Law. His article, by surveying the reaction of international scholars to the concept of humanitarian intervention, provides a roadmap of this divergence and conflict, and notes that this subject produces "an explosive mixture of ethics, politics, and law."

Professor Rogers provides the classical positivist perspective on humanitarian intervention by sketching how both the text of the U.N. Charter and its interpretation by the ICJ cabins the use of force to only individual or collective sell-defense or as a result of a U.N. mandate. Indeed, with respect to the ICJ, he notes that the Court "has said the respect for territorial integrity is an essential foundation of international relations," and is "skeptical about the use of force as an appropriate method to monitor or ensure respect for human rights." His survey of asserted, non-strictly charter-based permissible uses of force nonetheless includes preventing "an overwhelming humanitarian disaster." This approach, according to Professor Rogers, views international law as "not set in concrete," but as having to "adopt to meet new situations," including legitimating state intervention until the U.N. takes control "to prevent genocide or widespread crimes against humanity." Professor Rogers observes an open question created by such an approach: whether such law would sit "alongside the U.N. Charter to deal with situations not envisaged, or not adequately dealt with in the Charter," or whether it would effectively modify the Charter.

Delving into more specifics, Professor Rogers' survey of six legal approaches by international commentators to humanitarian intervention effectively provides a gradation of views from strictly positivist to more naturalistic. The third position he identifies regarding humanitarian intervention contains a naturalist bent, as it brings an external principle into the analysis: "there is an ethical imperative for law to permit humanitarian intervention in certain limited circumstances." He also identifies an approach to humanitarian intervention that hearkens back to the naturalist Cicero: "that authority to govern must be based on the will of the people," thus, where "a government does not have support of the population of or loses control over significant parts of its territory, such government has no power to represent that population or area. In a positivist move, Professor Rogers surveys state practice regarding humanitarian intervention, and concludes that States have started to follow a naturalist approach; he sees that a trend towards humanitarian intervention "has at least begun in the past ten years." This trend is not clearly identified as such in state practice, since, as Professor Rogers notes, only the U.K. set forth a clearly humanitarian reason for intervening in Kosovo, claiming that "it was the only means to avert an immediate and overwhelming humanitarian catastrophe." Professor Rogers concludes on a naturalist note, observing that "states cannot, on moral and policy grounds, simply sit back and watch the commission of genocide or persistent crimes against humanity." But he softens this conclusions by listing ten proposed limitations on humanitarian interventions.

9/11 and the Global War On Terrorism

Following the NATO military action in Kosovo, the dichotomy in discourse between the two approaches to international law was dramatically accelerated by the Bush administration's response to the September 11 terrorist attacks on the World Trade Centre and the Pentagon. Indeed, President Bush's ethical emphasis in both his "Axis of Evil" 2002 State of the Union address and the National Security Strategy of the United States of America (NSS), with their unambiguous moral tone and description of security strategy in the Global War on

Terror (GWOT), respectively, further focused the debate among conference participants.

Professor Michael N. Schmitt's article, US Security Strategies: A Legal Assessment, analyzes U.S. military actions during the GWOT, their doctrinal underpinnings, international precedent, and treaty law to answer five questions: when it is appropriate to use military force against terrorists; when it is legal to act without a mandate from the Security Council; when a State may act peremptorily in the face of future terrorism, Weapons of Mass Destruction (WMD) attack, or WMD transfer to terrorist; when counter-terrorist or counter-WMD operations can be conducted on foreign soil; and when a state sponsor of terrorism may be attacked. His article concludes that "there is no aspect of U.S. security strategy that is objectively illegal under international law." In reaching this result, Professor Schmitt uses a balanced and integrated approach to international law, utilizing an analysis that is both positivist and naturalist.

The naturalist approach manifests itself in his reasoned appeal to newly emergent facts in the GWOT and his call that all international legal practitioners account for "the constantly evolving security environment" in their interpretation of the applicable legal regime. He does just this, as elaborated below, when discussing anticipatory strikes and urging a fair balance between U.N. Charter Article 2(4)'s right protecting a State's territorial integrity and Article 51's right of a State to exercise self-defense. The positivist aspect of his article is best seen in the use of state practice (including state reaction or the lack thereof) to U.S. actions, his lack of an explicit discussion of an ethical basis for his interpretative approach incorporating the new security environment, and the need for a standard of evidence for anticipatory strikes.

Professor Schmitt's naturalist approach is apparent specifically in his description of the United States' new strategic environment, noting the Joint Chief of Staff's pre-September 11 Joint Vision 2020 prediction that opponents will counter the United States' "current conventional and nuclear advantages by adopting asymmetrical tactics and strategies," and how the NSS logically builds on this assumption by calling for disrupting and destroying terrorist networks by "direct and continuous action using all the elements" of power, thereby "taking the fight to the enemy by destroying the threat before it reaches the United States." Combined with the fact that the National Strategy for Combating Terrorism (NSCT) makes the point that "terrorism is no longer predominately secular and nationalistic or necessarily dependent on State-support... [making] traditional responses such as diplomacy or economic sanctions much less effective," and "some irresponsible governments—or extremist factions within them—seeking to further their own agenda may provide terrorists access to WMD," this new strategic environment is the foundation of his article's premise: "[t]hese changes in the nature of terrorism justify a new approach to the use of military force, pre-emption, and unilateral action."

In a positivist vein, to the extent it relies on state practice, Professor Schmitt views as significant the fact that the international community has grown "more tolerant of forceful responses to terrorism," contrasting the rejection by most of the world community to the 1986 U.S. air strikes against Libya (in response to the terrorist attack on a Berlin discotheque) with the mixed reaction to the cruise missile strikes into Afghanistan and Sudan (in response to the 1998 terrorist bombings of its embassies in Nairobi and Dar-es-Salaam) and the acceptance by the world community (after September 11) in numerous U.N. resolutions, which "by definition implicitly acknowledg[ed] the acceptability of using military force against terrorists under the law of self-defense." Professor Schmitt thus answers his first posed question: "[S]tate practice has unambiguously demonstrated that the use of military forces to combat terrorists, which the U.S. security strategy envisions, is no longer questionable as a matter of principle."

His treatment of the second question, regarding when it is legal to act without a mandate from the Security Council, first recognizes the "post-World War II positivist use-of-force paradigm" that admits only two U.N. Charter exceptions to the prohibition against the threat or use of force by any State: sell-defense and action authorized by the Security Council under Chapter VII. Illustrating, through use of the ICJ's opinion in

Military and Paramilitary Activities, how the most violent attacks by transnational terrorists would meet the threshold for "armed attack," Professor Schmitt then notes that strikes against al Qaeda (a group "that has planned or executed terrorist attacks against the United States for over a decade") are neither anticipatory nor punitive, they are rather "defensive responses to an armed terrorist campaign that is currently underway," comporting with the law of self-defense and consistent with the requirements of necessity and proportionality. He dismisses the question of whether it is appropriate to act, absent a U.S. Security mandate, as irrelevant in the context of Operation Iraqi Freedom, because the U.S. and the United Kingdom argue that Iraq's material breach of the cease-fire that ended the first Gulf War allowed them to use force pursuant to Security Council Resolution 678 authorizing military action by States cooperating with Kuwait following the Iraqi invasion. Nevertheless, in the absence of these prior Security Council resolutions, Professor Schmitt's discussion of self-defense establishes that the U.N. Charter right to self-defense permits the U.S. to act alone against terrorists and WMD "if the right to self-defense has matured," as in the case of al Qaeda's terrorist campaign against the U.S.

Turning next to pre-emption, Professor Schmitt decries the language in the NSS which suggests this concept needed to be refashioned in light of the capabilities and objectives of today's adversaries. Instead, he asserts, agreeing with Professor Novak's general approach discussed below, that pre-emption's legality turns on the "circumstances in which the pre-emptive strike is launched." Pre-emption must therefore comply with necessity and proportionality, and be in response to an imminent attack. Rejecting the temporal element of imminence as nonsensical in the era of terrorist attacks launched without warning, Professor Schmitt instead illustrates how interpreting "imminence" in light of its underlying purpose (permitting States to effectively defend themselves against attack) results in a reasonable interpretation "that allows a State to act anticipatorily (preemptively) if it must strike immediately to defend itself in a meaningful way and the potential aggressor is irrevocably committed to attack." When dealing with a terror group that has definite plans to conduct an attack, though the target, location, and exact timing is unknown, the use of anticipatory force to prevent these scenarios is lawful, because the last opportunity a State may have to foil an attack could arise "weeks, even months, earlier" than the attack.

One complicating factor raised by this conclusion is international law's failure to contain an express standard of proof regarding the quality of evidence necessary to justify an anticipatory strike.

Although, as noted by Dr. Cook below, an ethical approach would sketch a justification for requiring a standard, this evidentiary justification was not specifically addressed by Professor Schmitt, though he does recommend a "clear and compelling standard," drawn from the United States' October 2001 self-defense notification to the Security Council regarding the attacks on al Qaeda and Taliban assets in Afghanistan, to fill this gap in positive law. In any event, pre-emption is a moot issue with regard to the attacks on al Qaeda, Professor Schmitt writes, occurring as they do after al Qaeda attacked the US on September 11 in the course of an extended campaign.

The final two questions discussed by Professor Schmitt involve when counter-terrorist and counter-WMD operations can be conducted on foreign soil, and when a state sponsor of terrorism may be attacked.

The first question becomes problematic when counterterrorist operations are conducted without the consent of the State where the terrorists are located, due to U.N. Charter Article 2(4)'s prohibition against the use of force against the territorial integrity of a state. Pointing out that the right to self-defense would be meaningless if terrorist found sanctuary in a sympathetic State following an attack, Professor Schmitt reasons that a "lair balance" between these conflicting textual rights "must be sought." Regarding the question of when a state sponsor of terrorism may be attacked, he noted that the ICJ's judgment in Military and Paramilitary Activities setting the threshold of State involvement constituting an involvement in an armed attack has been lowered by state practice in the aftermath of the outpouring of support for Operation Enduring Freedom against the Taliban. What remains unclear, Professor

Schmitt observes, is the exact level of support that meets the lower threshold.

Professor Robert Turner's article, Operation Iraqi Freedom." Legal and Policy Considerations, like Professor Schmitt's contribution. utilizes both a naturalist and positivist approach to international law. Before doing so, however, Professor Turner also addresses perhaps the most perplexing question raised for non-legal specialists in the debate over Operation Enduring Freedom's legality: how can both sides in the debate base their position on "their preference for peace and their respect for the rule of law?" For Professor Turner, the answer is summed up in one word at the beginning of his article: "credibility." He explains up front that it is only when the rule of law is credible—that is, when international actors otherwise favourably disposed to resorting to aggression or other unlawful activity that threatens the peace perceive that the law will be enforced—that it has any chance of playing a serious role in keeping the peace.

Turning towards the "law" that needs to be "enforced," Professor Turner keys in on the relevant international legal principles related to "peace" by pointing out several principles embedded in the U.N. Charter relevant to the legality of state actions. First, the authors of the Charter vowed "remove 'threats to the peace'" even before aggression could occur, and that very vow finds expression in Article 1 of the U.N. Charter. Second, the Security Council has primary, not exclusive, responsibility for maintaining international peace and security. Finally, not every use of force by sovereign states in the absence of Security Council authorization is unlawful due to the Article 2(4) prohibition on threats or use of force against the territorial integrity or political independence of any state. Quoting Professor Phillip C. Jessup, a distinguished international scholar and ICJ judge, in support of his assertion that Article 2(4) does not prohibit force not aimed against territorial integrity or political independence of a state, Professor Turner finds Operation Iraqi Freedom thereby not prohibited by that section of the U.N. Charter.

Additionally, Article 2(4)'s reservation of "individual or collective self-defence," observes Dr. Turner, recognizes the legitimacy of state self defense, either individually or collectively, in the face of U.N. Security Council paralysis. Indeed, he notes, a senior member of the US delegation to the San Francisco conference that produced the U.N. Charter, Senator Arthur Vandenberg recognized this very scenario: "If the Security Council fails to act—or is stopped from acting, for example, by a veto—Article 51 continues to confound aggression. The United Nations is thus saved from final impotence. So is righteous peace." As recounted by Professor Turner, Operation Iraqi Freedom played out this scenario in reality. Describing in excruciating detail the futile attempts by the U.N. Security Council to convince Saddam that their Chapter VII threat of "severe consequences" was credible should he continue to flout U.N. resolutions, and noting the threatened Security Council vetoes by France and Russia, Professor Turner concludes that Operation Iraqi Freedom was thereby expressly permitted as an exercise of self defense to remove what the Security Council had recognized for "more than a dozen years" as a threat to peace.

Professor Turner's aforementioned discussion of the "purposes" of the U.N. Charter delves behind the text of that document, and this is where his naturalist approach to law is most evident. His long list of horrific humanitarian abuses by Saddam Hussein serves to illustrate his point that the U.N. Charter article 2(7) general prohibition against U.N. action in matters within the domestic jurisdiction of a state does not place these and similar perpetrators of terror beyond the reach of the law: "[I]f international law were so corrupt or wrong-headed that it immunized the slaughters of Stalin, Hitler, Mao, or Pol Pot from effective action by the world community, it would neither be worth studying nor supporting." By complementing his conclusion that Operation Iraqi Freedom was legal from a positivist perspective with his conclusion that Operation Iraqi Freedom was also ethically appropriate, Professor Turner provides international law with needed "credibility" while discerning its solid ethical basis. In short, by bringing to the debate a discussion of how Operation Iraqi Freedom comports not only with the text, but also the purpose, of the U.N. Charter, as well as international legal precedent,

Professor Turner's article provides one example of how ethical considerations are brought to bear in international legal analysis.

Capturing the Ethical Reality

Dr. Martin L. Cook's piece, The Ethical and Legal Dimensions of the Bush 'Pre-emption' Strategy, makes the case for ethics as an unapologetic element of international law. Urging international lawyers to view international law as kind of "stop-motion photograph of a much older and varied ethical tradition of reflection on the justifications for the use of military force," Dr. Cook posits that the "older ethical traditions [may well] provide useful insights and fundamental principles to guide the development of our thinking in times of change." After describing the current framework of international affairs that resulted from the Westphalian settlement, including a description of Michael Walzer's legalist paradigm, he notes that the Westphalian international system's concept of peace, the absence of aggression among those states, is essentially a positivist one, focusing exclusively on state-to-state interactions. This particular approach to international law, he implies, sits uneasily beside our moral sense:

> Normative legal and ethical thought has needed to accommodate exceptions to the paradigm to capture our considered moral intuitions about justified use of force precisely because some cases that do not fit the paradigm are clearly necessary and justified.... From a normative ethical perspective, however—as distinct from the legal perspective—there was always something deeply dissatisfying about the Westphalian compromise.

Dr. Cook identifies this "sharp dichotomy" between an international system built on equal states and their rights on one hand and the rights of actual human beings on the other, and how the Hague and Geneva movements, followed by international humanitarian law, were attempts to recognize the value and rights of human persons not "subsumed into their identity as members of the state." The NSS' suggestion that "sovereignty will not be a cloak beneath which terrorism and the development of Weapons of Mass Destruction can be developed" is not a "dramatic departure," Dr. Cook observed, from "the conceptual framework for overriding state sovereignty in the name of internationally agreed goals [that] has been in place for half a century." He opines that the NSS reduces the justification of pre-emption and self-defense to "a single test: capability," and as such, due to the State's self-judgment regarding this test, it "threatens to "destabilize the entire structure of restraint for use of force and respect for national sovereignty that lies at the foundation of the modern international system." This result disturbs Dr. Cook, for he envisions a "real and fundamental realignment" that apparently embraces a naturalist approach to international law, one in which "universalizing concerns with human rights and liberties, combined with the exigencies of the Global War on Terror," shifts the positivist foundation to a system that "rather than starting with state sovereignty as the bedrock, would instead start with the shared values and concerns of (for lack of a better word) the 'civilized' world." Dethroned from its privileged position in a positivist approach to international law, sovereignty would instead be "contingent on a state's willingness and ability to protect and preserve the lives and rights of its citizens and to participate meaningful in the struggle for the maintenance of global order against fundamental threats against it such as the aspirations of al Qaeda." Likening the current conflict with al Qaeda to the situation faced by Augustine, with both involving a foe committed to the collapse of the existing global civilization, Dr. Cook concludes by placing the responsibility for defense of the world's fundamental and shared concerns directly on the United States. He cautions the "sole remaining superpower" that its defense "transcends conventional issues of national interest of sovereign states." Instead, Dr. Cook views the critical defensive struggle as how to forge "a new, commonly understood, and generally embraced set of normative principles for the action of states in the international arena."

Professor Michael Novak, in his article, Just Peace and the Asymmetric Threat: National Self-Defense in Uncharted Waters, agrees with Dr. Cook's observation that the GWOT is a challenge to our civilization; "our concern," Prof Novak notes, "is the military threat to our nation and our civilization, and all the civilizations based upon law and rights, the threat quite starkly thrust upon us by Islamicist terrorists on September 11, 2001." Rather than directly urging ethics' inclusion in international law, as Dr. Cook did, Professor Novak instead makes ethics' role in international law self-evident by highlighting the current ethical and political context of the GWOT and providing an insightful historical discussion on the peculiar problems of asymmetrical warfare.

Drawing a sharp distinction between the religion of Islam and the political sect of Islamicism, Professor Novak identifies the latter as the West's enemy, willing "to use a distorted, anti-intellectual, and narrow version of religion to achieve their political purposes." The war in which the West is engaged is "not a war against the religion of Islam;" rather, notes Professor Novak, it is against Islamicism, whose leaders have "studied intensely the organizational methods and the political uses of terror perfected during twentieth-century political movements, such as those led by Lenin, Mussolini, Hitler, and Stalin," in order to fuse these into a distorted, secular version of primitive Islam. Describing the source of Islamicisim as resentment, and not transcendent religion, Professor Novak reminds the reader what one seldom finds in the popular media: "the sheer secular misuse of Islam by extremists is so severe that a great many Muslims around the world are prepared to give their lives rather than to accept them as rulers." In the GWOT, Professor Novak identifies three areas challenged by clandestine terror: first, just war concepts, second, political legitimacy, and third, military tactics. He devotes his article to the first two areas.

Drawing on just war tradition, Professor Novak notes that "when waged for the right purposes, with the right means, and in the right way, war may be an act required by justice." Rejecting the new mantra by "glib thinkers" that there is always a "presumption against war," Professor Novak notes that "justice sometimes requires the waging of war," for example, to come to the defense of one's own nation or of a weak nation under unjust attack by a stronger, to restore international order so that the rule of law and the protection of the rights of the people can flourish to punish terrorists and others who destroy civil order or employ violence to drive peoples apart, and the like. Professor Novak then reminds the reader that these ad bellum reasons have been used to justify past wars on terror, such as those against "organizations of pirates preying upon international shipping lanes," and identifies what is new in the current GWOT: "both the vulnerability of the modern city to clandestine terrorism and the terrible destructiveness of even small packages of modern weaponry." Thus, Professor Novak concludes that, under today's conditions of war, there is no such lead time, not at least when the destruction is wrought in such seemingly innocent events as a car driving into a hotel driveway... or a small briefcase being carried onto a train for explosion in a tunnel.... Sure knowledge that an aggressive attack is already underway is no longer easy to obtain in time for self-defense.

In making decisions to go to war preemptively or otherwise, Professor Novak emphasizes the need for phronesis, or practical wisdom, which entails the best possible choice one can make on what one knows at the time, and "must meet the highest standards of such reason." Professor Novak then finishes his discussion on just war by observing that "given the great destructive power available to terrorists today, pre-emption may be the only practical manner of self-defense."

Professor Novak's discussion of legitimacy underscores the economic, moral, and political nature of the division between Europe and the United States. He concludes that "Europeans consider themselves more secular and enlightened than Americans, and also more moral and politically advanced," despite the fact that the "collapse of socialism as an economic idea has failed to awaken the European left to a fresh appreciation of the resiliency and creative capacities of capitalism." Accordingly, these differences translate into the international legal sphere, with Europe trying to force the United States to submit to the U.N. in the name of legitimacy because Europe, particularly France, believes "it is better able than the United States to guide and control the U.N.," while in the U.S., the U.N. is a "source of division." Stating that "there is no utility in idealizing the United Nations," as it is "deeply flawed... mired in the muck of self-interest, disguised alliances, [and] double dealings" Professor Novak observes that "member states singled out for the special privileges of the Security Council in 1948 no longer represent the political realities of the twenty-first century." Dismissing the positivist argument, identified above by Professor Rogers, that strictly limits the use of force to individual or collective self-defense or as a result of a U.N. mandate, Professor Novak opines that the "canons of self-defense put forth in the U.N. Charter... sufficiently establish[] the moral legitimacy of the removal of Saddam Hussein from power by the Coalition of the Willing," and drives home this point by describing the unpalatable alternative. The question of how to achieve a legitimate and working government in Iraq after the war poses the second issue involving legitimacy. "The faster that the Iraqis take responsibility for their own self-governance, the better—with one major caveat," that it would be "a grave error to turn self-governance over to Iraqis until sufficient checks-and-balances are in place so that no one faction can seize total control over everybody and everything."

Both Professor Cook and Professor Novak view ethics as a vital element of international law, albeit one that is not yet directly acknowledged as such by many States or international officials. By discerning the pull of the ethical moral impulse on nations, justifying a use of force not strictly within the Westphalian positivist paradigm, and by emphasizing how ethics and the just war tradition can provide precedent and reasoning for states engaged with an asymmetrical enemy, Dr. Cook and Professor Novak respectively recapture the moral content of international law. In so doing, they illustrate how a less positivist, more naturalist, legal approach may better meet the critical challenges to, and gaps in, the positivist legal paradigm created by the end of the Cold War, the GWOT, and increasing humanitarian crises.

Between Peace and War: What Law Applies?

In contrast to the authors described above, Professor Wolf Heintschel von Heinegg takes a largely positivist approach to international law as he clarifies the law applicable to transitions from war to peace in his article, Factors in War to Peace Transitions. Attributing some of the misunderstandings that arise in this topic to reliance on political statements rather then on "a proper analysis of the relevant treaties," the theoretical theme that flows throughout Professor Heintschel von Heinegg's article is his insistence on a positivist approach, which he views as key to international order. "If international lawyers cease to remember one of their main tasks, i.e., the identification of rules and principles of international law as expressions of the consensus of States," he accordingly reminds his readers in his conclusion, "public international law will lose its credibility, and, most of all its legally binding force." In the face of today's dynamic legal order, Professor Heintschel von Heinegg counsels patience. This current attribute of the legal order does not 'justify calls for a modification of international law as soon as its application to a given situation creates problems." Rather, he states that existing law will produce operable solutions, especially if it includes "concepts of international law that may have been established a long time ago but that still continue to govern international relations." Any remaining disconnect between this existing law and new situation creates "inconveniences," but "that is a typical side effect of every legal order."

Professor Heintschel yon Heinegg's evidently tolerant attitude towards gaps in the positivist approach to international law created by current challenges is understandable, since, at least in his field of study, there are not many glaring gaps created by the lack of positive treaty law or state practice. As his article clarifies, the 1907 Hague Regulations, the Geneva Conventions of 1949, and the Additional Protocols of 8 June 1977 to the Geneva Conventions provide answers for determining the law applicable in various scenarios of state use of force and occupation. He notes that common Article 2 of the 1949 Geneva Conventions makes those humanitarian conventions applicable to every situation of armed conflict, whether recognized or not by a state, as well as to all "cases of partial or total occupation of the territory of a High Contracting Party, even if the said occupation meets with no resistance." Discussing the relationship between occupation and the cessation of active hostilities, Professor Heintschel von Heinegg notes that the beginning and end of international armed conflict do not necessarily have to coincide with the beginning and ending of occupation. He defines "positive peace" as "the reestablishment of the lull sovereignty of all belligerents," which is "based upon the principle of sovereign equality of States," thereby contrasting sharply with Dr. Cook's and Professor Novak's approaches to state's sovereignty as encompassing a justly constituted political order.

Professor Heintschel von Heinegg uses state practice, in addition to treaty law, to illustrate how armistices no longer suspend military operations but rather terminate wars, and how a ceasefire has the same effects as an armistice under the 1907 Hague Regulations. He also tackles the issue of how the ancient international legal concept of debellatio, the extermination in war of one belligerent by another through annexation of the former's territory after conquest and the annihilation of enemy forces, no longer provides valid title to territory but remains a valid term to describe a "factual phenomenon" of"the total defeat of one party to the conflict that has led to the extinction of most of that State's sovereignty." If followed by occupation or some form of exercise of authority by the victorious State, debellatio will not imply termination of war.

Professor Heintschel yon Heinegg's approach of his topic from a positivist perspective does not preclude his conclusion that Operation Iraqi Freedom was legal. When discussing ceasefires ordered by the U.N., he observes that Article 25 of the U.N. Charter makes ceasefires ordered by the Security Council binding upon the parties to the conflict, and if the ceasefire is made dependent upon unfulfilled conditions by one belligerent, the other belligerent is entitled to resume hostilities. Accordingly, Professor Heintschel von Heinegg notes, since "Iraq had been in material breach of the obligations imposed on it by Resolution 687, the allied forces regularly resumed armed hostilities in order to induce Iraq to comply with its obligations under the Security Council resolutions." Moreover, he adds "the extent and scale of armed force used in response to the breach of a ceasefire is immaterial." As one would expect in a positivist approach that strives to separate the moral from the legal, the immorality of Saddam Hussein's tyrannical regime does not factor into Professor Heintschel von Heinegg's analysis.

Instead, the legally significant "fact" in his article is the fact of Iraq's material breach of the UN's resolution.

The latter part of Professor Heintschel von Heinegg's article discusses the establishment of post-conflict law in a vanquished state, setting forth a useful chart to aid in his thorough discussion of how current treaties and state practice impact the exercise of sovereignty in a vanquished state by an occupying power. It is in his analysis of debellatio and occupation law, however, that one senses the gap in the positivist approach to the law of war to peace transactions, a gap that natural law unobtrusively fills. Specifically, Professor Heintschel von Heinegg observes that "[n]either the Hague Regulations nor Geneva Convention IV seem to have anticipated a situation of debellatio," since it does not reflect the reality of total defeat and the extinction of functioning governmental structures as in Iraq after Operation Iraqi Freedom. This lack of controlling international law does not result in international paralysis, rather, he states, "the victorious power that decides to establish and maintain an occupation regime have to be adapted to the special situation of debellatio," may, absent U.N. Security Council veto, "take all measures necessary to install functioning administrative, juridical, legislative, and social structures that are a prerequisite for the 'orderly government' of the territory concerned." Indeed, this is a right the U.N. acknowledges as going "beyond the traditional rules of occupation law." It is in this U.N.-recognized debellatio gap in existing positivist rules where natural law subtly but powerfully provides the reasoning for preserving the political sovereignty of the vanquished state and the moral dignity of its inhabitants. What Dr. Cook would describe as preserving "the lives and rights of its citizens," and what Professor Novak would assert is "the Iraqis tak[ing] responsibility for their own self-governance," is exactly the ethical reasoning the U.N. urged in U.N. Resolution 1483 when calling upon the United States and United Kingdom "to promote the welfare of the Iraqi people through the effective administration of the territory, including, in particular, working towards the restoration of conditions of security and stability and the creation of conditions in which the Iraqi people can freely determine their own political future."

IRAQ RESOLUTION

The Iraq Resolution or the Iraq War Resolution (formally the Authorization for Use of Military Force Against Iraq Resolution of 2002, Pub.L. 107-243, 116 Stat. 1498, enacted October 16, 2002, H.J.Res. 114) is a joint resolution passed by the United States Congress in October 2002 as Public Law No: 107-243, authorizing the Iraq War.

Contents

The resolution cited many factors to justify the use of military force against Iraq:

- Iraq's noncompliance with the conditions of the 1991 cease fire, including interference with weapons inspectors.
- Iraq's alleged weapons of mass destruction, and programs to develop such weapons, posed a "threat to the national security of the United States and international peace and security in the Persian Gulf region."
- Iraq's "brutal repression of its civilian population."
- Iraq's "capability and willingness to use weapons of mass destruction against other nations and its own people".
- Iraq's hostility towards the United States as demonstrated by the alleged 1993 assassination attempt of former President George H. W. Bush, and firing on coalition aircraft enforcing the no-fly zones following the 1991 Gulf War.
- Members of al-Qaeda, an organization bearing responsibility for attacks on the United States, its citizens, and interests, including the attacks that occurred on September 11, 2001, ARE (present tense) known to be in Iraq.
- Iraq's "continu[ing] to aid and harbor other international terrorist organizations," including anti-United States terrorist organizations.
- The efforts by the Congress and the President to fight terrorists, and those who aided or harboured them.

- The authorization by the Constitution and the Congress for the President to fight anti-United States terrorism.
- Citing the Iraq Liberation Act of 1998, the resolution reiterated that it should be the policy of the United States to remove the Saddam Hussein regime and promote a democratic replacement.

The resolution "supported" and "encouraged" diplomatic efforts by President George W. Bush to "strictly enforce through the U.N. Security Council all relevant Security Council resolutions regarding Iraq" and "obtain prompt and decisive action by the Security Council to ensure that Iraq abandons its strategy of delay, evasion, and noncompliance and promptly and strictly complies with all relevant Security Council resolutions regarding Iraq."

The resolution authorized President Bush to use the Armed Forces of the United States "as he determines to be necessary and appropriate" in order to "defend the national security of the United States against the continuing threat posed by Iraq; and enforce all relevant United Nations Security Council Resolutions regarding Iraq."

Passage

An authorization by Congress was sought by President George W. Bush soon after his September 12, 2002, statement before the U.N. General Assembly asking for quick action by the Security Council in enforcing the resolutions against Iraq.

Of the legislation introduced by Congress in response to President Bush's requests, S.J.Res. 45 sponsored by Sen. Daschle & Sen. Lott was based on the original White House proposal authorizing the use of force in Iraq, H.J.Res. 114 sponsored by Rep. Hastert & Rep. Gephardt and the substantially similar S.J.Res. 46 sponsored by Sen. Lieberman were modified proposals. H.J.Res. 110 sponsored by Rep. Hastings was a separate proposal never considered on the floor. Eventually, the Hastert-Gephardt proposal became the legislation Congress focused on.

Introduced in Congress on October 2, 2002, in conjunction with the Administration's proposals, H.J.Res. 114 passed the

House of Representatives on Thursday afternoon at 3:05 p.m. EDT on October 10, 2002, by a vote of 296-133, and passed the Senate after midnight early Friday morning, at 12:50 a.m. EDT on October 11, 2002, by a vote of 77-23. It was signed into law as Pub.L. 107-243 by President Bush on October 16, 2002.

United States House of Representatives

Party	Ayes	Nays	PRES	No Vote
Republican	215	6	0	2
Democratic	82	126	0	1
Independent	0	1	0	0
TOTALS	297	133	0	3

- 126 (61%) of 208 Democratic Representatives voted against the resolution.
- 6 of 223 Republican Representatives voted against the resolution: Reps. Duncan (R-TN), Hostettler (R-IN), Houghton (R-NY), Leach (R-IA), Morella (R-MD), Paul (R-TX).
- The only Independent Representative voted against the resolution: Rep. Sanders (I-VT)
  - o Reps. Ortiz (D-TX), Roukema (R-NJ), and Stump (R-AZ) did not vote on the resolution.

United States Senate

Party	Ayes	Nays	No Vote
Republican	48	1	0
Democratic	29	21	0
Independent	0	1	0
TOTALS	77	23	0

- 21 (42%) of 50 Democratic senators voted against the resolution: Sens. Akaka (D-HI), Bingaman (D-NM), Boxer (D-CA), Byrd (D-WV), Conrad (D-ND), Corzine (D-NJ), Dayton (D-MN), Durbin (D-IL), Feingold (D-WI), Graham (D-FL), Inouye (D-HI), Kennedy (D-MA), Leahy (D-VT), Levin (D-MI), Mikulski (D-MD), Murray (D-WA), Reed (D-RI), Sarbanes (D-MD), Stabenow (D-MI), Wellstone (D-MN), and Wyden (D-OR).

- 1 of 49 Republican senators voted against the resolution: Sen. Chafee (R-RI).
- The only Independent senator voted against the resolution: Sen. Jeffords (I-VT)

AMENDMENTS OFFERED TO THE HOUSE RESOLUTION

The Lee Amendment

Amendment in the nature of a substitute sought to have the United States work through the United Nations to seek to resolve the matter of ensuring that Iraq is not developing weapons of mass destruction, through mechanisms such as the resumption of weapons inspections, negotiation, enquiry, mediation, regional arrangements, and other peaceful means.

Sponsored by Rep. Barbara Lee (D-CA).

Failed by the Yeas and Nays: 72-355

The Spratt Amendment

Amendment in the nature of a substitute sought to authorize the use of U.S. armed forces to support any new U.N. Security Council resolution that mandated the elimination, by force if necessary, of all Iraqi weapons of mass destruction, long-range ballistic missiles, and the means of producing such weapons and missiles. Requested that the President should seek authorization from Congress to use the armed forces of the U.S. in the absence of a U.N. Security Council resolution sufficient to eliminate, by force if necessary, all Iraqi weapons of mass destruction, long-range ballistic missiles, and the means of producing such weapons and missiles. Provided expedited consideration for authorization in the latter case.

Sponsored by Rep. John Spratt (D-SC-5).

Failed by the Yeas and Nays: 155-270

The House Rules Amendment

An amendment considered as adopted pursuant to the provisions of H.Res. 574

Sponsored by House Rules.

Resolution (H.RES.574) agreed to by voice vote

Amendments offered to the Senate Resolution

The Byrd Amendments

To provide statutory construction that constitutional authorities remain unaffected and that no additional grant of authority is made to the President not directly related to the existing threat posed by Iraq.

Sponsored by Sen. Robert Byrd (D-WV).

Amendment SA 4868 not agreed to by Yea-Nay Vote: 14-86

To provide a termination date for the authorization of the use of the Armed Forces of the United States, together with procedures for the extension of such date unless Congress disapproves the extension.

Sponsored by Sen. Robert Byrd (D-WV).

Amendment SA 4869 not agreed to by Yea-Nay Vote: 31-66

The Levin Amendment

To authorize the use of the United States Armed Forces, pursuant to a new resolution of the United Nations Security Council, to destroy, remove, or render harmless Iraq's weapons of mass destruction, nuclear weapons-usable material, long-range ballistic missiles, and related facilities, and for other purposes.

Sponsored by Sen. Carl Levin (D-MI).

Amendment SA 4862 not agreed to by Yea-Nay Vote: 24-75

The Durbin Amendment

To amend the authorization for the use of the Armed Forces to cover an imminent threat posed by Iraq's weapons of mass destruction rather than the continuing threat posed by Iraq.

Sponsored by Sen. Dick Durbin (D-IL).

Amendment SA 4865 not agreed to by Yea-Nay Vote: 30-70

Weapons of mass destruction and Al-Qaeda

Two of the arguments used to justify the invasion of Iraq—the capability to produce and/or the possession of weapons of mass destruction and active links to al Qaeda — have been found to be incorrect according to all subsequent official reports.

The post-invasion Duelfer Report stated that Hussein had still not given up on trying to produce WMD in 2003. His strategy was to first bring UN sanctions to an end by demonstrating that he was cooperating with weapons inspectors and, once sanctions were lifted, to then revive Iraq's WMD program, including nuclear weapons. The report also stated that Hussein did not want to appear weak. To deter his enemies, he intentionally deceived the world into thinking he still had WMD. There was a "balancing act" between cooperating with the UN and keeping a "strategic deterrent".

A 2007 report by the Inspector General of the Department of Defense, declassified and released at the request of Senator Carl M. Levin (D-Mich), asserted that the claims of an operational working relationship between Iraq and al Qaeda, as put forth by a key Pentagon office in the lead up to the invasion of Iraq, were based on dubious or unconfirmed reports. President Bush has, since the invasion of Iraq, explicitly stated that Iraq was not involved in 9-11, which has also been concluded by subsequent reports, and al-Qaeda were operating in areas outside of Saddam Hussein's control. Also, the day before she voted on the resolution, Senator Hillary Rodham Clinton said during a speech on the Senate floor that there was no dispute that Hussein was not involved in the September 11th attacks. Nevertheless, BBC News, The Christian Science Monitor, the New York Times, the Washington Post, the Institute for Public Accuracy, and Media Matters for America contend that members of the administration repeatedly over the years made suggestive statements with the implied message there was a link between Saddam Hussein and the attacks.

The Bush administration initially suggested the discrepancy between the allegations and the subsequent findings was due to failure by the intelligence community. However, it became apparent that, prior to the invasion, these allegations had already been widely disputed, which had purportedly been reported to the U.S. administration. An in-depth investigation into the nature of these discrepancies by the Senate Intelligence Committee was frustrated, according to the New York Times. The Robb-Silberman Commission stated that the President's Daily Briefs from the intelligence community tended to repeat information in a misleading way. The National Intelligence Estimate (NIE) provided to Congress was more "nuanced" and less "alarmist" than information given to the President. However, the vast majority of Senators did not read the NIE and relied on briefings by the administration. Among those who have stated they did not read the NIE and voted positively for the Iraq Resolution are the former Senator and current United States Secretary of State Hillary Clinton, Senator John McCain, and former Senator John Edwards.

The assertion such weapons posed a threat towards the U.S. was not supported by the available evidence at the time, according to subsequent reports. The Bush administration asserted that two small trailers that had been found in Iraq were "weapons factories," despite the fact that U.S. intelligence officials possessed evidence to the contrary at that time. Weapon inspectors were given access to the alleged weapon factories, despite statements to the contrary by the Bush administration. Continuing these inspections was made impossible by the U.S.-led invasion of Iraq which forced the U.N. inspectors out, ignoring their requests for more time.

Skeptics argue that the administration knowingly distorted intelligence reports or ignored contrary information in constructing their case for the war. The Downing Street memo and the Bush-Blair memo are used to substantiate that allegation. Congressional Democrats sponsored both a request for documents and a resolution of inquiry.

LEGALITY OF INTERNATIONAL LAW

Debate about the legality of the 2003 invasion of Iraq under international law centers around ambiguous language in parts of UN Resolution 1441 (2002). The UN Charter prohibits any war unless it is out of self-defense or when it is sanctioned by the UN security council. If these requirements are not met international law describes it a war of aggression.

The position of the US and UK is that the invasion was authorized by a series of UN resolutions dating back to 1990. Resolution 1441 declared that Iraq was in "material breach" of the cease-fire under UN Resolution 687 (1991), which required cooperation with weapons inspectors. The Vienna Convention on the Law of Treaties states that under certain conditions, a party may invoke a "material breach" to suspend a multilateral treaty. Thus, the US and UK claim that they used their right to suspend the cease-fire in Resolution 687 and to continue hostilities against Iraq under the authority of UN Resolution 678 (1990), which originally authorized the use of force after Iraq invaded Kuwait. This is the same argument that was used for Operation Desert Fox in 1998. They also contend that, while Resolution 1441 required the UNSC to assemble and assess reports from the weapons inspectors, it was not necessary for the UNSC to reach an agreement on the course of action. If, at that time, it was determined that Iraq breached Resolution 1441, the resolution did not "constrain any member state from acting to defend itself against the threat posed by Iraq".

It remains unclear whether any party other than the Security Council can make the determination that Iraq breached Resolution 1441, as UN members commented that it is not up to one member state to interpret and enforce UN resolutions for the entire council. In addition, other nations have stated that a second resolution was required to initiate hostilities. John Conyers, Robert Parry and Marjorie Cohn assert that the Iraq war was a violation of the U.N. Charter and as such a war of aggression (a crime against peace) and therefore a war crime. Kofi Annan too has said the war in Iraq is an "illegal act that contravened the UN charter." Some scholars, including Columbia law professor Michael Dorf, have argued that treaties are binding on the U.S. under international law.

U.S. law

In early 2003, the Iraq Resolution was challenged in court to stop the invasion from happening. The plaintiffs argued that the President does not have the authority to declare war. The final decision came from a three-judge panel from the US Court of Appeals for the First Circuit which dismissed the case. Judge Lynch wrote in the opinion that the Judiciary cannot intervene unless there is a fully-developed conflict between the President and Congress or if Congress gave the President "absolute discretion" to declare war.

6

Control of Mercenaries and Private Military Companies

CHANGING THE LAW AND THE RISE OF MERCENARISM POST 1945

A long-standing problem with controlling the use of mercenaries has been the limit of modern legal analysis and precedent setting surrounding the problem. Some early legal writers did concern themselves with the practice of hiring mercenaries, but with mercenary forces playing such an integral part in the formation of European armies such concerns were largely ignored until the middle of the 19th century. It was a similar picture outside of Europe. Though, as a consequence of their use in colonial conflicts and other situations that served the national interests, their demise took longer, if it occurred at all. For example, the French Foreign Legion is a mercenary force that was originally recruited to protect French colonial possessions and yet it still exists today.

Prior to 1945, concerns to do with mercenaries were expressed largely through the development of the law of neutrality. A country that allowed its national territory to be used for the purpose of the recruitment or enlistment of mercenaries was deemed to be in support of a belligerent. This was a position that was likely to draw the neutral country into a conflict it had no interest in through retaliatory action by one of the belligerents. As a result, provisions were included in the 1907 Hague Convention prohibiting mercenary recruitment on national territory. Such obligations were limited to countries policing their own national territory, and were not extended to include the prevention of nationals crossing over to another country to enlist in the army of a belligerent as, for example, was the case of foreign individuals who enlisted in the International Brigades in the Spanish Civil War. A number of states did introduce domestic legislation to reinforce their international obligation, while a few sought to control the actions of its citizens wishing to enlist in foreign armies.

After the Second World War, significant changes were made to the law regulating the use of force in international politics. Even so, such changes to legislation that did occur did not address the question of the involvement of mercenaries in combat. Considering the numerous conflicts, including that of ideology that surfaced between the United States and the Soviet Union immediately after the war, the introduction of regulations concerned with controlling the activities of mercenaries was of minor concern to the international community. This indifference changed during the period of decolonisation in the 1960s. This period witnessed a marked increase in mercenary numbers and activities, especially in countries of central Africa. For example, mercenaries such as Mad Mike Hore, Jacques Schramme and Bob Denard all fought in the Congo in the 1960s. The concept of mercenaries now took on greater importance for the international community, but more so for those African countries directly affected by the presence of mercenaries involved in their wars of liberation. Even so, the response of the International Community was to do little more than re-affirm Article 2(4) of the United Nations (UN) Charter, explaining the logical implications of the Article.

It was not until the late 1960s that the use of mercenaries against national liberation movements fighting for independence in colonial territories was declared a criminal act by UN General Assembly Resolution 2465, thus designating mercenaries as outlaws. This position was further endorsed through subsequent resolutions concerned with colonialism. This, as Taulbee explains, marked a significant move away from the idea of collective liability of the traditional law toward individual criminal liability. These resolutions further called for third party states to observe traditional law prohibiting mercenary recruitment on their national territory, and to introduce laws forbidding their nationals from engaging in mercenary activities.

The OAU Convention, adopted in 1972, for the Elimination of Mercenaries in Africa mirrors those trends found in UN resolutions concerning mercenaries. The Convention also extended state obligation regarding the control of the activities of its nationals, by making states responsible for the prohibition and punishment of any activity connected with mercenaries that may occur within their jurisdiction. The move away from the traditional view that states are individually accountable, to a collective responsibility towards accountability is the result of the OAU Convention placing an obligation on individuals who meet its requirement. Individuals have to either fulfil the requirements in Article One, which defines what a mercenary is, or the requirements regarding those people who recruit or assist mercenaries through training, financial help, or protection of prosecution. Further to this departure is the adoption of obligations by contracting States to stop their nationals from participating in mercenary activities as defined by the above Convention. As such, contracting States must endeavour to prosecute any person, whatever nationality, within their jurisdiction, who is accused of mercenary activity. The relevant Article One reads as follows:

- [A] 'mercenary' is classified as anyone who, not a national of the state against which his actions are directed, is employed, enrols or links himself willingly to a person, group or organisation whose aim is:
- (a) To overthrow by force of arms or by any other means the government of that Member State of the Organisation of African Unity;
- (b) To undermine the independence, territorial integrity or normal working of the institutions of the said State;
- (c) To block by any means the activities of any liberation movements recognised by the Organisation of African Unity.

Even with these provisions, the OAU Convention does not totally forbid the recruitment of mercenaries. In accordance with Article One, governments, or any other groups, are prohibited from employing mercenaries to defend themselves from those actions carried out by a liberation movement recognised by the OAU. The aim of the Article was primarily to stop European mercenaries fighting for the minority governments of Rhodesia and South Africa. However, non-nationals that fall outside the defined category of mercenary may be employed by a government to defend itself from dissident groups within its own borders, as in the case of the Cuban troops that fought on the side of the Popular Movement for the Liberation of Angola (MPLA) during the Angolan civil war. The reason for this was to allow African governments to give support to movements of national liberation, without allowing conditions to emerge in their own country that might encourage such dissident groups to operate against them. At the same time, African governments wanted to deny the opportunity to mercenaries to operate against the same movements of national liberation.

The capture and subsequent trial of thirteen mercenaries in Angola in 1976 again focused international attention on mercenary activity. All the accused were charged with the crime of being a mercenary. Of the thirteen accused, four were sentenced to death, and the others to long prison sentences. As a result of the trial, the Luanda Draft Convention on the Prevention and Suppression of Mercenaries (1976) was issued. The Luanda Draft Convention again stressed the responsibility of individual states to prevent their nationals from taking part in mercenary activities, as well as those individual persons defined as mercenaries. State responsibility, as such, is conveyed in Article 319 that makes government officials who undertake to employ, aid, or recruit mercenaries liable for criminal prosecution. Thus, failure by a State to carry out the prosecution of officials who had undertaken such activities would, argues Taulbee, 'create international responsibility on the part of the offending State'. Article 5 represents the attitude of the members of the Popular Revolutionary Tribunal who presided over the trial, in that, 'a mercenary bears responsibility both for being a mercenary and for any other crime committed by him as such'. Possibly the most important Article was Article 4, which deprived mercenaries of the status of being a lawful combatant.

Captured mercenaries were, as such, not given the protected status of prisoners-of-war. This, as Hampson explains, 'violated the principle of equality of belligerents and confused the *jus ad bellum* and *jus in bello*'. This provision was later incorporated into the 1977 Geneva Additional Protocol I. However, the definition of mercenary as decided upon by the Geneva conferees is more limited in scope than that expressed in the Luanda Draft Convention. At the same time, Additional Protocol I does allow for States to offer to mercenaries prisoner-of-war status if they so wish. What is clearly understood, and addressed in Additional Protocol II, is that mercenaries are entitled to the basic humanitarian treatment and protections provided for persons in the power of a party to the conflict who are not otherwise entitled to more favourable treatment.

A Legal Definition

How then should we define a mercenary? The traditional notion of a mercenary is 'a soldier willing to sell his military skills to the highest bidder, no matter what the cause'. Mockler, on the other hand, believes the true mark of a mercenary is 'a devotion to war for its own sake. By this, the mercenary can be distinguished from the professional soldier whose mark is generally a devotion to the external trappings of the military profession rather than to the actual fighting'. While such general definitions may be true, they do not address the question of a precise definition. The task of addressing such a question is essential if individual persons are to be denied important legal rights as a consequence of falling into a particular category. But also, as international law covering mercenaries evolves, States will have no option but to take on the obligation to control those activities determined by the scope of the definition.

The definition that finally emerged, set out in Additional Protocol I to Article 47 of the Geneva Convention (1949), only did so after states ensured their political interests were looked after. As such, the definition has allowed for competing state interests, while it has also had to balance precision with significance. As Taulbee notes, it has had to strike a balance between a need to provide general parameters for evaluating contextual elements, and requirements that attempt rigorous and exhaustive descriptions of persons, situations and activities. A definition that is too detailed might be too rigid, and thus unable to accommodate changes as circumstances demand. On the other hand, a brief definition that allows a judgement in its application leaves open the possibility of abuse. A very general definition would allow the interpretation of the terms to be too openly susceptible to political or ideological calculations.

The actual definition in international law as set out in Additional Protocol I to Article 47 of the Geneva Convention (1949) classifies a mercenary according to the following criteria:

- Is specially recruited locally or abroad to fight in an armed conflict;
- Does, in fact, take part in activities;
- Is motivated to take part in hostilities essentially by the desire for private gain
- Is neither a national of a Party to the conflict nor a resident of a territory controlled by a Party to the conflict;
- Is not a member of the armed forces of a Party to the conflict;
- Has not been sent by a State, which is not a Party to the conflict on official duty as a member of its armed forces.

The wording of the definition is such as to exclude those foreign nationals in the service of the armed forces of another country, as with those individuals that served in the International Brigades in the Spanish Civil War, and where the international community is willing to tolerate such persons, from falling within the definition of mercenary. Furthermore, Article 47 of Protocol I ignores foreign military personnel integrated into the armed forces of another state. Included here would be the French Foreign Legion, and Gurkhas. The definition also leaves out those induced by ideology or religion, and those who may not participate directly in the hostilities. Finally, those foreigners employed as advisors and trainers are also not included in the definition.

Without a clear working definition, the problem arises of how to ensure states comply with international laws relating to the control mercenaries. While states accepted in principle, through the adoption of General Assembly resolutions, not to permit by way of action or omission an armed group launching an invasion of another state from within its own borders, member states still failed to restrain their citizens from enlisting in mercenary groups. As a result of this failure, the international community recognised the need for a multilateral convention. During the course of the thirty-fifth session of the General Assembly it was therefore decided to draft an International Convention against the recruitment, use, financing and training of mercenaries. The Convention was presented to the General Assembly for signature and ratification in December 1989. The Convention adopts a more inclusive definition than that found in the Additional Protocol I. As a result, the recruitment, use, financing and training of mercenaries are also declared to be offences. But, while such an inclusive definition is not in itself a problem, there is a problem in policing the activities of individuals engaged in the above activities. We will return to the Drafting of an International Convention against the recruitment, use, financing and training of mercenaries later. First, there is a need to examine the issues connected with the problems of constructing an adequate legal definition of the term mercenary.

The Additional Protocol I must still rely on motivation when making a distinction between mercenaries and other types of combatants. Western States have been highly critical of this point. The motivation for mercenaries is money. Thus explains Abraham, 'a mercenary is motivated ... essentially by the desire for private gain'. However, as the Diplock report, which was published in 1976 following the involvement of British mercenaries in Angola, makes clear the chances of determining the motivation of combatants is virtually impossible:

"... any definition of mercenaries which require positive proof of motivation would either be unworkable, or so haphazard in its application as between comparable individuals as to be unacceptable. Mercenaries, we think, can only be defined by reference to what they do, and not by reference to why they do it."

While motivation should not comprise the sole definitional element, objections to its use as part of the definition are also unconvincing. In domestic law, critical distinctions based upon motivation are regularly made. There also appear to be no grounds for objecting to the evidence needed to establish motivation under the test in Additional Protocol I. The point being made here is that it is very difficult to obtain the necessary evidence to prove the first five elements of Taulbee's list, included below, since it means having access to the records of the opposing party to the conflict, a situation unlikely to occur.

Taulbee identifies 6 issues relating to the problem of distinguishing mercenaries from other foreign volunteers. They are:

- (1) Whether a distinction should be drawn between non-nationals and resident non-nationals;
- (2) Whether a "mercenary" includes all who meet certain operative tests, or whether some overt actions directly related to hostilities are necessary;
- (3) Whether outside private forces and national troops should be considered different from third party states;
- (4) Whether individuals recruited for a specific conflict should be distinguished from those recruited under other circumstances;
- (5) Whether motive should be defined through objective tests;
- (6) Whether a legal distinction should be drawn between legitimate and non-legitimate movements for national liberati

However, the problem of obtaining evidence necessary for a prosecution exists with all statutes that provide for extraterritorial jurisdiction over nationals, and, as such, there are no real grounds to object to matters of this concern. More important is the question of compensation, which is seen as essential to establishing a distinction in motivations. For African states, compensation by way of private gain distinguishes mercenaries from non-resident non-nationals who volunteer to aid legitimate liberation movements. If the drive for private gain is removed from the definition, then the definition holds no substantive content. The term mercenary would simply describe all non-resident non-nationals that have chosen to fight for whatever reason, including political and religious ones. This therefore appears to be an important test in determining the status of a combatant in war. Though at present it is unclear how states would test for compensation that might take a number of forms other than monetary.

Origin also serves to define the term mercenary. A mercenary is neither a national of a party to the conflict nor a resident of a territory controlled by a party to the conflict. Instead they are generally 'bands of professional soldiers ... temporarily united, under leaders of strong personality, fighting for pay and the [spoils of war], but not entirely indifferent to claims of honour and legality, or to the interests of their country of origin'. The idea of using origin in international law to help determine the apportionment of rights and obligations of a national may not necessarily be the most effective way of linking an individual to a specific territory. Non-nationals often reside in territories where conflicts erupt. As such, even as a non-national, they may feel they have a substantial interest to protect. Such a person might also have important skills, as well as local knowledge, that one of the parties to the conflict may be prepared to pay a premium wage for. Yet under the OAU Convention and the Luanda Draft Convention, this particular type of individual could be deemed a mercenary. Their status is wholly dependent on the party they choose to fight for in a conflict. The critical test being whether such a person opposes movements for self-determination, or liberation.

The definition of mercenary as noted above in Additional Protocol I gives conservative answers to the above questions. Furthermore, for a person to qualify as a mercenary they must meet all of the tests in the definition consecutively. As previously discussed, any person deemed a mercenary has no right to the protected status of a combatant, or prisoner-of-war that a soldier serving in a state military will have. The purpose of Additional Protocol I and II is to ensure that those participating in struggles against colonial domination, racist regimes, or alien domination are given protected status, while the provisions also apply to the use of mercenaries in general. The enlistment of mercenaries in national liberation movements is, again, not singled out. This point is interesting since the Additional Protocol I definition does not mirror the general thrust of the language of previous UN resolutions or of the OAU and Luanda Draft Conventions.

The Additional Protocol I definition represented a compromise in that members of the Organisation for Economic Cooperation and Development (OECD) emphatically argued that criminal liability can only come from the performance of specific acts of war while the majority of other nations wanted a broader definition of mercenary to include the idea that status alone was also a criminal act. Those states that sought a more inclusive definition pointed to the fact that by voluntarily enlisting in a mercenary force the person was signifying intent, and, as such, enlistment should automatically subject the individual to criminal liability. Thus, placing an emphasis on the voluntary act of enlistment meant that the determining of mercenary status carries an additional onus. Any person carrying out those acts listed above in the draft conventions, including the Convention against the Recruitment, Use, Financing and Training of Mercenaries, would be liable for prosecution, thereby supplying a necessary deterrent upon such an individual.

African states have also attempted to extend the definition of mercenary to include those mercenaries not covered under the definition in Additional Protocol I. A number of states have argued that Additional Protocol I only covers those mercenaries engaged in armed conflicts of an international nature. The Protocol does not cover civil wars where mercenary activity is most prevalent. As such, any useful definition of mercenary must include situations of intrastate wars, as well as meet the criteria of international armed conflict.

Delegates from the West have agreed that the 1977 Nigerian Draft Convention for the Elimination of Mercenaries in Africa should address those situations that fall outside those covered by Additional Protocol I. In agreeing to this position, Western states assert two principal positions be met. First, that the definition in Additional Protocol I does not apply only to situations of international armed conflict, and second, any definition set out in future conventions remains consistent with the Additional Protocol I definition so as to maintain the integrity of the regime established in Additional Protocols I and II. Any additional circumstances that do not fall under international armed conflict should be presented in a form that is in line with the Additional Protocol I definition. Western states argue that the correct way of addressing the above problem is to prohibit certain acts and activities within a carefully specified context. These delegates, argues Taulbee, must widen the contingencies to which the Additional Protocol I definition would apply, rather than expanding the classes of activities and individuals included in the definition proper.

The result of these discussions, to reconcile opposing views between different member states of the UN, was, as mentioned previously, the introduction of the International Convention against the Recruitment, Use, Financing and Training of Mercenaries on the 4th December 1989.46 The articles included in the Convention embrace more closely those ideas advocated by African states. The Convention diverges somewhat from the conservative emphasis of Additional Protocol I. The approach adopted is the specific offences approach for extending the definition of mercenarism to situations that fall outside international armed conflict. Thus, those acts mentioned in the Convention's title become equivalent to direct participation within the meaning of the provisions of Additional Protocol I.

The International Convention against the Recruitment, Use, Financing and Training of Mercenaries is not beyond criticism. Abraham points to three areas where the Convention is deemed problematic:

- (1) Only when the crime of mercenarism is committed within the boundaries of a state or by a national of a state is that state accorded jurisdiction to deal with the crime;
- (2) In the event of conflict, the Convention denies to the aggrieved state the right to proceed against an offending state;
- (3) The Convention provides for no monitoring mechanism of its provisions, thus placing that responsibility on the individual member states.

Since 1989, when the Convention against the Recruitment, Use, Financing and Training of Mercenaries was signed, The United Nations General Assembly has continued to pass resolutions concerned with the activities of mercenaries. Such resolutions, as previously explained, have, in general, reflected the restricted nature of the ban on the use of mercenaries, as well as those traditional worries expressed by the international community towards the activity of individuals engaged in mercenary activities, while also dealing with the actions of mercenaries in a variety of different circumstances. These include the destabilising of neighbouring states, acting as the vanguard for a coup in a small state, the hindering of movements of national liberation in their drive towards independence, and the violation of human rights. The object of these resolutions is to highlight the fact that the actions of mercenaries contravene basic principles of international law, including non-intervention in the internal affairs of states, and territorial integrity, and independence. This type of mercenarism is described by Marie-France Major as 'an international wrongful act'.

Again there is no total ban on the use of mercenaries under international customary law. Those conventions introduced by the international community have focused on the prohibition of mercenary activities aimed at the sovereignty of legitimate states, the suppression of movements of national liberation, or national self-determination. Those activities undertaken by PMCs in Africa and other parts of the world have, in the majority of cases, fallen outside of this characterisation. We will return to this issue later. But briefly, they have not been seen to challenge the sovereignty of states, oppose movements of national liberation, or been directed against movements of self-determination. As Zarate argues, in Africa there has developed 'a clear distinction between foreign support of legitimate African regimes and individualised mercenary attempts to wreak havoc in the region'.

The continued effort to condemn mercenarism through the different political institutions of the UN is seen by some, whose objective is to interpret that part of international law concerned with mercenary activity, as constituting evidence of a rule, 'that states have a legal obligation, which goes beyond the traditional constraints of international law, to control the recruitment of its nationals in situations where a threat to peace and security exists'. Those that support this argument fail to recognise that such condemnation and resolutions have been directed at specific conflicts, which have seen mercenaries pose a potential threat to international peace and security. As such, these resolutions and condemnations do not necessarily constitute a blanket opposition to the use of mercenaries.

Expanding on this argument, even where the condemnation and resolutions expressed have been more general in their range and meaning, the statements do not endorse customary international norms. In this instance, the General Assembly does not have the authority, under the UN Charter, to enact, alter, or to terminate rules of international law. Thus, the proliferation over the last four decades of resolutions and repetition of recommendations regarding mercenaries does not amount to evidence of practice on the part of states, and *opinio juris* that would be necessary for such practice to constitute international law. All such resolutions and recommendations that originate from the General Assembly or those regional organisations including the OAU can do is to contribute to the eventual establishment of a future customary rule of international law. Further to this argument is the issue of ratification. For the International Convention against the Recruitment, Use, Financing and Training of Mercenaries to constitute settled international law the Convention must be ratified. As the Convention stands at present, only sixteen states have become signatories. Of these, three, Angola, Congo, and Nigeria, have all hired, or had direct dealings with PMCs. The Convention needs twenty two signatures for it to pass into law. In this respect, the legal impact of the Convention is further reduced, giving additional weight to attempts to undermine the above claim regarding customary rule of international law.

Mercenaries and State Responsibility

The notion that states have responsibilities has in the past been linked to the idea of territorial sovereignty. While a state can demand that it receives the same rights of independence and territorial integrity as any other state that is a member of the international community, holding such rights necessitates an obligation on the part of all states to respect and protect these rights when applied to other states. Taulbee notes that there are two areas of responsibility a state recognises when it violates international law. First, loss and damage resulting from the act; and second, delinquency imputed to the state. The validity of these propositions has been rarely disputed.

The topic of the debate has primarily been the connection between non-performance of duties and consequent liability. The point of contention is realising a standard of performance required by states within the context of the extent of its own legal authority in protecting the rights of other states. A state's standard of performance in controlling mercenary activities, as well as PMCs, is only one part of this ongoing debate. The idea of statehood suggests states are able to perform certain functions. One function that is presumed to be within the capacity of the incumbent government, since they have absolute authority over their territory, is to police the activities of its own nationals within its own borders. Garcia-Mora argues that a '[s]tate which fails to prevent a harmful act against another state has violated an international obligation to preserve world order. Furthermore, even if a state has clearly used all of its means to prevent an unlawful act against a foreign state, but has not remedied the situation, it has failed to discharge its obligation and will remain liable'.

The implication for states of failing to carry out their international responsibilities to other member states is that there be imposed on them, through arbitral tribunals and courts, an absolute standard of liability. In the past, relative standards have been imposed and have sought to include two components: knowledge and capacity. The fact that a state knows of a harmful act, or one that is to be carried out is not in or of itself sufficient to establish responsibility. Even so, traditional international law does require states to demonstrate good intentions by extending all reasonable efforts to protect member states from acts of aggression by their nationals, and or, to punish offenders.

The issue as to the extent a state can, or should, be held responsible for its nationals engaged in mercenary activity is a contentious one. This is even more so now that there is a reliance on motivation in the definition of mercenary found in both the Additional Protocol and the International Convention against the Recruitment, Use, Financing and Training of Mercenaries. In this respect, both conventions ignore the accountability of states regarding the actions carried out by their nationals. Indeed, as Abraham points out, '[t]hose peremptory norms which do in fact exist continue to shy away from imputing responsibility to a state for the actions of its citizens'. This reluctance is, in part, related to 'the international community's fear of mercenaries, ... in that they are wholly independent from any constraints built into the nation state system'. Thus, it is argued that states are extremely limited as to what they can actually do to prevent nationals from carrying out mercenary activities, and should therefore not be held responsible for those nationals that undertake such activities. A state that accepts such a proposition ignores its own obligations of respect for territorial integrity and political independence of other member states in the international community, and as such neglects its responsibility to ensure its own nationals behave in a manner that serves not to undermine those obligations. If this problem is to be addressed, then international law will have to have incorporated within it the power to attribute responsibility to states for the actions of its nationals. Such responsibility would arise from the acknowledgement by states of the fact that membership of the international community accords such a responsibility on the modern state.

Ultimately, the core of this argument is not whether a state has a responsibility ascertaining to obligations to the international community, this is not disputed, but how far this responsibility reaches. The law has in the past deemed it unreasonable to attempt to attach responsibility to a state where there has been a satisfactory attempt by that state to stop those actions caused by their own nationals that might lead to an act of injury on another state. Thus, without the state concerned having prior knowledge of those actions, there is limited action it can take to prevent such actions occurring, and, as such, the international community has not felt it appropriate to punish the state concerned over those actions carried out by its nationals. Furthermore, many states, especially less developed ones, do not have the necessary resources to control the movements and actions of their nationals. It is not surprising therefore that the international community has supported attempts by individual states to introduce legislation and administrative measures to control the actions of their nationals, which they see as the easier route. Such legislative action is within the capability of most member states, including most of the less developed, of the international community.

The driving force for legislation against mercenaries has on the whole come from Third World states. African states, in particular, have sought to negotiate a multilateral convention concerning the use of mercenaries in armed conflicts around the world. This is not surprising. If we trace the history of mercenary involvement in armed conflicts since the 1960s we see that most have taken place on the African continent, and are continuing to do so. As a result of this, most recent commentaries have argued that there is now the need to strengthen existing laws concerning all aspects of mercenary activities, as well as to make states more accountable for the actions of their citizens. While the International Convention against the Recruitment, Use, Financing and Training of Mercenaries has addressed the need to prohibit the activities of individual mercenaries, or groups of mercenaries, it has failed to apportion blame to states for the actions of its citizens who conduct such activities. As such, the impact the Convention has had on preventing mercenaries from applying their trade has been much reduced. The meaning of the Convention can therefore be seen as more symbolic than substantive. Current efforts and concerns might also be directed at a phenomenon that is in reality transitory in nature.

PRIVATE MILITARY COMPANIES OR CORPORATE MERCENARIES

The argument so far has been with regard to the problems associated with constructing a legal definition of mercenarism, and a state's responsibility in preventing their nationals from participating in mercenary activities. Thus, we have seen how difficult it is to give an exact legal definition of mercenarism that covers every eventuality of mercenary activity, and which states accept and are therefore willing to subscribe to. In such a difficult environment any attempt to brand those working for private military companies (PMCs) as mercenaries only further complicates the issue of definition. David Shearer draws on this, pointing out the significant problems of applying the criteria of Article 47 to the personnel of military companies. Shearer highlights four major areas of contention:

Employees of PMCs, whose job it is to provide military support, are frequently accused of being mercenaries, but with a smart business veneer to hide this fact, and are therefore seen as operating illegally. Although problematical, establishing the legal status of PMCs is therefore important since it has implications for the conduct of employees of PMCs involved in the promotion of international security in general. While such exclusions, as commented on by Shearer, are in reality technicalities, with each section left sufficiently open so as to be able to question its actual meaning, taken together they render Article 47 unworkable for both the individual mercenary and PMCs. This is of course intentional. African states have in their construction of the legal definition of mercenarism, been careful to ensure that such a definition is sufficiently open to dispute, and this allows them the opportunity to employ whatever military force they deem necessary to maintain power.

Should we therefore define those working for PMCs as mercenaries? This is more of a political than legal question in that reasons for deciding either way will invariably be politically driven. Those opposed to any private military involvement in war argue that those who work for PMCs should only be described as mercenaries and that no other label should be attached that might conceal this fact. For this group, state armies, or national liberation movements, representing political communities, are the only forces that should be allowed to conduct war. War is the domain of these two groups, and, as such, they are responsible for the physical protection of the communities they represent. PMCs, on the other hand, are often seen as representing the economic interests of a minority group, normally Western interests that share nothing in common with those they are charged with protecting. Those that carry out the work of PMCs should therefore be classified as mercenaries, in that they represent an organisation willing to sell military skills to the highest bidder, no matter what the cause. The only exceptions are those foreigners that choose to fight because of their political convictions. Such a person or group of persons receive no economic benefits from fighting, unlike those working for PMCs, and are therefore described as volunteers.

Those opposed to this argument point to the political agendas of those who describe PMCs as representing nothing more than corporate mercenaries. This is especially the case of those military forces that see themselves as victims of the success of PMCs, whether they are themselves legitimately recognised by their own people or not. In the end it is left up to the conscience of the individual, influenced by his own political beliefs and values, as to whether a person contracted to give military assistance to a foreign army is a mercenary, volunteer, or security advisor. Finally, regarding the issue of regulating PMCs, if the international community is that unclear as to its intentions about whether the actions of PMCs should be made illegal, then the alternative is to control them through regulation.

The problem of definition is clearly related to the political problems associated with the reluctance of states to exclude the use of mercenaries. The result of this reluctance has seen the emergence of tension between African states in particular, and the West, especially Europe. While African leaders have been the driving force behind shaping international law regarding mercenaries, the West remains cautious. Such tensions are noticeable in The Additional Protocol 1 definition. Indeed, as where OECD countries see criminal liability coming from the performance of specific acts in war, the majority of nations have sought to include the idea of status alone as a criminal act, thus establishing a more inclusive definition. Attempts to resolve these tensions are proving difficult.

Current International Legislation on Mercenaries

Current international legislation on mercenaries is very limited in its effectiveness. The weakness of the law is of course intended. Governments, but notably African governments, see no reason to deny themselves access to a potentially valuable source of military expertise. All the international community has wanted to do for the last 5 decades is to remove freelance mercenaries from those wars it would prefer them to stay out of. This is particularly so of African governments who have been the target for these freelance mercenaries in the majority of cases, and still are today.

Finally, international law at present makes no mention of PMCs. This is not surprising considering the recent appearance of these organisations on the international stage. The problem now is if, in the future governments do allow PMCs to actively engage in civil wars on their behalf, failure to achieve a legal separation could see the employees of PMCs having their combat status legally challenged by the other side, leading to dire consequences for any employee unlucky enough to be taken captive. In this respect, international law has two important roles to play if PMCs are to act on behalf of the international community. First, it must protect the combat status of PMCs employees actively engaged in fighting. Second, it must allow PMCs go about their lawful business, while prohibiting the activities of the classic mercenary. These will not be easy tasks to achieve, but they must if PMCs are to work for the international community.

7

War on Terrorism and International Law

A BRIEF HISTORY OF THE GUANTANAMO DETAINEES

Seven days after the terrorist attacks of September 11, 2001, President George W. Bush signed into law Congress' Authorization for Use of Military Force (AUMF). In Section 2(a) of the AUMF, Congress granted the President the power to: use all necessary and appropriate force against those nations, organizations, or persons he determines planned, authorized, committed, or aided the terrorist attacks that occurred on September 11, 2001, or harboured such organizations or persons, in order to prevent any future acts of international terrorism against the United States by such nations, organizations or persons.

Following this Congressional mandate, the President ordered the United States military to engage in combat operations to oust the Taliban government from Afghanistan on October 7, 2001 in Operation Enduring Freedom. The Taliban government was accused of not cooperating with the United States Government in its War on Terrorism due to its refusal to hand over members of Al Qaeda who were suspects in the September 11th terrorist attacks.

After the first three months of combat operations, the United States military detained more than 7,000 Taliban soldiers and Al Qaeda suspects and fighters. On January 11, 2002, the United States Government began airlifting detainees from

Afghanistan to Camp X-Ray, a prison located at the United States Naval Base in Guantanamo Bay, Cuba. On March 27, 2002, there were 300 detainees in Camp X-Ray. On April 28, 2002, these detainees were transferred to Camp Delta, a newly constructed prison at the United States Naval Base in Guantanamo Bay, Cuba. More detainees from Operation Enduring Freedom were periodically transferred to Camp Delta, and by August 5, 2002 there were 598 detainees being held there, most of whom were still detained in June 2004.15

The humanitarian conditions of Camps X-Ray and Delta have been extensively documented by journalists and human rights activists around the globe. The International Committee of the Red Cross has been allowed access to the facility in order to monitor the Government's treatment of the detainees. Generally, detainees are kept in fenced cells measuring 1.8 meters by 2.4 meters with a height of 2.4 meters. Detainees are each issued a sleeping mat, blanket, buckets, a canteen, two orange boiler suits, one pair of flip-flops, two bath towels, toiletries, a copy of the Koran, and meals, medical visits, mail services, and exercise periods.

The primary reason for the detainees' detention at Guantanamo Bay is to elicit information that may be helpful in the War on Terrorism. As President Bush stated in response to questions about Guantanamo Bay, " We want to learn as much as we can in this new kind of war about the intention, and about the methods, and about how these people operate." During their detention, the detainees have been subjected to various interrogation methods designed to elicit such valuable information in connection with the Government's War on Terrorism. These interrogation techniques include placing prisoners in uncomfortable interrogation cells and deceiving them into thinking they are in the hands of Middle East interrogators who knew all about their culture, giving uncooperative prisoners cold food, and isolating uncooperative prisoners from their peers. In February 2002, nearly two-thirds of the detainees staged a hunger strike after a guard stripped a detainee of an improvised turban while he was praying in his cell, illustrating the strict nature of the confinement of the detainees designed to elicit valuable intelligence.

In October 2003 the International Committee of the Red Cross found that detainees were suffering from "a worrying deterioration" in mental health as a result of the uncertainty surrounding their future. On June 28, 2004, the United States Supreme Court relieved some of uncertainty surrounding the future of the detainees when it issued its decision in *Hamdi v. Rumsfeld.* In *Hamdi*, the Court held that a United States citizen captured by Northern Alliance forces in Afghanistan, transferred to the United States Government, and later held as an "enemy combatant" without access to counsel at Camp Delta and later on a naval brig outside Norfolk, Virginia, was entitled to "meaningful opportunity to contest the factual basis for [his] detention before a neutral decisionmaker." On the same day, the Court in *Rasul v. Bush* held that the federal habeas corpus statute, 28 U.S.C., conferred jurisdiction on federal courts to hear habeas corpus petitions from the Guantanamo detainees.

Nine days later, the Department of Defense announced the establishment of the Combatant Status Review Tribunal (CSRT), which would give the Guantanamo detainees an opportunity to contest the factual bases for their detentions as "enemy combatants" before three neutral military officers with the presence of another military officer as a "personal representative." In addition, the detainees were to be notified of their right to seek a writ of habeas corpus from federal courts in the United States under 28 U.S.C. § 2241 in accordance with *Rasul.* As of August 22, 2005, the CSRTs found that 38 of the detainees were not properly classified as enemy combatants and later released. 68 others were transferred to other governments, and as of August 22, 2005 there were 505 detainees at Guantanamo classified as enemy combatants. However, in September 2005, more than one-third of the detainees staged a hunger strike to protest conditions and their prolonged confinement without a trial.

It should be noted that a strict construction of *Hamdi* would limit its application to United States citizens captured and/or detained abroad engaged in military activity against the Government, as the Government has argued. On the other hand, critics view the CSRTs as insufficient to satisfy the mandates of *Hamdi*, which many believe applies to all detainees without regard to citizenship or place of capture or detention.

THE GOVERNMENT'S POSITION ON THE STATUS OF THE GUANTANAMO DETAINEES

The Government has maintained from the start that the Guantanamo detainees are not entitled to the protections granted to POWs under the Third Convention. In particular, the Government contends that since Al Qaeda is not a state party to the Third Convention, its captured members are not entitled to POW protection under the Third Convention. More intriguing is the Government's argument that, although the Taliban government was never recognized by the United States, Afghanistan is a party to the Third Convention and the Taliban detainees are therefore protected by the Third Convention, but the Taliban detainees are not entitled to POW status under the Third Convention because they did not "effectively distinguish themselves from the civilian population of Afghanistan," "have not conducted their operations in accordance with the laws and custom of war," and because Afghanistan is a "failed state" to which the Geneva Convention does not apply. Nevertheless, in a secret memorandum issued on February 7, 2002, the President stated that "[a]s a matter of policy, the United States Armed Forces shall continue to treat detainees humanely and, to the extent appropriate and consistent with military necessity, in a manner consistent with the principles of Geneva."

Before delving into a detailed analysis of the Third Convention's applicability to the Guantanamo detainees, it will be helpful to briefly outline the history and relevant provisions of the Third Convention. The Third Convention was prepared in Geneva, Switzerland during the Diplomatic Conference for the Establishment of International Conventions for the Protection of Victims of War, and ratified by the United States on August 12, 1949.41 It was intended to revise the 1929 Geneva Prisoners of War Convention based on lessons learned during World War II, and there are currently 192 countries that are parties to the Third Convention. American courts have frequently relied upon the Third Convention in the disposition of their cases, as have courts of parties to the Third Convention around the world.

The Third Convention gives a relatively detailed description of who is to be given the protections granted to POWs under the Third Convention. Article 4(A)(1) of the Third Convention states that POWs include "members of the armed forces of a Party to the conflict, as well as members of militias or volunteer corps forming part of such armed forces." In addition, Article 4(A)(2) includes as POWs:

Members of other militias and... volunteer corps, including those of organized resistance movements, belonging to a Party to the conflict... provided that such militias or volunteer corps, including such organized resistance movements, fulfil the following conditions: (a) that of being commanded by a person responsible for his subordinates; (b) that of having a fixed distinctive sign recognizable at a distance; (c) that of carrying arms openly; (d) that of conducting their operations in accordance with the laws and customs of war.

Finally, Article 4(A)(3) also includes as POWs "members of regular armed forces who profess allegiance to a government or an authority not recognized by the Detaining Power."

The Government's conclusions regarding the status of the Al Qaeda detainees seem to be a straightforward interpretation of the Third Convention. Because Al Qaeda was not a state party to the Third Convention and the Al Qaeda detainees do not profess allegiance to a government or authority not recognized by the United States, the status of the Al Qaeda detainees is governed by Article 4(A)(2) of the Third Convention. Although it is undeniable that Al Qaeda maintained a structure with commanders and soldiers and there is evidence that members openly carried arms in Operation Enduring Freedom, there is no evidence that Al Qaeda has a symbol recognizable from a distance. The final prong of the Article 4(A)(2) test, whether Al Qaeda conducted its operations in accordance with the laws and customs of war, is a rather amorphous test that can be argued either way with respect to the Al Qaeda detainees. Nevertheless, because Al Qaeda did not have a fixed sign recognizable from a distance, the Government is on strong ground in denying POW status to the Al Qaeda detainees in Operation Enduring Freedom. However, as will be discussed in Section V, it seems disingenuous for the United States to refuse to grant the Al Qaeda detainees at Guantanamo Bay POW status and protection due to the mere fact that they do not belong to an organization with a fixed sign recognizable at a distance.

The Government's argument that the Taliban detainees are not entitled to the protections granted to POWs in the Third Convention is weak at best. The fact that the United States did not recognize the Taliban government is irrelevant in determining whether the Taliban detainees are entitled to POW status under Article 4(A)(3) of the Third Convention. Therefore, the Taliban detainees were not required to distinguish themselves from the civilian population in Afghanistan or conduct its operations in accordance with the laws and customs of war in order to be entitled to POW status under the Third Convention as required by Article 4(A)(2). Furthermore, under the Article 4(A)(1) of the Third Convention, it is enough that the members of the Taliban were members of "an armed party to the conflict," and it was clear that the United States was in conflict with the Taliban and understood it to be the rogue government of Afghanistan. In addition, as noted by Judge Joyce Hens Green of the United States District Court for the District of Columbia in *In Re Guantanamo Detainees* in holding that the Taliban detainees were covered by the Third Convention, "[n]othing in the Third Convention itself... authorizes the President of the United States to rule by fiat that an entire group of fighters covered by the Third Convention falls outside of the Article 4 definitions of 'prisoners of war.'" In short, the Government's refusal to grant POW status to the Taliban detainees can be seen as a direct refusal to apply international law with respect to the Guantanamo detainees.

The most contentious element of the Government's application, or lack thereof, of the Third Convention to the Guantanamo detainees is the fact that POW treatment was denied to all detainees without regard to the particular circumstances of each individual detainee. In particular, Article 5(2) of the Third Convention provides that:

Should any doubt arise as to whether persons, having committed a belligerent act and having fallen into the hands of the enemy, belong to any of the categories enumerated in

Article 4, such persons shall enjoy the protection of the present Third Convention until such time as their status has been determined by a competent tribunal.

It was not until February 8, 2002 that a spokesperson of the State Department indicated that the United States would be prepared to review its determination about the applicability of Article 4 of the Third Convention should any doubt about status arise in individual cases. To this date, the Guantanamo detainees have not been placed before any tribunal to determine their status under the Third Convention. The only tribunals that have passed judgment on the detainees are the CSRTs, which determined whether the detainees were "enemy combatants," not POWs. In fact, as illustrated in Section II, 38 detainees were ultimately released after the CSRTs due to insufficient evidence of their status as enemy combatants. The fact that there was insufficient evidence to hold 38 of the detainees as enemy combatants supports the conclusion that there was and is significant doubt about the status of the individual detainees at Guantanamo Bay. The failure of the Government to establish a competent tribunal to this date to individually determine the status of the Guantanamo detainees is therefore in direct violation of Article 5(2) of the Third Convention.

In refusing to grant the Al Qaeda and Taliban detainees the protections afforded to POWs under the Third Convention, the Government is dramatically increasing its ability to interrogate the detainees. In particular, Articles 17 and 118 of the Third Convention state that detainees recognized as POWs cannot be compelled to give any further information than their name, rank, date of birth, and identification number and must be released and repatriated after the cessation of hostilities. In arguing that the Guantanamo detainees are not entitled to POW status, the Government is legitimizing its interrogation techniques at Guantanamo Bay. Although it is undoubtedly desirable that the Government obtain information from terrorist suspects, and in all likelihood many of the detainees at Guantanamo contain such information, such interrogation does not comport with the principles underlined by Articles 17 and 118 of the Third Convention. In addition, the failure to grant the Guantanamo detainees POW status makes them vulnerable to indefinite detention, also directly in contrast to the principles underlying Articles 17 and 118 of the Third Convention.

In any case, the Guantanamo detainees, if not afforded POW status, are entitled to the protections granted to civilians under the Fourth Geneva Convention, which include the right to due process in the event of criminal prosecution, freedom from physically or morally coercive interrogation, the right to repatriation (including the right to leave the enemy territory voluntarily) unless reasons of security prevent it, and the right to limited internal camp governance. However, these protections may be derogated to the detainees in either Afghanistan or the United States' territories "in those cases where absolute military security requires," but full rights must be granted "at the earliest date consistent with the security of the [United States]." There has been no effort by the Government to determine if each detainee is a security threat and when each detainee may be released "consistent with the security of the [United States]" and afforded the protections granted to civilian detainees under the Fourth Convention. Therefore, the Government has flouted the Fourth Convention while refusing to grant the Taliban and Al Qaeda detainees at Guantanamo Bay the protections afforded to POWs under the Third Convention.

Finally, Additional Protocol I to the Geneva Conventions, derived from the 1974-1977 Diplomatic Conference on International Humanitarian Law Applicable in Armed Conflict, also lends support to the conclusion that the Taliban detainees should be granted POW status. Although the United States rejected Additional Protocol I in 1987, many argue that it still provides the basis for binding customary international law. Article 43(1) of Additional Protocol I broadens the Third Convention's definition of combatants entitled to POW protection as "all organized armed forces, groups and units which are under a command responsible to that Party for the conduct of its subordinates, even if that Party is represented by a government or an authority not recognized by an adverse Party." Article 44(3) of Additional Protocol I qualifies that "combatants are obliged to distinguish themselves from the civilian population while they are engaged in an attack or in a military operation preparatory to an attack," but states that a combatant that "carries his [or her] arms openly" shall still be permitted to claim POW status, a significantly lower standard than the aforementioned test adopted by the Third Convention. In addition, Article 45 of Additional Protocol I states that there shall be a presumption that anyone who "takes part in hostilities and falls into the power of an adverse Party shall be presumed to be a prisoner of war," and that any person who has taken part in hostilities and who is not entitled to POW status is entitled to a laundry list of protections, including prohibitions against all kinds of torture and outrages upon personal dignity.

The broad definition of those entitled to POW protection under Article 43(1) of Additional Protocol 1 clearly encompasses the Taliban detainees, whose government was allegedly not recognized by the United States. Furthermore, Article 44(3)'s qualification of Article 43(1) that combatants "carry arms openly" covers most, if not all, of the Taliban detainees at Guantanamo that were captured on the battlefield in Afghanistan. Finally, Article 45's presumption of POW status of those who took part in hostilities in Operation Enduring Freedom was clearly not applied to the Taliban detainees, and the indignations against the Guantanamo detainees described in Section II clearly violate the protections afforded to those combatants who took part in hostilities who are not entitled to POW status. Therefore, Additional Protocol I lends additional support to the contention that the Taliban detainees at Guantanamo deserve POW status under customary international law, which has been recognized by the United States.

THE GOVERNMENT'S USE OF INTERNATIONAL LAW IN THE WAR ON TERRORISM

The Government has used international law to its advantage in several other cases in the War on Terrorism. In particular, the Government has used the principles of international law at length in its arguments before the United States Supreme Court in *Hamdi v. Rumsfeld.* In its reply brief in *Hamdi*, the Government appealed to general principles of international law in arguing that it had the authority to capture and detain enemy combatants during wartime, at least during the period of conflict, In the same brief, the Government cited Article 105 of the Third Convention and general principles of international law in contending that the laws of war do not grant enemy combatants the right to meet with counsel to contest his or her wartime detention unless formal charges have been filed.

In addition, in its arguments before the United States Supreme Court in *Hamdan v. Rumsfeld.* the Government contended that the Geneva Third Convention was not a self-executing treaty, another way of arguing that the Third Convention could not be enforced by federal courts. In making this argument, the Government relied centrally upon the fact that the "corrective machinery" in the Third Convention is primarily non-judicial, pointing specifically to Articles 1 (it is the responsibility of the High Contracting Parties to ensure compliance with the Third Convention), 8 (the Third Convention shall be applied with the cooperation and under the scrutiny of the Protecting Powers), 11 (in the event of conflict over application of the Third Convention, each Protecting Party shall send a representative to meet on a neutral territory to resolve the conflict), 78 (POWs have the right to inform their captors and the representatives of the Protecting Powers of their treatment), and 132 (an enquiry shall be conducted at the request of a Party to the conflict concerning any alleged violation of the Third Convention, and if an agreement is not reached, the parties shall agree upon a neutral umpire to resolve the conflict with the least possible delay) of the Third Convention.

The Executive Branch is not the only branch of the government that uses international law in the War on Terrorism. The United States Supreme Court in *Hamdi* cited Article 118 of the Geneva Third Convention and Article 20 of the Second Hague Third Convention on Laws and Customs in War on Land in stating in dicta that detention of POWs cannot be held past the cessation of active hostilities. The federal circuit courts of appeal have followed the Supreme Court in utilizing international law to assist in the disposition of its terrorism cases. In *Hamdan*, the District of Columbia Circuit relied heavily upon the Geneva Third Convention, particularly Articles 111 and 132, in holding that the Third Convention was not judicially enforceable. The District of Columbia Circuit in *Hamdan* also relied upon Article 4 of the Third Convention in stating in dicta that the defendant, a member of Al Qaeda, was not entitled to POW status because he did not carry a "fixed distinctive sign recognizable at a distance." In a decision that was later overturned on other grounds, the Ninth Circuit in *Gherebi v. Bush* condemned the Government's failure to grant the Guantanamo detainees POW status, noting that "the government's position here is at odds with the United States' longtime role as a leader in international efforts to codify and safeguard the rights of prisoners in wartime" and citing Article 5 of the Third Convention.

The federal district courts have also utilized international law to substantiate their dispositions in the war on terrorism cases. In *In re Guantanamo Cases,* Judge Joyce Hens Green of the United States District Court for the District of Columbia cited Article 4 of the Third Convention in holding that the Taliban detainees were entitled to POW status under the Third Convention, while the Al Qaeda detainees were not entitled to such protection. In *Hamdan v. Rumsfeld.* later overturned by the D.C. Circuit, Judge Robertson of the United States District Court for the District of Columbia cited the Geneva Third Convention in holding that it was a self-executing treaty enforceable in federal courts. Judge Robertson also cited Article 2 of the Third Convention (the Third Convention covers "all cases of declared war or of any other armed conflict which may arise between two or more of the High Contracting Parties, even if the state of war is not recognized by one of them.") in holding that the Third Convention covered defendant Guantanamo detainee and Al Qaeda suspect. In *Padilla ex. rel. Newman v. Bush,* later vacated on other grounds by the Supreme Court, Judge Mukasey of the United States District Court for the Southern District of New York cited Article 2 of the Third Convention in holding that the laws of war applied whether or not war was formally declared, and the Hague Third Convention and Article 118 of the Geneva Third Convention in holding that defendant Al Qaeda and United States citizen captured on United States soil was not entitled to POW protection under the laws of war.

The analysis of the Government's tenuous position on the applicability of the Third Convention to the Guantanamo detainees, specifically the Taliban detainees and in light of the federal courts' increasing use of the Third Convention and international law to substantiate its decisions in the War on Terrorism, its use of the Third Convention and international law to define its wartime powers in the War on Terrorism, and its refusal to grant the Guantanamo detainees the protections afforded to civilian detainees under the Fourth Convention leads one to pose the following question: Is there a way to reconcile the Government's use of the Third Convention and international law to define the scope of its powers during wartime while failing to permit all of the Guantanamo detainees the protections offered to POWs under the Third Convention or civilians under the Fourth Convention?

There are two ways that one can answer this question. First, one can take the skeptical approach that the Government is strategically using international law in order to justify its actions in the War on Terrorism, here the detentions of terrorist suspects at Guantanamo Bay and their inability to appeal to POW status under the Geneva Third Convention or civilian status under the Fourth Convention. Second, one can understand the Government as sincerely attempting to abide by its treaty obligations under international law and the Third Convention, and coming to the conclusion that all of the Guantanamo Bay detainees are not covered by the Third Convention or the Fourth Convention.

Although the second conclusion may very well be true, it is difficult for the Government to substantiate its claims that it is sincerely attempting to abide by its treaty obligations under international law and the Third Convention in light of its denial of POW status to the Taliban detainees, a clear violation of the Third Convention, its denial of POW status to the Al Qaeda detainees for the mere fact that they represent a group that does not carry a fixed, distinctive sign or insignia, and its denial of Fourth Convention rights to all of the detainees. The veil of insincerity surrounding the Government's application of the Third Convention and international law is also heightened in light of its use of the Third Convention and international law to justify its detention of enemy combatants, denying enemy combatants access to counsel, and arguing that the Third

Convention is not a self-executing treaty enforceable in federal courts.

The fact that the Government's position on the status of the Taliban detainees in Guantanamo Bay goes against two federal district courts that have analyzed the issue also lends doubt to the Government's purported application of the Third Convention and international law in the War on Terrorism. In short, regardless of whether or not the Government is sincerely attempting to abide by its treaty obligations under the Third Convention and international law, its use of the Third Convention and international law with respect to the Guantanamo detainees and enemy combatants rings of insincerity to outside observer.

Finally, it should be noted that Congressional authorization for Executive action in the War on Terror is limited by the AUMF, which specifically limits permissible Executive action in the War on Terror to: necessary and appropriate force against those nations, organizations, or persons he determines planned, authorized, committed, or aided the terrorist attacks that occurred on September 11, 2001, or harboured such organizations or persons, in order to prevent any future acts of international terrorism against the United States by such nations, organizations or persons.

As is widely taught in Constitutional Law courses across the country, Justice Jackson's opinion in the Supreme Court's decision in *Youngstown Sheet & Tube Co. v. Sawyer* held that " When the President acts pursuant to an express or implied authorization of Congress, his authority is at its maximum, for it includes all that he possesses in his own right plus all that Congress can delegate."

In their seminal article *Congressional Authorization and the War on Terrorism,* Professors Curtis A. Bradley and Jack L. Goldsmith rely upon the Supreme Court's decision in *Hamdi* in arguing that " courts should give content to the AUMF by looking to prior Executive Branch wartime practice and the international laws of war." In particular, Bradley and Goldsmith rely upon an extensive amount of historical case law and the use of international law in *Hamdi* in contending that "the AUMF should be read as authorizing the President to do what the laws of war permit." Therefore, in accordance with Bradley and Goldsmith's article, under the aforementioned arguments that the Third and Fourth Conventions grant the Taliban detainees POW status and the Al Qaeda detainees civilian status not only apply pursuant to the United States' treaty obligations, but also pursuant to the AUMF, which inherently limits the Executive's ability to act in the War on Terror under *Youngstown*. Without consideration as to one's belief as to whether or not the Government is genuinely attempting to abide by its treaty obligations under the Third Convention and international law in the War on Terrorism, it is clear that the divergent manner in which the Government has used the Third Convention and international law in the federal courts raises questions as to the sincerity of the Government's motives behind its application of the Third Convention and international law in the War on Terrorism. Three possible ramifications of the Government's ostensible failure to abide by the Third Convention and international law in good faith in the War on Terrorism.

First, the Government's strategic use of the Third Convention and international law leaves it in danger of a lack of reciprocity in applying the Third Convention and international law from other countries involved in conflicts around the world. The fact that the military and economic superpower of the world, and perhaps the main threat in enforcing compliance with the Third Convention, applies the Third Convention and international law only when convenient leaves less reason for countries around the world to comply with the Third Convention and international law in its treatment of POWs and detainees in future wars and international conflicts.

Second, related to the potential breakdown of the Third Convention is the increased threat that other international agreements will break down as a result of the United States' strategic use of the Third Convention and international law in the War on Terrorism. As with the Third Convention, the United States is the main enforcer of compliance with international organizations such as the World Trade Organization, International Monetary Fund, World Bank, and international agreements with respect to arms and the environment such as the Nuclear Non-Proliferation Treaty, Convention on the Prohibition of the Development, Production, Stockpiling, and Use of Chemical Weapons and on Their Destruction, and the Convention on International Trade in Endangered Species of Wild Fauna and Flora. The Government's ostensible insincerity in the application of the Third Convention and international law leaves open the possibility that other countries around the world will be more willing to flout their obligations under important international organizations and agreements to the detriment of all in the international community.

Third, and most significant, is that the global perception of the United States as an insincere international citizen may lead to an increase in terrorism directed at the United States as well as strained foreign relations. An international poll conducted by The Pew Research Centre For the People and the Press found that the favourable opinion of the United States from 2002 to 2005 has dropped in 9 of the 12 countries polled, including Great Britain, France, and Germany, by an average of 14.8%. Although the United States' actions in Operation Iraqi Freedom are a substantial reason behind this significant decline in international perception, the manner in which the United States has treated the Guantanamo detainees has also been cited as one of the central reasons behind the decline. The marginal increase in international dissatisfaction with the United States as a result of the Government's lackluster application of the Third Convention and international law in the War on Terrorism has the danger of inciting more individuals on the margin to join terrorist groups aimed at conducting operations against the United States. In addition, the marginal increase in global hostility against the United States as a result of the Government's ostensible insincerity in applying the Third Convention and international law to the Guantanamo detainees could also strain foreign relations, making it more difficult for the United States to succeed in its numerous other foreign policy objectives. 118 Indeed, 75% of French citizens, 77% of German citizens, and 64% of British citizens had a negative opinion about the President's re-election; much of this resentment undoubtedly comes from the manner in which the

President has conducted the War on Terrorism. Thus, the Government's aggressive use, or misuse, of the Third Convention and international law against the Guantanamo detainees in order to gain more information through interrogation techniques may actually be decreasing the national security of the United States and disabling it from pursuing its alternative foreign policy objectives.

Nevertheless, it must be noted that the potential harm that could result from a release of the Guantanamo detainees could outweigh the marginal increase in terrorism that may result from the declining perception of the United States around the world. The White House has reaffirmed the notion that "The individuals who are at Guantanamo Bay are dangerous terrorists who seek to do harm to the American people. And the President is committed to doing everything he can to keep America safe and protect the American people. Vice President Dick Cheney has also maintained that " The [Guantanamo detainees] are people we picked up on the battlefield primarily in Afghanistan. They're terrorists. They're bomb-makers. They're facilitators of terror. They're members of Al Qaeda and the Taliban... For the most part, if you let them out, they'll go back to trying to kill Americans." For the sake of the security of the American people, one can only hope that the White House and Vice President Cheney are right, and that the benefits of the continued detention of the Guantanamo detainees outweighs the ramifications of their detention.

INTERNATIONAL LAW : FUTURE OF WEAPONS AND TECHNOLOGY

One type of new weapons technology in particular stimulated the debate and highlighted the complexities with regard to international law. Non-lethal weapons have recently been the focus of much research. Peter Herby argued that the name 'non-lethal' is misleading and much of a weapon's lethality depends on its intended use. A supposedly non-lethal weapon used at the wrong distance, with the wrong amount of ammunition, and directed at the wrong target can be just as deadly as a regular gun. For example, a teaser gun used on a child with the voltage intended for an adult may cause death. Even if used correctly, a weapon's impact on the target may not be foreseeable. The use of pepper spray, or other chemical compound, may cause severe allergic reactions and death.

A legal review process should consider the correct use of the weapon, i.e. its intended target, the distance of application, and the amount of 'ammunition' to be applied.

Whether the target is an individual or a crowd also matters for legal purposes. The indiscriminate use of weapons is in principle not accepted under international humanitarian law, i.e. in war times. The means that the use of weapons directed at a crowd of civilians is not allowed, except where military advantage is proportionate to the civilian costs. This could be the case, when insurgents hide in civilian crowds.

At the same time, international law does not outlaw the use of 'non-lethal weapons' by the police in situations of domestic protests. Many states have set legal parameters for the use of 'non-lethal' weapons for crowd control. The distinction between domestic policing activities and conflict involving military force is relevant, especially in conflict situation where the lines between the two get blurred.

In the ensuing discussion, many representatives from the military services voiced support for more clarification and guidelines on the use of such weapons, including better training. They were pointed out, however, that 'non-lethal' weapons constituted an important tool in their ability to protect their soldiers and capture and neutralize suspects.

INTERNATIONAL TERRORISM AND INTERNATIONAL LAW

The events of 11 September and the subsequent military response by the United States and its allies raise some difficult issues in international law. Does an attack by a non-state terrorist group give rise to the right of self-defence as understood under international law? Under what circumstances was the Taliban regime as the Afghani government itself a legitimate target for military action under the self-defence doctrine? To what extent was the United States entitled to dictate the terms by which the Taliban regime should act before the military action would cease against it and Al Qaeda bases on Afghani soil?

Only the first issue can be answered-yes-with any degree of confidence. The others are clouded with uncertainty. To some extent this uncertainty reflects the shift of international law away from an emphasis on regulating relations between sovereign states (countries) towards having to incorporate the actions of non-state groups within the legal framework. As part of this shift, the responsibility of governments for the actions of non-state groups such as the international terrorist network Al Qaeda is receiving increasing attention. The periodic use of military force by the United States against such organizations and so-called 'state sponsors of terrorism' during the 1990s appears to be forcing a change in accepted state practice and hence (arguably) influencing the boundaries of international customary law. However, given that the United States is likely to be motivated primarily by national interests, it would be useful for the United Nations General Assembly to authorise the International Law Commission to codify exactly what are the principles applying to the doctrine of self-defence under international law.

This paper begins with a short chronology tracing the major relevant events from 11 September through to the ongoing airstrikes by the United States and its allies during October. This is followed by a review of the status of terrorism under international law. It then looks at the question of legal responsibility for the 11 September attacks, including under what circumstances the Taliban might be deemed to share some form of responsibility. The paper goes on to examine the legal use of force, and whether the events of 11 September give rise to the right of self-defence. Finally it considers what the practical limits of self-defence are in the present case, including role of the United Nations Security Council.

Chronology

11 September-Four commercial United States jetliners on domestic routes are hijacked. The hijackers issue no demands to authorities. Two of the jets are flown into the twin towers of the World Trade Centre in New York, one into the Pentagon in Washington DC and another crashes in rural Pennsylvania. Around 3 000 people are killed. No organisation claims responsibility for the hijackings. Representatives of the Taliban

government of Afghanistan immediately condemn the attacks. Later, Osama bin Laden also denies involvement.

12 September-The United Nations General Assembly and Security Council pass resolutions condemning the events of 11 September as acts of terrorism. The resolutions call for the 'perpetrators, organizers and sponsors' to be '[brought] to justice' and states that those responsible for 'aiding, supporting or harbouring' such persons 'will be held accountable'.

14 September-the United States Congress authorises the use of military force against those involved in the attacks, including those who 'harboured' such persons or organisations 'so as to prevent any future acts of international terrorism'. Also on 14 September, the Australian Government announces the activation of the ANZUS treaty.

17 September-Both Houses of the Australian Commonwealth Parliament pass a resolution which, amongst other things, states that Parliament 'fully endorses the commitment of the Australian Government to support within Australia's capabilities United States-led action against those responsible for these tragic attacks'.

20 September-In an address to a Joint session of Congress, United States' President George Bush states that 'the evidence we have gathered all points to a collection of loosely affiliated terrorist organizations known as Al Qaeda...they are the same murderers indicted for bombing American embassies in Tanzania and Kenya, and responsible for bombing the USS Cole'. Osama bin Laden is named as the leader of Al Qaeda. President Bush demands that the Taliban must 'deliver to the United States authorities all the leaders of Al Qaeda who hide in your land...immediately and permanently close every terrorist training camp in Afghanistan, and hand over every terrorist, and every person in their support structure, to appropriate authorities'. Failure to immediately hand over the 'terrorists' would result in the Taliban 'sharing their fate'. According to President Bush, the 'war on terror begins with Al Qaeda, but it does not end there. It will not end until every terrorist group of global reach has been found, stopped and defeated.'

21 September-The Taliban refuse to comply with the United States demands unless evidence is produced. The United States rejects the Taliban's position, stating that bin Laden has already been indicted in the United States for the bombings of United States embassies in Kenya and Tanzania in 1998.

6 October-The Taliban offers to detain bin Laden and try him under Islamic law in Afghanistan if the United States makes a formal request and presents them with sufficient evidence. This proposal is rejected by the United States who insist on the fulfilment of their 20 September demands.

7 October-Airstrikes by United States and British planes commence against Al Qaeda training camps and military installations of the Taliban regime in Afghanistan. According to President Bush, 'these carefully targeted actions are designed to disrupt the use of Afghanistan as a terrorist base of operations and to attack the military capability of the Taliban regime'.

7 October-The United States representative to the United Nations delivers a letter to the President of the United Nations Security Council citing the right of self-defence as justification for the airstrikes. The latter states that 'from the territory of Afghanistan, the Al Qaeda organization continues to train and support agents of terror who attack innocent people throughout the world and target United States nationals and interests in the United States and abroad'. It also states that 'we may find that our self-defence requires further actions with respect to other organizations and other States'.

12 October-The United States ceases strikes for one day, pending a response to a renewed demand to hand over Osama bin Laden and the Al Qaeda members. The demand is refused.

13 October-Ongoing airstrikes resume.

November/December-Taliban and Al Qaeda forces are progressively driven out from former strongholds by a combination of Afghani anti-Taliban forces and United States airstrikes. By the end of December, anti-Taliban forces effectively control Afghanistan. Neither the Taliban leader, Mohammed Omar, nor bin Laden are captured or confirmed as killed and their whereabouts are unknown.

14 November-the United Nations Security Council pass a resolution expressing 'strong support for the efforts of the Afghan people to establish a new and transitional administration leading to the formation of a new government'.

22 December-A transitional Afghani administration is sworn in Kabul.

INTERNATIONAL TERRORISM AND INTERNATIONAL LAW

The international community has never succeeded in developing an accepted comprehensive definition of terrorism. During the 1970s and 1980s, the United Nations attempts to define the term foundered mainly due to differences of opinion between various members about the use of violence in the context of conflicts over national liberation and self-determination.

Terrorism is defined by the Australian Defence Force as:

The use or threatened use of violence for political ends, or any use or threatened use of violence for the purpose of putting the public or any section of the public in fear.

This is broadly consistent with most definitions in academic literature which generally require two elements:

1. actual or threatened violence against civilians or persons not actively taking part in hostilities, and
2. the implicit or explicit purpose of the act is to intimidate or compel a population, government or organisation into some course of action.

International law has traditionally dealt with the duties and rights of states in their relations with each other. This is reflected in the fact that most international law dealing with international terrorism concentrates on the duties of states to prevent and punish terrorism. Certainly terrorism in all its forms is considered a criminal act under international law, but historically terrorists have generally been punished under the domestic law of the country harmed by the specific act in question. This said, the mass-murders committed on 11 September by the hijackers probably constituted a crime against humanity under Article 7(a) of the Rome Statute of the

International Criminal Court (ICC). However as the ICC only has jurisdiction over crimes committed *after* the Rome Statute comes into force-it is still seventeen ratifications short of the sixty required-the ICC has no immediate relevance to the current situation.

The first major step in the modern era in outlawing terrorism under international law was made through the *Convention for the Prevention and Punishment of Terrorism*, developed by the League of Nations in the 1930s. However, the Convention never came into force. A number of conventions were developed during the 1960s and 1970s to address specific types of violent acts such as aircraft hijacking, kidnapping of diplomats and the taking of hostages. These generally obligated parties to the Convention to either prosecute offenders or extradite them to countries in which the act in question took place. The aircraft hijacking conventions in particular have a large number of parties to them, including Australia, Afghanistan and the United States.

In spite of its failure to define terrorism, in 1985 the United Nations General Assembly adopted a resolution: unequivocally condemn[ing], as criminal, all acts, methods and practices of terrorism wherever and by whomever committed... [and calling]s upon all States to *fulfil their obligations under international law* to refrain from organizing, instigating, assisting or participating in terrorist acts in other States, or acquiescing in activities within their territory directed towards the commission of such acts. [Italics added by author]

Similar language can be found in any number of subsequent General Assembly and Security Council resolutions over the last fifteen years. Many of these resolutions also state that terrorism is contrary to the purposes and the principles of the United Nations and represent a 'threat to international peace and security'.

From the mid 1990s, there has been a concerted effort by the United Nations to develop a more comprehensive approach to combating terrorism and this has resulted in the 1997 *International Convention for the Suppression of Terrorist Bombings* (the Bombing Convention) and the 1997 *International Convention for the Suppression of the Financing of Terrorism* (the Financing Convention). The Bombing Convention came into force in May 2001. Australia, Afghanistan and the United States are not parties to this convention, although the United States has signed but not ratified it. Under this Convention, a person commits an offence if they unlawfully and intentionally use an explosive or lethal device against a public place, a government facility, infrastructure, or transport craft or system either with the intent to cause death or serious bodily injury or extensive destruction of such a place, facility or system resulting in major economic loss. However, acts that occur within the boundaries of a country and do not involve foreign nations do not come within the Convention, nor do acts by armed forces involved in armed conflict.

The Bombing Convention aims to deny safe havens to persons wanted for terrorist bombings (including accomplices) by obligating each state party to prosecute such persons if it does not extradite them to another state that has issued an extradition request. A country cannot decline to extradite a person on the basis that a bombing within the meaning of the convention was a 'political offence'. Importantly, parties to the Bombing Convention are also obliged to take all practical measures to prevent preparation of terrorist acts where they take place within their territories.

The Financing Convention is not yet in force and again, Australia, Afghanistan and the United States, are not parties to this Convention, although Australia and the United States have signed but not ratified it.

The Financing Convention provides that an offence occurs where a person unlawfully provides or collects funds with the intention that the funds should be used or in the knowledge that they are to be used to carry out various acts. These acts include an offence under the other various 'terrorist conventions' or any other act intended to cause death or serious bodily injury to a civilian, or to any other person not taking an active part in the hostilities in a situation of armed conflict, when the purpose of such an act is to intimidate a population, or to compel a government or an international organization to do or to abstain from doing any act. Accomplices, defined in a similar way as in the Bombing Convention, are also deemed as committing an offence. Again, acts that occur within the boundaries of a country and do not involve foreign nationals do not come within the Convention, nor do acts by armed forces involved in armed conflict.

The Convention obligates states parties either to prosecute or to extradite persons accused of funding terrorist activities, and requires banks to enact measures to identify suspect transactions. It also forbids the use by a country of its bank law secrecy laws as an excuse for not providing assistance to other Parties in their investigations of possible offences.

Individual and State Legal Responsibility for 11 September

Since early October, the United States has maintained that it has firm evidence that Osama bin Laden and the Al Qaeda network were responsible for the attack. However, perhaps the fullest account of the evidence has been released by Britain. In summary, this evidence includes the apparent ringleader of the hijackers as being a member of the largest constituent group within Al Qaeda, a senior Al Qaeda lieutenant planning the details of the attack, and intercepts of various telephone calls and money trails. Since then, the most potent evidence has been has been the (poor quality) video that features bin Laden discussing how the 11 September attacks were planned. Items such as flight-simulator programs and lists of United States flight schools have also been recovered in Afghanistan as anti-Taliban forces progressively captured various Taliban and Al Qaeda facilities during November and December.

The Australian Prime Minister described the evidence shown to him in October by the US Ambassador to Australia as 'collectively [amounting] to a very compelling case in support of the allegations concerning bin Laden and his terrorist organisation'. Around the same time, Pakistan, one of the few countries to maintain regular diplomatic relations with the Taliban, has been reporting as acknowledging the strength of the evidence against Osama bin Laden. Bin Laden has denied involvement in the 11 September attacks, as well as earlier attacks against United States nationals. However, for the purposes of argument, it is assumed that the evidence mentioned above exists that indicates that at least certain elements of the senior Al Qaeda hierarchy, including bin Laden, may have been involved in the planning and facilitation of the 11 September attacks.

But what responsibility does the Taliban regime have? It seems clear that Al Qaeda have established training camps in Afghanistan with the acquiescence of the Taliban. The Taliban have failed to comply with Security Council resolutions demanding the closure of all camps where terrorists are trained and the surrender of Osama bin Laden to stand trial for the bombings of United States embassies in Kenya and Tanzania in 1998. Immediately after the 11 September attacks, the Taliban denied that they have permitted Osama bin Laden to use Afghan territory 'to launch any attack on any government around the world'. While the United States has not directly asserted that the Taliban leadership, or elements of it, knew of the attacks beforehand, can they nonetheless be held responsible under international law for the attacks?

In the case of *Nicaragua v United States of America,* the International Court of Justice found that the United States government provided weapons, finance and other logistical assistance to guerilla forces who carried out ongoing attacks against both Nicaraguan armed forces and civilians in Nicaragua. The Court ruled that the actions of the United States did not constitute an attack by it on Nicaragua. The Court found for the United States to have legal responsibility under international law for the attack, it must have effective control over the group or groups carrying out the attacks. However, the Court did not provide any real guidance on what constitute the lower limits of effective control.

More recently, the issue was considered by the Appeals Court of the International Criminal Tribunal for the former Yugoslavia in *The Prosecutor v Dusko Tadic,* where the question was whether the armed forces of Serbian Bosnia were under the control of the former Yugoslavian Republic. The Court found that the 'effective control test' used in *Nicaragua* was 'at variance' with judicial state practice in relation to the activities of paramilitary groups. Unfortunately again the Tribunal does not provide any real detail on what the test should be. However, it did comment that: on the basis of the International Law Commission's Draft on State Responsibility, [the Tribunal] found that international law on State responsibility is founded on a realistic concept of accountability which transcends legal formalities. A State is responsible for acts by individuals who make up an organised group under its overall control irrespective of whether or not it issued specific instructions.

This comment is likely based on Article 8 of draft articles on Responsibility of States for Internationally Wrongful Acts which states: The conduct of a person or group of persons shall be considered an act of a State under international law if the person or group of persons is in fact acting on the instructions of, or under the direction or control of, that in carrying out the conduct.

Is worth noting that the 'State' does not necessary mean the duly authorised activities of the government or its authorities. Under Article 7 of the draft articles, the actions of a government official or entity, even when exceeding their authority, are considered to be an act of the government under international law. It can be argued that at least bin Laden and some other senior Al Qaeda figures were a de-facto part of the Taliban government. Al Qaeda is generally accepted as providing the Taliban with significant financial and military support. Morever, according to the report of the United Nations Secretary General, the Al Qaeda leadership exercised a markedly increased degree of influence over Taliban political, social and military policy during the course of 2001 by means of significant participation in the Taliban's decision-making processes. This influence manifested itself in matters such as the Taliban's supreme leader stating his support for a global Jihad, as advocated by bin Laden. It is also hard to argue the Taliban leadership were not clearly aware of the potential implications of hosting Al Qaeda. For example, the United Nations Secretary General has said: my Personal Representative time and again exhorted the Taliban to hand over Bin Laden in compliance with [the Security Council resolutions], and repeatedly spelled out the consequences that were likely to ensue from their continued refusal to do so. He specifically warned them that any incident similar to those attributed to Osama bin Laden in the past would have catastrophic consequences for the Taliban and for the Afghans.

This all suggests that, although the Taliban leadership may have been completely unaware of the planning of the 11 September attack, their failure to act in the face evidence of past Al Qaeda attacks and of binding Security Council resolutions means that there must bear significant responsibility under international law for 11 September. This conclusion is supported by discussion in academic writings as to whether the *Nicaragua* effective control test should be modified in cases like the attacks of 11 September. For example, it has been suggested that an attenuated (lowered) standard: may be particularly appropriate when the non-state actor is known by all to be a highly dangerous and readily capable and willing of initiating attacks.

It appears that Al Qaeda would readily fit into 'capable and willing' category, particularly if we assume Osama bin Laden is truly the leader or primary backer of the organisation.

THE LEGAL USE OF FORCE IN INTERNATIONAL LAW

The Charter of the United Nations is one of the world's most important treaties. Ratification of the Charter is a prerequisite to membership of the United Nations. The Charter sets out the obligations of members and, amongst other matters, establishes the Security Council.

Article 2(4) of the Charter states: All Members shall refrain in their international relations from the threat or use of force against the territorial integrity or political independence of any state, or in any other manner inconsistent with the purposes of the United Nations.

Essentially, this eliminates the concept of a 'just war'. The use of force, or the threat of it, by a state is no longer a legitimate means of dealing with a dispute with another state.

However, Article 2(4) does not prevent a country from defending itself in response to acts of aggression. Article 51 states: Nothing in the present Charter shall impair the *inherent right of individual or collective self-defence if an armed attack* occurs against a Member of the United Nations, until the Security Council has taken measures necessary to maintain international peace and security. Measures taken by Members in the exercise of this right of self-defence shall be immediately reported to the Security Council and shall not in any way affect the authority and responsibility of the Security Council under the present Charter to take at any time such action as it deems necessary in order to maintain or restore international peace and security.

Alternatively, force may be used by a state or coalition of states in order to 'maintain peace and security' if this is specifically authorised by the Security Council under Article 42 of the Charter. Article 42 was used, for example, to authorise the military response by the United States and its allies against Iraq to drive it out of Kuwait in the so-called 'gulf-war' of 1990-91. More recently, force has been used without express Article 42 authorisation in so-called 'humanitarian intervention', where NATO conducted sustained airstrikes against the Federal Republic of Yugoslavia during 1999 in reaction to the civil conflict in Kosovo and the widespread killing of Kosovo Albanians.

Is the Doctrine of Self-Defence Applicable?

The United States has said that its military action (use of force) in Afghanistan constitutes acts of self-defence rather than being reprisals or punishment. This is not the first time the US has taken military action in response to a terrorist act ostensibly for the reason of self-defence. In 1998, it launched missile strikes on Afghanistan and Sudan in response to the 1998 bombings of its embassies in Kenya and Tanzania. In that case, about 100 tomahawk missiles were fired at seven alleged training camps in Afghanistan and an alleged biological weapons plant in Sudan. In these cases, American officials justified these attacks as required to prevent Al Qaeda from being able to launch further attacks as 'there was evidence that they were planning operations against specific (unnamed) US targets'.

There has been some academic debate as to whether the concept of 'armed attack' as contained in Article 51 must originate from a State (government) rather than a non-state group like Al Qaeda. Security Council resolution 1368 of 12 September is ambiguous on the issue. In its preamble, the resolution 'recogni[ses] the inherent right of individual or collective self-defence in accordance with the Charter', but in the operative part of the resolution describes the attacks as 'terrorist attacks' (not armed attacks) which 'represent a threat to international peace and security'. In summary, the resolution does not explicitly recognise that the right of self-defence applies in relation to any parties as a consequence of the 11 September attacks.

In the author's view, well-organised terrorist groups with the means to reach across international borders to inflict significant damage on a country on a ongoing basis (which Al Qaeda arguably have) must represent the sort of threat against which self-defence is legitimate if the doctrine is to have any practical contemporary value. There are no obvious examples of United Nations members claiming that the 1998 missile strikes against Al Qaeda camps could not be acts of self-defence because the alleged perpetrators of the embassy bombings were a non-state group. State practice would therefore seem to support the hypothesis that an Article 51 armed attack may be by a non-state group. In any case, the symbiotic relationship of Al Qaeda in Afghanistan and the Taliban means that at least the Al Qaeda leadership cannot be seen as purely as a 'non-state' entity and that the Taliban shares significant responsibility for Al Qaeda's actions in the 11 September attack.

Limits of the Right of Self-Defence

The right of self-defence is not an open-ended right. To be a valid act under international customary law, as set down by the classic formulation by the United States in the 1837 *Caroline* incident, it is generally required to conform with three elements:

- was the response necessary?
- was the response proportionate?
- was the response immediate?

The last point, the question of immediacy, seems to be of lesser importance in contemporary practice. State practice suggests that a reasonably delayed response is acceptable where there is a need to gather evidence of the attackers identity and or collect the intelligence and military force in order to strike back in a targeted manner.

So, was a military response necessary? It seems clear that the diplomatic actions through the United Nations in the late 1990s such as the various Security Council resolutions and development of the Bombing and Finance Conventions have been largely ineffective in combating the terrorist ability of Al Qaeda, although why this is so is beyond the scope of this paper. As already mentioned, following the 11 September attacks, the United States demanded that Osama bin Laden and members of the Al Qaeda network within Afghanistan be surrendered to the United States. They also demanded that all terrorist training camps be shut down and access given to United States personnel to verify this. It appears the United States refused to share the evidence regarding Al Qaeda's alleged guilt with the Taliban to the extent this was shared with its allies. The Taliban refused to comply with the United States demands, initially saying they were prepared to try him in Afghanistan under Islamic law if sufficient evidence of his guilt was provided, although later they said they were prepared to surrender him to a neutral country. These options were dismissed by the United States.

If the United States objective was to protect itself from the possibility of further Al Qaeda attacks in the immediate future, was their 'no negotiation' position the only way of likely achieving this? Ultimately this must be a subjective question. Earlier in this paper, it has been argued that the actions of the Taliban before 11 September mean that the regime shares significant responsibility for the attacks under international law, even if the circumstances do not neatly fall within the *Nicaragua* 'effective control' test. However, it was Al Qaeda rather than the Taliban that represented the *direct* threat to the United States. The Taliban's failure to at least take steps to detain bin Laden and any senior Al Qaeda leaders present in Afghanistan pending agreement on how to proceed could be said to render the United States military actions necessary to eliminate this direct threat, at least in the absence of any useful guidance on what are the limits of international law in this area. However, a more difficult question is whether the United States was justified under the self-defence doctrine in pursuing a policy aimed at assisting the Afghani anti-Taliban forces to completely oust the Taliban. However, this question became academic after Security Resolution 1378 of 14 November which expressed support for the Afghan people to establish a transitional administration. Resolution 1378 effectively cut the feet out from under the Taliban in terms of them being the lawful government of Afghanistan.

Finally, was the military response proportional? There are two main aspects to this. Firstly, was the scope of the response proportional to the 11 September attack? Secondly, as the humanitarian laws of war apply, have noncombatants been properly protected?

The first issue is mainly bound up in the discussion above about necessity in that it is questionable whether the purpose of military campaign against the Taliban was proportional because the Taliban did not of themselves represent a direct threat to the United States. If the Taliban's acquiescence to the presence of Al Qaeda was a threat to international peace and security, it is properly the role of the Security Council to deal with this, including through the mandating of the use of force under Article 42 of the United Nations Charter. The possibility that the international politics of the Security Council may not have allowed the United States as broad-ranging a mandate to deal with the Taliban is it might wish for does not change the position in international law.

In relation to the second issue, there are no strict limits as to when non-combatant deaths through so-called collateral damage become excessive. International customary law forbids the use of weapons that are incapable of distinguishing between civilian and military targets. A question may arise whether, in targeting any Al Qaeda training camps, all persons present can be classified as combatants. However, the author has no information on this.

Collective Self-Defence

As previously mentioned, Article 51 of the United Nations Charter recognises the right of both individual and collective self-defence. Australia's committal of military force to the campaign in Afghanistan is consistent with Australia's right to participate in the collective defence of the United States if requested to do so following an armed attack on that country. This right is unaffected by the existence or otherwise of any treaty obligations to provide military or other support, such as under the ANZUS Treaty.

The Role of the Security Council

Under Article 51, the right of self-defence ceases once the Security Council has taken measures necessary to maintain international peace and security. In theory, the question arises whether the measures taken would have to be demonstratively effective before the right of self-defence ceases. However, given the United States is a permanent member of the Security Council, it could veto any measures it deems contrary to its national interests. Thus it is unlikely a situation would arise where the Security Council was at odds with the United States on whether a right of self-defence continued to exist or whether that right was being exercised within the limits set down under international law. Once the right of self-defence arises, the only legal obligation the United States has is to report to the Security Council on what measures it has taken in self-defence. It has no obligation to seek authorisation under Article 42 for the use of force so long as the force it is using is consistent with the right of self-defence as previously outlined.

THE RELATION BETWEEN INTERNATIONAL HUMANITARIAN LAW AND INTERNATIONAL CRIMINAL LAW

One of the greatest paradoxes of International Law is the one related with war; even if nowadays the use of force is forbidden as a breach to the international legal order since it constitutes a massive violation to human dignity and contravene elemental considerations of humanity, there is a whole normative set which is to determine how hostilities have to be conducted. For that reason, and looking to establish a balance between these two extremes, the distinction between combatants and civilians is the cornerstone of all humanitarian law, and therefore, has a tremendous influence on the regime of international individual penal responsibility, as in practice by far the most numerous crimes are committed against civilians. The purpose of this article is to establish the content, scope and pragmatic problems of the Principles of Distinction and Proportionality, inspirational elements of the so-called category of war crimes under International Criminal Law.

In order to do that, section II will briefly raise two topics; first, illustrate some basic aspects of the relation between International Humanitarian Law (IHL, henceforth) as a *norme de comportement*, and International Criminal Law while a branch of international law which its primarily task is to ascertain individual criminal responsibility; and second, as a way to understand the practical implications of those Principles in the context of a punitive sanction, due attention will be regarded to the content and scope of Distinction and Proportionality, showing the process which lead to get to their modern formulation through the rules of IHL.

Consequently, and provided that the focal point of the article is the influence of those principles into the modern system of individual criminal responsibility, it will be analyzed first, various common matters which influence the structure of war crimes, and second, the content of the legal provisions related to war crimes under the Statute of the International Criminal Court (the ICC Statute, hereafter), specifically those directly inspired by the universal formulations in comment, which may be divided in a general prohibition, on one hand, and their concrete application in the sphere of methods and means of warfare, on the other.

This is so in order to identify their basic penal structure, that is to say, the objective and subjective elements, and some circumstances which might lead to the exclusion of the unlawfulness of the conduct or the criminal responsibility. Hence, the study will address some problematic issues arising from the way the Statute was set forth, as it reflects the political position of the States tending to limit the possibility to punish some conducts provided the nature of modern armed conflicts and the subjects which take part on them. Finally, there will be displayed some conclusions on the challenges for International Criminal Law in respect of these specific situations.

As a transversal resource, relevant international jurisprudence will illustrate the way that International Criminal Law has understood the Principles of Distinction and Proportionality on concrete situations of armed conflict, and the important role which has been assumed to clarify the content and scope of those legal rules.

PRELIMINARY MATTERS ON THE RELEVANT LEGAL BRANCHES

Following the ICTY's (International Criminal Tribunal for the former Yugoslavia) considerations on *Tadic case*, the elements which permit the identification of a war crime are (i) a serious infringement of an international rule that belongs to the corpus of a customary law or to be part of an applicable treaty, and (ii) that this conduct entails criminal responsibility for breaking the rule.

Such precision permits to identify the nature of the relation between the rules of IHL and the ones of ICL; the former are *normes de comportement* or primary rules concerning a description of what is prohibited in case of an armed conflict, and the latter are secondary rules which complementary may adjudge criminal responsibility as an effect of the above mentioned breach.

It is clear then that an act which is not prohibited under the primary rules can not constitute a war crime. However, should it be noted that "*not every act prohibited under the primary rules also constitutes a war crime as the definitions contained in the various items in the catalogue are sometimes narrower than the primary norms*," although they might give rise to state responsibility.

As this is not the main purpose of this paper, it will just be mentioned that the reasons for this unbalanced situation are basically political, in the sense that the consequences to determine international criminal responsibility are touching, at least tangentially, the sovereignty of States. However, the notion of war crime is a dynamic concept, as it is bound to change with the development of the primary substantive rules relating to that behaviour. Why then an international criminal jurisdiction if regardless of the existence of a solid set of primary rules developed by the International Community, States are reluctant to include a broader number of war crimes?

"Despite these rules, however, the need remains for an international criminal court since many States have proved unwilling to fulfil their duty to exercise their jurisdiction. Though the States continue to have the primary role to play in prosecuting war criminals, the ICC is being set up precisely to step in for national courts when these are unwilling or genuinely unable to do so."

B. The Principles under the framework of International Humanitarian Law

Distinction and Proportionality

According to Jean Pictet, the Principles which inspire the framework of IHL can be found expressly formulated on conventions or implicitly captured inside its substance, acting as *l'ossature du corps vivant*, and characterized by a high level of abstraction and generalization. In that sense, even if they are considered as fundamental elements, Distinction and Proportionality are not explicitly laid down in any normative provision.

Nevertheless, a systematic interpretation of the relevant rules could be useful to identify their presence as an influence on every likely disposition, provided that they personify the essence of modern IHL on one hand, as well as codifications are just the development and expression of such principles, on the other; that is in general terms, the balance between humanity and military necessity, values which normally can't be weighted up as they represent different scales of measurement.

Under the particularities of modern armed conflicts the possibility to make a fair application of the principles is problematic, as *"The protection of civilians from military operations is not absolute, [since] attacks made against military targets that lead to incidental damage to civilians are not prohibited."* This would result, then, into an incomplete protection to civilians and civilian population.

However, it has to be pointed a specific relation of complementarily as Proportionality appears to be the way by which Distinction is concretely implemented when hostilities are considered from a pragmatic point of view; the rules related to targeting, collateral damage and collateral civilian casualties, among others, are derived from Distinction, and form part of the core content of Proportionality. This is the way these two principles are going to be treated through this study.

Location of the Principles on International Humanitarian Law

It has been suggested that even Distinction and Proportionality were present on the content of IHL since the first legal attempts to codify the rules of IHL it wasn't until the emergence of the 1977 Additional Protocols to the Geneva Conventions Protocol I and II that they were finally laid down in proper sense.

Those legal instruments combined both branches of IHL (conduction of hostilities and protection to certain individuals and objects), creating a comprehensive vision of the law of armed conflicts, which notice the particularities of war, but at the same time purports for the protection of human dignity no matter the causes or mobiles for war to take place.

Distinction as a general principle is consecrated in article 48 of Protocol I for the case of an international armed conflict. Such disposition shall be read in accordance to article 50, which defines the personal scope of application, by creating a dichotomy *par exclusion* between civilians and combatants, the latter comprehensively defined on several dispositions of IHL, even if at the end there is no vestige of a clear definition of who is protected, but who is not. Regarding on Proportionality, article 51 establishes a comprehensive protection of civilians against dangers arising from military operations in all circumstances, and develops concrete provisions to limit means (especially weapons) and methods of warfare resulting on indiscriminate attacks or which may cause incidental injuries. Following this approach, article 57 develops the concept and content of precautionary measures to the case of military operations which, provided their scale and magnitude, are subject to planning.

In the case of non-international conflicts the rules concerning Distinction and Proportionality are limited as Protocol II doesn't contain any provision consecrating the principles nor defining who is legitimized to take part into hostilities, and consequently, who is protected from them. In addition, article 13.2 contains a similar but limited statement in relation with article 51 of Protocol I, as it lays down the general clause of protection from military operations and the prohibition to be treated as military objectives, and points the prohibition for a civilian to take direct part in hostilities. No mention on indiscriminate attacks, precautionary measures or prohibition of indiscriminate weapons is made.

GENERAL ISSUES ARISING FROM THE STRUCTURE OF ARTICLE 8 OF THE ICC STATUTE

The debate on Distinction and Proportionality as principles which influence the structure of war crimes reflects some of International Law's modern challenges, while the actors-parties (States) involved into its dynamics (creation, interpretation, application) are assuming political positions which give content to those legal institutions, norms and procedures according to their main aim; sovereignty to defend their interests when recourse to force is concerned.

Hence, such problematic can be condensed in three points which have an influence over the jurisdiction of the ICC on war crimes related with Distinction and Proportionality provided their general character; the ambiguity of the pairing civilian/ combatant, the limitation of the jurisdiction of the Court in the case of a noninternational armed conflict, and the relevance of customary law in order to extend the applicability of war crimes to specific situations vis à vis the certainty on the applicable law which a punitive legal system has to own.

Issues Around the Dichotomy Civilian/combatant

The most immediate outcome of Distinction is the insertion into the legal texts of two categories of individuals which are related with the development of hostilities; civilians, the ones which are subject of protection, and combatants, which due to their status are legitimized to take part in hostilities.

Therefore, coming from humanitarian law, this vague pairing influenced the structure of war crimes in the same way that it created lacunas in the application of the *norms de comportement* on IHL, specifically on the applicability of criminal descriptions to certain kind of individuals.

Thus, the nature of some of the involved individuals or groups in the light of penal responsibility is not cle" as possible perpetrators of war crimes on one hand, and the possibility to exclude criminal responsibility in the case of an individual which causes injuries to a civilian who has lost protection as have taken active part into hostilities.

However, this problematic is directly linked with the jurisdiction of the ICC in the case of non-international armed conflicts, while the unqualified actors are the ones which perform as the counterpart of States in this type of hostilities.

War Crimes in the Context of a Non-international Armed Conflict

As it was discussed, the standardization of the relevant actors on a conflict plays a relevant role not just as a protective measure, but in the determination of who is legally authorized to take part in hostilities (and who is not). Therefore, the scenario where those actors are performing is relevant as well when assessing which unlawful conducts are criminally reproachable.

While most of modern armed conflicts have a non-international character, surprising and regrettable omissions were made in this case when including criminal descriptions, specifically on the behaviors related with the prohibition of indiscriminate attacks (method of warfare) and the use of certain weapons (means of warfare), both of them coming from the Principle of Proportionality.

One possible explanation is that the omission comes from the primary rule, as by the last phases of the Geneva Diplomatic Conference where Protocol II was negotiated, States refrained from including such legal provisions to the case of an internal conflict because they considered their sovereignty to be particularly threatened in this area..

Therefore, it would look like a *real* war between belligerents having equal rights.

However, the result was a dramatic simplification of the text, although for others, the sole inclusion of the provisions related to this type of conflict is one of the greatest achievements of the Conference. Even more, this is shocking when it is brought what the International Criminal Tribunal for the former Yugoslavia (ICTY) stated on this respect while "*the rule that civilian population as such, as well as individual civilians, shall not be object of attack, is a fundamental rule of international humanitarian law applicable to all armed conflicts*," and as we saw, Distinction and Proportionality are inseparable as they are a pairing constituted by a general aim and a provision of concrete application.

Issues on the Customary Nature of the Primary Rules

Following what the ICJ has stated in its case law, the Principles of Distinction and Proportionality have a customary character, so they should be applied to any type of armed conflict as they represent basic values to the international community, and which are concretized through a systematic practice. This means, then, that the humanitarian norms are flexible, and are able to be adapted to new circumstances whether the conditions to verify their customary character are met.

Nevertheless, the problematic described in the first sections of the paper showed that even if the secondary rules are feed from the *normes de comportement* in order to define which conducts inside an armed conflict could be criminally sanctioned, the former don't represent exactly the latter, creating a limited system of criminal responsibility in comparison with IHL.

Moreover, according to the principle *Nullum crimen, nulla poena sine praevia lege poenali*, a person shall not be criminally responsible unless the conduct in question constitutes a crime within the jurisdiction of the Court, and that the definition of a crime shall be strictly constructed and shall not be extended by analogy. In other words, "*the principle of legality promotes a legal system's legitimacy by limiting the interventions of its criminal process to those which have been clearly prescribed by law in advance.*"

Such provision would be subsequently a wall for customary international law to influence from a flexible point of view the content and scope of war crimes, in order to promote legal certainty as one of the cornerstones of the international penal system. In other words, that the judges do not have the right to supplant the authoritative law-maker.

Then, a conclusion *a priori* would be that the jurisdiction of the ICC is restricted to situations literally described in the Rome Statute. The question which raises here, provided the customary character of the principles in comment is whether the flexible performance of such humanitarian rules could be extended to the lists of crimes under the Statute, in order to adapt the latter to the changing structure of armed conflicts, as well as the need to protect universally some values vindicated by the international community. As it will be seen henceforth, this proposal is one of the possible alternatives to clarify the case of the applicability of proportionality in war crimes related to non-international armed conflicts, specifically on the prohibition of indiscriminate attacks and the use of certain means of warfare, and in some way could assist the jurisdiction to clarify situations related with civilians taking active part in hostilities.

PRAGMATIC ISSUES ON DISTINCTION AND PROPORTIONALITY

Taking into account the theoretical issues displayed on section 3, it will be described the way that the Statute deals with war crimes related to the Principles of Distinction and Proportionality, firstly describing general common elements, and therefore analyzing each conduct.

Structure of War Crimes

Article 8 of the Statute establishes four categories of war crimes which are determined by two variables; the type of armed conflict (international or non-international) and the legal source where the conducts come from; on one hand "*grave breaches*" of the Geneva Conventions, and "*other serious violations*" of the laws and customs applicable in armed conflict on the other. Consequently, the Court may dispose of four lists of war crimes which describe diverse criminal actions related to the limits of the conduct of hostilities and the protection of certain persons and goods.

Hence, even if the Principles of Distinction and Proportionality have a global influence on the whole branch of IHL, and therefore, on every war crime, their direct manifestation can be found in one general prohibition applicable either to situations of international and internal armed conflicts (section B), and two complementary criminal conducts in relation the methods and means of warfare which are disproportionate (section C), following the way they were developed from the normes de comportement of the 1977 Additional Protocols to the Geneva Conventions, without prejudice of complementary rules coming from another legal instruments, for instance, in the case of means of warfare. Even though each criminal behaviour will be analyzed separately in order to address the specificities of each conduct, four common elements to the crimes can be identified in order to establish practical consequences for the determination of criminal responsibility:

- The conducts shall be unlawful in relation to a norme de comportement (primary rule) coming from the framework of International Humanitarian Law.
- Even if the results vary depending on each case, the conducts have to be concretized in an attack, *i.e.* the offensive or defensive use of violence against an adversary, which reflects the display of a military operation in the context of an armed conflict (nexus).
- The civilians individually considered or civilian populations are the passive subject of the criminal conducts, *i.e.* the effects of military actions resides on them, directly (8.2 (b) (i)) or indirectly (8.2 (b) (iv; xx)).
- Notwithstanding subjective specificities for each criminal conduct, intent and knowledge from the perpetrator have to be verified when determining the mental element of the crimes.

Prohibition to Intentionally Direct Attacks against Civilians

The Statute of ICC recognizes that according to the Principle of Distinction, civilians cannot be considered as a legitimate objective, which means that a direct action against them is not justified in order to obtain a military advantage, and likewise, that it is forbidden provided that it constitutes a breach to the most *elemental considerations of humanity*.

Thus, as a manifestation of its customary character there is an identical rule applicable to both types of conflicts even if reproduced on different lists; thus, articles 8.2 (b) (i) and 8.2 (e) (i) states such prohibition as it follows:

"Intentionally directing attacks against the civilian population as such or against individual civilians not taking direct part in hostilities."

Moreover, the International Criminal Tribunal for the former Yugoslavia has confirmed that *"the rule that civilian population as such, as well as individual civilians, shall not be object of attack, is a fundamental rule of international humanitarian law applicable to all armed conflicts."*

The general elements of crimes described above apply without any additional provision, save for the occasional problematic situation for the judge to identify who is protected in cases where civilians take direct part into hostilities, and the criminal conducts are committed against them (this will be treated in section IV-D), and the discussion on if the perpetrator should have the "*purpose*" of committing attacks against civilians, or just "*been aware*" of the civilian status of the object of attack, thesis stated by the ICTY.

Principle of Proportionality

As it was pointed on what the ICJ has said about the relation between distinction and proportionality, the former cannot be easily disassociated from the rules inherent to its implementation, which includes specifically the prohibition of indiscriminate attacks and the use of weapons with the same potentiality to cause incidental injuries to civilians and civilian population.

However, and relying on section III-B, no rule on the Statute was found in order to expressively establish criminal responsibility for the commission of disproportionate attacks in the case of a non-international armed conflict, despite of two lists of prohibited conducts dedicated to this factual situation. Hence, actions contrary to the Principle of Proportionality would only be punishable in the case of an international armed conflict.

Nonetheless, it is suggested that the general prohibition of attacks to civilians and civilian population included in article 8.2 (e) would be sufficient to include such behaviors in the case of an internal armed conflict, as they form a unity under the customary primary rules of IHL; however, and taking into account on the other hand what was pointed on the principle of legality, this issue is open to further discussion as the ICC develops relevant jurisprudence.

METHODS OF WARFARE (INDISCRIMINATE ATTACKS)

Article 8.2 (b) (iv) lays down the prohibition to launch an attack which will cause incidental injuries to the protected entities, as it follows:

"Intentionally launching an attack in the knowledge that such attack will cause incidental loss of life or injury to civilians or damage to civilian objects or widespread, long-term and severe damage to the natural environment which would be clearly excessive in relation to the concrete and direct overall military advantage anticipated."

Alternatively to the description of article 8.2 (b) (i) which dealt with direct attacks against civilians, this article develops the case of an operation which was initially directed to a legitimate military objective, but under certain conditions generates unlawful collateral effects to protected entities. Therefore, it implicitly recognizes that in terms of criminal responsibility, there's a "*thin red line*" in order to determine when some incidental injuries during hostilities are not reproachable provided the reality of armed conflicts, and when they are.

In that sense, as the ICTY pointed, *"The protection of civilians (...) may cease entirely or be reduced or suspended in exceptional circumstances: (...) (ii) when, although the object of a military attack is comprised of military objectives, belligerents cannot avoid causing so-called collateral damage to civilians."*

Such delimitation deserves further discussion, as it is important to point some specificities of this criminal description:

A priori, *particular results coming from the launch of the attack are not required to verify the material element, as the reproach comes from the fact of committing the action which would cause incidental loss of life or injury to civilians*. This is so provided that in the Elements of Crimes, the word will, inside the original article, was replaced by *would*.

Consequently, there is a special qualification of the mental elements –intent and knowledge–, as it is specifically required that the perpetrator had conscience of the effects of the attack before it was launched, as well as of the factual circumstances that established the existence of an armed conflict. Specifically, the knowledge element implies that the perpetrator should make a value judgment based in the information available to him at the time the military action is being planned, and following the parameter of a *"reasonable commander"* when taking the commented decisions.

Special controversy is provided by the phrase *"which would be clearly excessive in relation to concrete and direct overall military advantage anticipated,"* whether it is the one which determines to what extent military operations which generate incidental damages to civilians are disproportionate, and then, subject to criminal responsibility.

Departing from the primary norm which was displayed in articles 51.5 (b) and 57.2 (a) (iii) of Protocol I, the article of the Statute includes the words *"clearly"* and *"overall"*. This is relevant in order to point that whether by the time the IHL instrument was negotiated there were divergences in the way this provision had to be interpreted, in the case of the Rome Statute concerns were even greater and recalled the old discussion under the Diplomatic Conference; so the flexibility of such new expressions pretended to contribute to solve the tension between states, finally letting it to the *bona fides* of the parties and a wide margin of appreciation to the judge. This argument shall be elaborated:

Firstly, regarding on the content of the expression *"clearly excessive,"* the negotiating history of Protocol I indicates that the term *disproportionate* was proposed initially but, as it was strongly challenged by several countries because of its subjectivity, it was replaced by the term *excessive*.

It can be inferred then an attempt to include an objective scale of proportionality to the results of a military action, as it pretends the evaluation of its effects in terms of the amount of force required to achieve an advantage, having as limit the protection of civilians and civilian population which occasionally might be affected.

Therefore, the determination of the excessiveness in an action results difficult as well, provided that the quantities being measured are dissimilar; then it is not possible to establish any reasonably exact proportionality equation between them. Moreover, the adjective clearly is vague in the sense that attributes an even wider margin of appreciation to an equation per se complex, turning the criminal description even more hardly applicable.

Secondly, reference to "*concrete and direct overall military advantage*" constitutes a subjective scale of proportionality. Trying to interpret the meaning of "*overall*," a footnote to the Elements of Crimes was included in order to explain that the warfare benefit should be "*foreseeable by the perpetrator*," and that the advantage, as it has to be considered as a whole, "*may or may not be temporally or geographically related to the object of attack*" suggesting that the military benefits which supports an action must be considered with regard to military actions in general.

In that sense, this term results dangerous provided that modifies the normal interpretation of the requirement that the military advantage shall be "concrete and direct," as it is contradictory to demand a general view of the armed conflict to determine a circumstance which is visibly specific in the context of a military action. However, the Committee which drafted the Elements of Crimes tried to get over this contradiction saying that whether the article suggested the possibility of lawful injuries it was not justifying any violation of the law of armed conflicts, it was just reflecting the proportionality element in order to determine the legality of a military activity in the context of an armed conflict. In the same way, according to the ICC the term "*overall*" is redundant provided that its pretended meaning is included in the existing wording of Additional Protocol I.

At the end, unless further case law clarifies the text, it will be really difficult for the Court to address criminal responsibility for the case of violations of the Principle of Proportionality as but certainly it constitutes a possibility to use abusively the provision. Moreover, it gives great latitude to the belligerent and renders judicial scrutiny almost impossible, reflecting the political impact of law, and the way States consider their sovereignty to be threatened by an international criminal jurisdiction.

However, the judge will have to examine each case in order to determine the final impact of military operations, and if excess on incidental injuries to protected entities (individuals and objects) can be identified from the factual circumstances, and to "*construe as narrowly as possible the discretionary power to attack belligerents and, by the same token, so as to expand the protection accorded to civilians.*"

Means of Warfare (weapons)

The application of the Principle of Proportionality on individual criminal responsibility is also projected to the case of the indiscriminate use of means of warfare during an international armed conflict, as can be inferred from Article 8.2 (b) (xx):

"*Employing weapons, projectiles and material and methods of warfare which are of a nature to cause superfluous injury or unnecessary suffering or which are inherently indiscriminate in violation of the international law of armed conflict, provided that such weapons, projectiles and material and methods of warfare are the subject of a comprehensive prohibition and are included in an annex to this Statute, by an amendment In accordance with the relevant provisions set forth in articles 121 and 123*".

The consequences of the use of certain weapons could be so grave that their use should be restricted, even if they might be effective against the enemy. Therefore, weapons can be qualified as indiscriminate in the case that they can't be directed to a specific military objective, as well as when even if they can do it so, they cause incidental injuries to civilians or protected objects.

Consequently, according to the phrase "*inherently indiscriminate in violation of the international law of armed conflict*," there are two elements which have to be taken into consideration in order to establish such restriction; a comprehensive prohibition and their inclusion into an annex to the Statute which will determine the prohibited methods of warfare.

Concerning the first element, it can be inferred from the Statute that poison, poisoned gas and certain types of ammunition are clearly forbidden, as they are expressly mentioned as unlawful in articles 8.2 (b) (xvii, viii, xix). Nevertheless, it should be taken into account what the ICJ stated in the Advisory Opinion on the legality of the Threat or Use of Weapons of Mass Destruction, as it was stated that under certain conditions, the prohibition of certain weapons of mass destruction such as nuclear chemical and biological military hard-ware is a customary principle, applicable even to non-international armed conflicts.

Regarding on the second element, given that so far no annex to the Rome Statute including the list of forbidden weapons, projectiles and material of warfare exists, it wouldn't be possible for the Court to adjudge criminal responsibility for the commission of this war crime until such list were developed as an amendment to the treaty, as there is a lack of specific material elements for this crime.

FINAL REMARK ON CIVILIANS TAKING ACTIVE PART IN HOSTILITIES

It is important to address as a corollary, a relevant common point to all the criminal behaviors analyzed, when establishing the consequences of attacks to civilians and civilian population in terms of criminal responsibility. This is the case of civilians taking active part in hostilities, whether according to the primary rules they inherently lose their protection status, and moreover, they could be subject of the jurisdiction of the ICC.

Hence, civilians who take active part in hostilities are not anymore the passive subject of the criminal behaviors intended to protect them, as they lose the status coming from the primary rules. Therefore, they become legitimate military objectives and no criminal responsibility related with distinction can be attributed in case of attacks against them.

This is especially problematic in the case of non-international armed conflicts, where civilians are involved in several ways with non-state actors; the internal armed conflict in Colombia should be a relevant example, as peasants have familiar relations with members of the guerrillas, and in various occasions national authorities have stated that those persons, even if civilians, are collaborating with the dissident armed forces. Would an attack against them contribute to gain a military advantage? Moreover, incidental injuries against them could be considered legitimated provided they are not any longer protected by the status of civilians?

Finally, it has to be formulated the question whether civilians which effectively take active part in hostilities can be judged by the Court for the commission of criminal conducts, or just as common delinquents into national criminal systems, provided that they can't be treated as belligerents with equal rights in the context of an internal armed conflict due to the consideration of sovereignty made by States when adopting the Statute in articles 8.2 (d) and 8.2 (f).

8

International Law: Use of Military Forces and Accountability

The debates that arose about North Atlantic Treaty Organization's Operation Allied Force in Kosovo in 1999 brought into sharp relief the fundamental issues involved in using force for purposes other than to repel a cross border invasion. Is authorization by the UN Security Council essential for general acceptance of the legitimacy of the use of military forces? Can the authorization of a body like the North Atlantic Council be sufficient for those taking part in the operation? How about for non-NATO members? When do national legislative bodies of countries have to take specific action to authorize participation of their country's military forces in international operations? To whom are military commanders responsible? Practice in these areas has outpaced scholarly analysis and understanding of the issues involved.

TENETS OF DEMOCRACY: PARTICIPATION IN DECISION MAKING AND ACCOUNTABILITY

Democracy as a matter of international law is perhaps most firmly rooted in Article 25 (a) of the International Covenant on Civil and Political Rights that: "Every citizen shall have the right and the opportunity ... to take part in the conduct of public affairs, directly or through freely chosen representatives." Article 25 stems from Article 21 of the Universal Declaration of Human Rights that states: "Everyone has the right to take part in the government of his country, directly or through freely chosen representatives." Democracy further assumes constraints on government power vis a vis its citizens. Since this study is focused on countries that are already democracies, we are not addressing the question of whether democracy commands any special status as a form of international governance. Our focus is on how democracy and international obligations interact.

Since democracy can be used to mean specific things in particular political contexts, we find it useful to start from an abstract and theoretical standpoint. As a concept, democracy means "government by the people." Elaborating this basic notion, Robert A. Dahl, one of the foremost contemporary democratic theorists, stated that "a key characteristic of democracy is the continuing responsiveness of the government to the preferences of its citizens, considered as political equals." (Endnotes)

Dahl has identified five criteria that a process for governing an association should meet to be regarded as democratic.

Effective participation. Before a policy is adopted by the association, all the members must have equal and effective opportunities for making their views known to the other members as to what the policy should be.

Voting equality. When the moment arrives at which the decision about policy will finally be made, every member must have an equal and effective opportunity to vote, and all votes must be counted as equal.

Enlightened understanding. Within reasonable limits as to time, each member must have equal and effective opportunities for learning about the relevant alternative policies and their likely consequences.

Control of the agenda. The members must have the exclusive opportunity to decide how and, if they choose, what matters are to be placed on the agenda. Thus the democratic process required by the three preceding criteria is never closed. The policies of the association are always open to change by the members, if they so choose.

Inclusion of adults. All, or at any rate most, adult permanent residents should have the full rights of citizens that are implied by the first four criteria. Before the twentieth century this criterion was unacceptable to most advocates of democracy.

The five criteria include items that most democratic theorists consider essential. Using more familiar language democratic theorists would speak of freedom of information, association, assembly, participation, and speech. It is through these political rights that Dahl's criteria of effective participation and enlightened understanding are met. They would also speak of equality and majority rule. They would discuss forms of representation, periodic elections, and voting rules. These are the ways that the criteria of inclusion of adults, control of the agenda, and voting equality are met.

By the late 1990s more than 115 states had governments that by broad criteria could be called democratic. As late as 1987 there were fewer than 70 democratic states. The trend toward democracy was one of the most prominent developments of the late twentieth century. Established and aspiring democracies constituted more than half of the states in the world. The basic tenets of democratic rule as embodied in the International Covenant on Civil and Political Rights are likely a factor in this development. As of 1999, 144 states were party to the Covenant.

In all democratic states elected representatives make policies that affect individual lives. The formal arrangements for making these decisions vary, but broadly divide into two types, parliamentary systems like that of the United Kingdom, and presidential systems like that of the United States. In the former type executive and legislative authority is fused, and while parliamentary assent is necessary for the adoption of laws, this frequently can be assured through disciplined political parties. In the latter type, particularly when the executive and legislative branches are under the control of different political parties, legislative assent is much more problematic. But in both types of systems, accountability is thought to be assured through regular elections. Citizens vote for individuals to be their representatives on the basis of their expectations about the decisions that these individuals would make if they were in office, and they can remove from office representatives who take decisions with which they do not agree.

It is unclear how to ensure that decisions made under international auspices are made with the same attention to democratic criteria that is applied when they are made within states. Dahl's criteria are helpful in thinking about the problem because they are stated in general terms, not in those tied to particular institutions and practices associated with particular governments. Just as creating democracies within states required the invention of new institutions, making decisions at the international level accountable to democratic institutions have also required new practices.

Dahl is pessimistic that international institutions can take decisions in ways that accord with his criteria for democracy. He believes that decisions in international institutions come about primarily through bargaining among political and bureaucratic elites. "Bargaining, hierarchy, and markets determine the outcomes. Except to ratify the results, democratic processes hardly play a role." Dahl is particularly pessimistic that opportunities can be provided to citizens for "political participation, influence, and control roughly equivalent in effectiveness to those already existing in democratic countries." He is also skeptical that citizens could become as concerned and informed about decisions taken in international institutions as they now are about decisions taken by the governments of their own countries. And he doubts that an appropriate scheme for representation could be created that would give equal weight to all citizens without creating a situation in which smaller democracies with particular interests and problems would be constantly outvoted.

Not all democratic theorists are as pessimistic as Dahl. David Held is a democratic theorist who has thought and written about democracy and international institutions. He acknowledges that the existing ensemble of international institutions fall short of meeting democratic criteria but he is hopeful that cosmopolitan democracy could be established through what he regards as attainable transformations of these institutions. He describes cosmopolitan democracy as: "an ensemble of organizations, associations and agencies pursuing their own projects, whether these be economic, social or cultural; but these projects must always also be subject to the constraints of democratic processes and a common structure of political action."

The question of applying democratic procedures is not just an abstract issue. It also relates to the effectiveness of the decisions. Popular support is essential. Unless there is popular support the decisions and actions taken for using military forces under the auspices of international institutions it is unlikely that sufficient resources will be provided for a sufficient length of time for the forces to accomplish the goals that have been collectively agreed upon. Lack of popular support could not only jeopardize the actions, if popular attitudes became not just apathetic but hostile, it could jeopardize the international institution itself. Popular support is unlikely to be gained among educated populations unless they feel that the decisions have been taken in ways that accord with democratic accountability. This implies clear information about the purposes of the action, ample debate, and participation in the decisions by officials who are accountable.

The shift of authority to processes and institutions outside of the framework of nation states is particularly evident in the realm of economics, and the shift has been most pronounced in the European Union (EU) which functions by delegation of authority from EU member states. A significant literature has developed about the "democratic deficit" in the European Union, and there are many suggestions about how the deficit might be met. The shift of decision-making authority is also going on, however, with respect to military matters.

In all political systems, decisions to deploy and use military forces are among the most important that can be taken. Gaining a monopoly of authority over the use of force has been a key element in the creation of states and the establishment of sovereignty. Democracies have therefore gone to great lengths to ensure democratic accountability in decisions about the use of military forces. National constitutions frequently contain special provisions specifying how the decisions are to be made.

The experience of the United States highlights this. The constitution makes the president commander-in-chief of the armed forces. It assigns congress the power to appropriate funds for the maintenance of the armed forces and to declare war. These provisions, however, provide only a framework for establishing democratic accountability. Issues relating to the precise ways of maintaining democratic accountability with respect to the use of military forces have been debated throughout American history. It was a major factor explaining the enactment of the War Powers Act in the United States.

The United States experience may be extreme, but all democratic countries have been concerned with establishing and maintaining democratic accountability regarding the use of military forces, and all have developed procedures to achieve this goal. Lori Fisler Damrosch has documented that in the closing decades of the twentieth century there has been a general trend "toward subordinating war powers to constitutional control, and that this trend includes a trend toward greater parliamentary control over the decision to introduce troops into situations of actual or potential hostilities."

Whatever the constitutional situation, the political reality is that citizens have become increasingly concerned about the purposes to which their countries' military forces are used and may be reluctant to have them used when the interest for doing so is not sufficiently clear or understood. This broad sentiment was evident in the French reaction to the war in Algeria, the American reaction to the war in Vietnam, and the Soviet reaction to the war in Afghanistan. Factors which contribute to these reactions include the cost in lives and other resources and can change if the desired result is not achieved within a period of time. This broad sentiment has been a factor contributing to the trend that Professor Damrosch identified.

How do the trends toward democratization within nation states and these basic constitutional understandings about the use of military forces and the debate and developments about them fit with efforts to use military forces collectively?

MILITARY FORCES UNDER INTERNATIONAL AUSPICES

Generalizing from the experience of the UN and NATO since World War II, the uses of military forces under international auspices can be placed in five broad categories described by their general purposes. The categories are based on the number of military personnel involved, their mandate and their rules of engagement, and whether or not they enter the territory of the state where they operate with the consent of that state. The five categories are:

- Monitoring and Observation
- Traditional Peacekeeping
- Peacekeeping plus State-building
- Force to Ensure Compliance with International Mandates
- Enforcement.

Monitoring and Observation is a preventive military response involving the positioning of troops, military observers and related personnel on one or both sides of a border between entities that are or have been in dispute or where there is an emerging threat of conflict, with the primary object of deterring the escalation of that situation into armed conflict.

Eighteen of the deployments of military forces under the auspices of the United Nations have been for the purpose of monitoring and observation. Eleven of these missions were started before 1990 and seven after 1990. Monitoring and observation missions constituted more than 60 percent of the UN's deployments before 1990, but only slightly more than 30 percent of the deployments after 1990.

Traditional Peacekeeping involves unarmed or lightly armed military contingents being engaged in the monitoring, supervision and verification of cease-fire, withdrawal, buffer zone and related agreements with the consent of the parties. It presumes cooperation and neutrality, and its methods are peaceful: the use of military force, other than in self-defense, is incompatible with the concept.

In all there have only been four traditional peacekeeping forces, UNEF I and the United Nations Force in Cyprus (UNFCYP), UNEF II, and the United Nations Force in Lebanon (UNIFIL). All of these forces were originally deployed prior to 1990.

Peacekeeping plus State-building involves supplementing traditional peacekeeping with activities such as election monitoring or organization, human rights protection, and assisting or exercising civil administration functions during transition to independence or democracy.

There have been 25 cases of peacekeeping plus state-building, and all but two of these were deployed after 1990.

Force to Ensure Compliance with International Mandates involves the use of force to ensure the safety of peacekeepers and to enable a peacekeeping mandate, which is being frustrated, to be carried out. Military forces engaged in such operations usually also perform state-building tasks.

Five of the fifty-four military forces deployed under UN auspices fall in this category, as do all four of those deployed by NATO. All of the forces deployed by the United Nations and the North Atlantic Treaty Organization in the former Yugoslavia would be in this category. NATO's International Force (IFOR) was the largest of these military operations. It included more than 60,000 personnel. Of the deployments of force in this category, only ONUC occurred before 1990.

Enforcement involves the threat or use of military forces in pursuit of efforts to maintain or restore peace, in response to conflicts or other major security crises. The classic example of such a use is that to prevent or repel an attack on the territorial integrity of a state.

The UN authorized operations in Korea and Kuwait are the two cases of enforcement action. The Korean operation involved close to a million personnel, and the Kuwait operation more almost 800,000. UN forces suffered 95,000 fatalities in the Korean War, but only 240 in the Gulf War.

In popular and scholarly discourse peacekeeping is often used as a generic term to cover all of the first four uses of military forces listed above. We feel that the uses are so different in so many ways that for analytical purposes it is important to make the distinctions that we have made

The increasing frequency with which military forces have been used under the auspices of the UN and NATO and the increasing seriousness of the military operations since the end of the Cold War are key factors in making the issues of democratic accountability a more pressing matter than it was in the immediate years after World War II. Although military forces were used during the Cold War years, the uses outside of the UN context raised issues of accountability that could be addressed within established procedures of national governments.

We can conclude several things from this experience:

- The international community has become more sophisticated about the use of force than it was when Wilson and others first sought to give effect to a system of collective security in the early years of the twentieth century. Proposals and practices have evolved.
- The absence of means directly available to the United Nations to carry out collective actions puts it at the will of contributing states to determine what will or not will not be done to give effect to UN mandates.
- The emphasis on human rights and the increased number of intra-state conflicts that have been deemed worthy of international concern and action has "lowered" the barriers that exist in the UN Charter against interference in a state's internal affairs. Widely accepted processes for judging the appropriateness of international action, however, seem not yet to exist and certainly seem not to exist outside the UN framework.

ISSUES OF DEMOCRATIC ACCOUNTABILITY

The history and experience with the use of military forces under international auspices have produced questions with regard to forms for authorization, national responsibility, and individual responsibility for the conduct of operations in the field. As the forms of the use of military forces have multiplied, so have the questions of authority and responsibility in deciding to deploy troops, to select military and political objectives, and to incur risk. These raise issues of applying democratic tenets to decisions and actions taken internationally and collectively.

Five forms of authorization and responsibility can be identified. We use the term democratic accountability to mean ways by which democratic tenets are fulfilled. We use the term democratic accountability to cover the following five sets of issues.

- International Authorization to Use Military Forces

- National Authorization to Use Military Forces
- Civilian/Political Control of Military Personnel and Operations
- Civilian Responsibility to the Military for Their Safety
- Responsibility to Comply with Norms Governing the Conduct of Military and Other International Personnel in the Field.

Democratic governments over time have developed procedures that cover the last four of these issues. These procedures are embedded in constitutions, internal conditions, and political and military traditions. A considerable body of moral doctrine that can be used to guide choices with respect to these issues has also been developed. The first issue is newer and arises as a consequence of the effort to shift the legitimate use of force from states acting alone to international institutions and it is compounded by the increasing emphasis on intra-state as opposed to inter-state conflict. While there are bodies of doctrine with respect to the last four issues, it is not clear how these should be applied when forces are being used under the auspices of an international institution.

The relevance of Dahl's five criteria to international and national authorizations to use military forces does not require explanation. The criteria are also relevant to the latter three issues. These three issues concern the implementation of policy. They are intended to ensure that policies are implemented in accordance with the decisions to adopt them. Dahl's criterion of control of the agenda is particularly important with respect to them.

INTERNATIONAL AUTHORIZATION TO USE MILITARY FORCES

The first condition for a war to be just under the catholic just war doctrine is that the authority deciding to engage in war must be legitimate. This is also a test demanded by the constitutions of nation states. With the effort to move away from unilateral uses of force and to manage conflict under international auspices, what are accepted international auspices? Which institutions can authorize the use of force and what legal and political implications flow from this authorization? The intent of the UN Charter was to centralize this authority in the Security Council. Under Article 42, the Security Council could authorize the use of military forces. The voting arrangements in the Security Council were intended to insure that military action would have broad international support and that action would not be taken against the wishes of one of the permanent members.

Under Article 51 of the UN Charter states could individually or collectively take military action in their own self-defense, but this action had to be reported to the Security Council and the authorization was limited until the Security Council had taken action. NATO was created under the authority of Article 51. Under Chapter VIII of the Charter regional organizations could deploy military forces but only with the authorization of the Security Council.

In practice the United Nations Security Council, the United Nations General Assembly, and the North Atlantic Council all have given authorization to use military forces. The legal grounds for authorization in the fifty-eight cases that have occurred have varied from threats to the peace as established under Chapter VII of the UN Charter to the necessity of preventing genocide and violations of humanitarian law.

National Authorization to Use Military Forces

Democratic governments have firmly established procedures for authorizing the use of military forces. Some are embedded in constitutional provisions, others in tradition. There are differences between governments that have presidential and parliamentary forms. In all cases though over time popular support is crucial if a democratic government is to persevere in a military operation. Elected officials must periodically face voters, and this is the way in which accountability is ultimately enforced. Voters may reject officials who have used force in ways that they do not approve. Karen Mingst has identified areas of political culture, political relationships, and societal factors that shape popular sentiment and perceptions of national interest.

In the late twentieth century an important trend in the complex arrangements that govern the use of military forces is emerging. Lori Fisler Damrosch has shown an increasing tendency of legislative bodies in established democracies and countries aspiring to become democratic to insist on being involved in decisions about the use of military forces. They are less and less content to leave these matters to the executive who may rely on an international undertaking in deciding to act rather than on the views of the legislature.

As military forces have been used under the auspices of international institutions, democratic governments have struggled to fit established procedures into these new situations.

CIVILIAN/POLITICAL CONTROL OF MILITARY PERSONNEL AND OPERATIONS

Civilian/political control of military personnel and operations is a firmly established principle in all democracies, and it is one that many authoritarian governments also seek to enforce. In the United States the constitutional provision that the president is the commander-in-chief symbolizes this principle, and there have been numerous episodes in U.S. history when the principle has been upheld.

The clear lines of control when military forces are used nationally become complicated when force is used under the auspices of international institutions. Who is or are the civilians to whom a commander of UN or NATO forces is responsible? What about subordinate commands, the commander of a brigade in a multinational operation whose immediate superior has a different nationality?

Civilian Responsibility to the Military for Their Safety

Consideration of the purposes and objectives of a mission, the availability of intelligence to determine appropriate arms and deployment based on an informed estimate of the situation, and agreement on the rules of engagement are all areas where civilian decision makers make decisions about the potential risk to personnel deployed in a mission. Elected officials in democratic countries who put military forces unnecessarily at risk would likely face electoral punishment. But what if military forces deployed under the auspices of the UN or NATO were given a mandate but not provided with sufficient personnel and equipment effectively to carry out the mission and put in serious risk? How would accountability be established and who would be held accountable? Establishing responsibility in the way that responsibility is established in democracies might prove to be impossible. Who should and could voters punish? Would there be enough transparency for responsibility to be assigned? Would the decision have been, as Dahl feared, the result of bargaining among elites?

Conduct of Military and other International Personnel in the Field

The laws of war contain clear directives about the conduct of military personnel in the discharge of their missions and their responsibility towards the population and property of their adversary. The provisions of these laws are included in the codes of military conduct of national military establishments. How do these norms apply to military and civilian personnel who are operating as part of international operations? Who is responsible for insuring that the norms are upheld?

Force under International Auspices

A basic hypothesis undergirding the analysis is that the greater the risk to the lives of the military personnel, the more ambiguous the basis for action, the longer the duration of the operation, and the less certain its outcome, the greater the demand will be to ensure democratic accountability. Thus enforcement operations will raise issues of democratic accountability more acutely than the use of force to ensure compliance with international mandates and so on. Monitoring and observation operations will be the least likely to raise complex issues of democratic accountability.

We examine the historical experience with these issues in nine countries: Canada, France, Germany, India, Japan, Norway, the Russian Federation, the United Kingdom, and the United States.

All are members of the United Nations. Four, France, the Russian Federation, the United Kingdom, and the United States are permanent members of the United Nations Security Council.

Germany, Japan, and India aspire to permanent membership on the Security Council. Six, Canada, France, Germany, Norway, the United Kingdom, and the United States are members of NATO.

All nine have contributed their military forces to operations conducted under the auspices of international institutions. Canada and Norway have been among the states that have contributed military forces to the largest number of UN missions. India has contributed more military forces to UN operations than any other state. Together these nine states accounted for more than sixty percent of the world's military expenditures in 1998 and had almost a quarter of the world's military personnel. Their combined assessments for UN peacekeeping operations constitute more than eighty percent of the total.

The nine differ in important ways. Six have parliamentary systems, two have presidential systems, and one is a mixed presidential-parliamentary system. Five, France, India, the Russian Federation, the United Kingdom, and the United States have used their military forces unilaterally since World War II. Four, Canada, Germany, Japan, and Norway have only used their military forces under the auspices of international institutions during this period.

The position of the United States stands out among the nine. U.S. military expenditures were larger than those of the other eight countries combined and its military personnel accounted for a third of the total personnel of the nine. It alone had a significant air and sea transport capacity, and thus it alone had a global military reach. Its military technology vastly exceeded that of any other state. The United States military power was overwhelming. Because of the size of U.S. military expenditures particularly in research and development, the United States led the Revolution in Military Affairs, the introduction of high technology, especially new forms of sensors and information technology into battlefield situations. Some of this technology was used in the Gulf War and Operation Allied Force in Kosovo to the increasing dismay of other countries.

The experience of the twentieth century with regulating the use of force and building international institutions has created several conditions that touch on understanding the concept of democratic accountability that we develop in this study.

- Decision making based on some form of democratic procedure is increasingly regarded as a measure of the legitimacy of the decision. This poses special challenges for democracies when they are constrained or bound by the decisions of institutions that are not democratic. This raises questions of effective participation in international decision making.
- Democracy as generally practiced and understood is that of a system of governance functioning within defined territories.
- The present requirements of protecting human rights and self-determination are lowering the barriers of non-interference into the affairs of states, so that uses of military forces to protect these rights may be regarded as permissible.

These forces combine to place democracies in the difficult position of ensuring accountability when decisions are made beyond the reach of state-based electoral and participatory structures, but are taken to safeguard the rights and freedoms of individuals that are the foundations of democracy.

The objective of this study is to try to understand the extent to which the criteria for democracy like those set forth by Robert Dahl have been met through actions at national and international levels in decisions to use military forces under the auspices of international institutions and if there is a shortfall, as surely there is, what might be done to improve the situation.

There are strong reasons for Dahl's pessimism about the difficulty of ensuring that decision making in international institutions accords with democratic criteria. Yet if movement cannot be made toward establishing democratic accountability when military forces are used under the auspices of international institutions, the twentieth century project of placing limits on the unilateral use of force and establishing mechanisms so that force can be used under the auspices of international institutions for collective purposes is likely to be severely constrained.

TOWARD A MIXED SYSTEM OF DEMOCRATIC ACCOUNTABILITY

Two important political developments of the twentieth century are featured in this study. One is in the international and domestic restraints placed on coercive power. The other is in the growing acceptance of international rights and protections for individuals even against actions taken by their own governments. Scholarly attention has rightfully focused on both of these within the context of international institutions – itself an important phenomenon of the twentieth century in their number and scope. However, the experiences of the nine countries in this study demonstrate that developments within countries during this period have also been significant in contributing to these trends.

The mixing of the international and domestic decision making and governing systems that has resulted from these developments has raised questions for democracies both in practice and theory. On a theoretical basis, Dahl identified this as the challenge of internationalization for democracy. He wrote: "...from a democratic perspective the challenge posed by internationalization is to make sure that the costs to democracy are fully taken into account when decisions are shifted to international levels, and to strengthen the means for holding political and bureaucratic elites accountable for their decisions. Whether and how these may be accomplished is, alas, far from clear." How a select group of countries have handled this question is the basis for this study.

This challenge is particularly acute in the important area of the use of military forces. Outlawing the unilateral and unrestrained use of military forces was an important success of the first half of the twentieth century, a success finally achieved with the entry into force of the United Nations Charter in 1946. Since World War II states have largely come to accept the norm that the use of force unilaterally against the territorial integrity of another country would violate international law and could be countered by a collective response on behalf of the international community.

Gaining equal prominence in the international arena has been the growth of international human rights, first as an aspiration and then as a body of law now with a full set of institutions charged with its development and implementation. This international system is further supplemented by regional systems that are more developed in Europe and in the western hemisphere, and less developed in Africa. If restraining the use of force can be regarded as the achievement of the first half of the twentieth century, wide acceptance of human rights norms is surely an achievement of the second half of the century.

The founding and development of international institutions have also made progress in using military forces under international auspices for collective purposes. While the League of Nations and the United Nations were given the power to authorize the use of military forces, they were not provided direct means to carry out their decisions. Nevertheless, since World War II states individually or in concert with others have been willing to have their military forces used within frameworks established by international institutions.

Democracy both as a concept and as a form of government has also made progress as it has been adapted to fit territories of varying sizes and social and cultural complexity. Institutions of democracy have also changed to adapt to new circumstances including the practice of implementing decisions made by international institutions to use a country's military forces.

Governments of democratic states and their citizens have therefore sought to maintain democratic accountability through a mixed system that involved relying on the authority of international institutions as a basis for national action and review by national institutions and political processes. This system has provided a limited capability to use military forces under the auspices of international institutions. The extent to which this mixed system meets the challenge posed by Dahl needs to be examined.

As the twentieth century drew to a close military forces were increasingly being placed under the auspices of international institutions in situations where borders had not been violated, but where violent civil conflicts raged or human rights were seriously violated. The legal status of these humanitarian interventions as they have come to be known is contested. This has compounded the problem of maintaining democratic accountability when efforts are made to use military forces under the auspices of international institutions.

INTERNATIONAL AUTHORIZATION TO USE MILITARY FORCES

The intent of the UN Charter was to centralize authority concerning the use of military force in the Security Council. Under Article 42, the Security Council could authorize the use of military forces. Under Article 51 states could individually or collectively take military action in their own self-defense, but this action had to be reported to the Security Council and the authorization was limited until the Security Council had taken action. Under Chapter VIII of the Charter regional organizations could use force but only with the authorization of the Security Council. The voting arrangements in the Security Council were intended to ensure that military action would have broad international support and that effective action would be feasible, that is action would be taken only with the consent of the five permanent members, the states that at the end of World War II were assumed to have the greatest capacity to enforce the peace.

In practice, the United Nations Security Council, the United Nations General Assembly, and the North Atlantic Council have all given authorization to use military forces. The General Assembly's role was not foreseen in the Charter. Whether or not any institution other than the UN Security Council can authorize the use of military forces for purposes other than self-defense has been contested, as have the legal bases for deploying forces.

Decisions involving monitoring and observation missions have not been controversial. The practice became well established in the early years of the United Nations, and the League had undertaken similar tasks. Monitoring and observation missions have had the consent of the host states. The UN Security Council authorized all of the eighteen monitoring and observation missions.

Debates have arisen with respect to decisions about the other uses of military forces. Nevertheless, thirty-seven of the forty uses of military forces under the auspices of the UN and

NATO in the other four categories have had the authorization of the UN Security Council. The only three instances when the Security Council did not authorize the initial deployment of military forces were UNEF I in 1956—a traditional peacekeeping operation, the United Nations Security Force in West New Guinea (West Irian – UNSF) in 1962—a peacekeeping plus state-building Operation, and NATO's Operation Allied Force in 1999—a force to ensure compliance operation. The General Assembly authorized the first two, and the North Atlantic Council the third. Although the Security Council authorized the initial deployment of military forces in the Korean case, subsequent decisions about the military operation were taken by the General Assembly under the Uniting for Peace Resolution. This was true also in the case of the UN Operation in the Congo. In all, the UN Security Council authorized fifty-five of the fifty-eight uses of military forces, or almost ninety-five percent of them.

The United States and the United Kingdom were early proponents of the view that when the Security Council cannot act because of the veto decisions of the UN General Assembly or the North Atlantic Council constitute appropriate authorization for the use of military forces. The United States and the United Kingdom were co-sponsors of the Uniting for Peace Resolution in 1950, which allowed the General Assembly to act in crisis situations when the Security Council could not act because of the inability of the permanent members to reach unanimity. The UK's position, however, changed with the use of the Uniting for Peace Resolution to authorize UNEF I following the British and French attack on the Suez Canal in 1956. Even their Western allies have opposed this view on occasion, and the People's Republic of China and the Soviet Union and later the Russian Federation consistently opposed it. India abstained from voting on the Uniting for Peace Resolution, but voted for the authorization of UNEF I and UNSF. Japan's peacekeeping law explicitly accepts General Assembly authorization.

The essential question is under which if any circumstances should the UN structure and law be bypassed keeping in mind that the system exists precisely to restrain the use of force?

And if it should be bypassed, then on whose authority and judgment? And how much force is authorized? Are regional organizations valid sources for authorization? Can states act unilaterally?

UN Secretary-General Kofi Annan expressed the dilemma clearly in a contribution to the *Economist*. He wrote:

> To those for whom the greatest threat to the future of international order is the use of force in the absence of a Security Council mandate, one might say: leave Kosovo aside for a moment, and think about Rwanda. Imagine for one moment that, in those dark days and hours leading up to the genocide, there had been a coalition of states ready and willing to act in defence of the Tutsi population, but the council had refused or delayed giving the green light. Should such a coalition then have stood idly by while the horror unfolded?
>
> To those for whom the Kosovo action heralded a new era when states and groups of states can take military action outside the established mechanisms for enforcing international law, one might equally ask: Is there not a danger of such interventions undermining the imperfect, yet resilient security system created after the second world war, and of setting dangerous precedents for future interventions without a clear criterion to decide who might invoke these precedents and in what circumstances.

If the United Nations were a democratic institution these questions would be less vexing. A body that was democratic might be able to act in a way that would be broadly regarded as legitimate. It could subject proposed policies to public scrutiny, debate the issues, and take decisions by some form of majority vote. However, the UN structure is not democratic. The Security Council was set up to provide an effective response to threats to the peace by those states that were assumed in 1945 to have the most powerful military forces. Unanimity among these states was seen as an essential condition for collective action. Because of this, the veto was given to the five permanent members of the Council. While these states remained militarily powerful in 2000, other states such as Germany, India, and Japan were at least as powerful if not more powerful than some of them. The justification for giving the five the special privilege of the veto had eroded. All organs of the United Nations further fail to meet the democratic criterion requiring the inclusion and equality of all adults. Representation and voting in the United Nations are based on the doctrine of the sovereign equality of states not the inclusion and equality of all adults. China with more than 1.2 billion people and Liechtenstein with only 31 thousand each have one vote in the UN General Assembly. According to this criterion, neither the Security Council nor the General Assembly provides democratic representation. Even if one took a broader notion of representation grouping states by their geographical regions, the Security Council would fail the test. Asia the most populous region of the world is seriously underrepresented.

Finally, more than a third of the 188 member states of the United Nations do not have governments that even under the most lenient interpretation could be regarded as democratic. Their representatives may or may not represent the wishes of the citizens of these countries.

Yet on issues of war and peace, the United Nations is at the apex of the international political and legal structure. There is no other organization that has universal membership and a mandate to deal with issues of war and peace. States clearly prefer to have the Security Council's authorization when they use military forces. Because of the importance of the UN in the legal and political decision-making processes within states, Security Council authorization bestows a legitimacy that cannot be gained in any other way. This legitimacy is important for gathering domestic support for using of military forces.

The legal grounds for authorization in the fifty-eight cases that have occurred have varied from measures to facilitate the pacific settlement of disputes under Chapter VI of the UN Charter, through threats to the peace as established under Article 39, Chapter VII of the UN Charter, to the necessity of preventing genocide and violations of humanitarian law. When Article 39 of the UN Charter and Article 5 of the North Atlantic Treaty were drafted, threats to peace were generally conceived as cross border military attacks. The North Korean attack on South Korea and the Iraqi attack on Kuwait involved clear violations of Article 2, Paragraph 4 of the United Nations

Charter. The international law involved in the other fifty-six cases in which military forces were deployed under the auspices of the UN and NATO has frequently been less clear and has sometimes been contested. The humanitarian concerns that have compelled the deployment of international operations within states and without clear authorization by the UN Security Council have raised the most difficult questions as Operation Allied Force in Kosovo demonstrated.

That many contemporary conflicts stem from intra-state rather than inter-state violence tests a key assumption of international law — that states are sovereign within their own territory. However, if the international law prohibiting genocide and providing for human rights protection appears to overcome, or even requires overcoming, the concerns of intervention in the internal affairs of states, new standards and procedures must be developed if international relations are not to revert to the unregulated unilateral great-power interventions of the nineteenth century. As the international community explores this issue, it may be useful to recall that the initial impulse to control the cross-border use of military forces came from within states. The debates at the dawn of the 21st century taking place within states as to the level of commitment to humanitarian operations may provide a basis for building an international consensus on the purpose and scope of these operations. The controversy surrounding NATO's out of area operations demonstrate the complexities of this problem. The central question is whether NATO can legitimately take decisions to use military forces in out of area operations without authorization by the UN Security Council. NATO's decisions relating to the International Force (IFOR), the Stabilization Force (SFOR), and the Kosovo Force (KFOR) were all taken within a framework provided by UN Security Council resolutions. Operation Allied Force, the air war against Serbia, did not have this mandate. As in the UN Security Council's expansion of the concept of threats to peace, in NATO's out of area operations what constitutes a basis for intervention is also an issue.

The debate in October 1998 in NATO and preparation of the Activation Order authorizing the air strikes that started in March 1999 in Kosovo highlighted these issues. The legal basis for NATO's taking action was a central concern. France, Germany, and Italy initially maintained that explicit authorization by the UN Security Council would be required for the NATO Council to authorize any out of area military operation.

Russia, China and many other countries including India have maintained this consistently. Britain, in contrast to its allies, felt that international humanitarian law provided an adequate legal basis. The U.S. assumed adequate authority from Resolution 1199 in which the Security Council acting under Chapter VII demanded that all parties in Kosovo "cease hostilities."

NATO countries eventually were able to build the required consensus to take a decision, and at its 50th anniversary summit in 1999, NATO adopted the Alliance's Strategic Concept, which called on the alliance to make "full use of every opportunity to help build an undivided continent by promoting and fostering the vision of a Europe whole and free." This suggested that NATO might again take such action. Yet, it remains uncertain whether NATO could ever again achieve the consensus required to repeat such an operation in Kosovo or elsewhere. Moreover, the legitimacy of NATO's decision was contested by states, particularly those who were not members of the alliance.

The broad issues of whether any institution other than the UN Security Council can authorize the deployment of military forces and what constitute legitimate grounds for intervention thus are far from resolved.. See the debate in countries whose policies have been examined in this study have taken on the issue of international authorization. As can be seen, there is disagreement about the legitimacy of General Assembly and North Atlantic Council authorizations. Further unresolved are the legal bases for deploying military forces in operations that do not involve repelling cross border attacks.

Is progress in resolving these issues unlikely until the UN Security Council has been reformed? Will making the Security Council more representative of the world's population and changing its procedures so that the majority will could be implemented enhance its authority for the majority of states:

Are these essential conditions for moving the Security Council and its procedures toward conformity with democratic tenets?

NATIONAL AUTHORIZATION TO USE MILITARY FORCES

Once an international institution decides that military forces should be used, the issue of authorization then shifts to the national level. The concept involved in Article 43 of the United Nations Charter was that military forces made available under these agreements would be committed without further national authorization. Since NATO has maintained standing military forces in the territory covered by Article 5, these forces would automatically become engaged if an attack occurred. However, the Article 43 agreements were never put in place and NATO forces have never been attacked in the territory covered by Article 5. The issue of national authorization thus has arisen every time that the UN or NATO has decided that military forces should be used.

The nine countries in this study have handled the issue of national authorization in different ways. As we expected, in all nine countries the debate at the national level has been deeper and more extensive the larger and more risky the military operation and the murkier the legal basis for action. Some of the nine have developed explicit formal guidelines. Norway and Japan have enacted laws that govern their participation in military operations conducted under the auspices of the United Nations. The United States has enunciated policies. While the others have not done this, their actions have followed implicit guidelines. The extent to which the legislature has been involved in the decisions to assign countries military forces to international military operations has varied across the nine countries and with the type of operation. Another issue that has varied among the countries is the conditions under which their political authorities are willing to assign military forces to international operations.

Except in the cases of Japan and Germany, monitoring and observation missions have been handled relatively simply. Executives in countries other than Japan and Germany have routinely assigned military personnel to such missions acting on their own authority. Frequently, however, they have only felt free to assign those personnel that volunteered for these missions. Until the passage of the peacekeeping law in 1992, Japan's governments felt that they could not assign personnel of Japan's Self-Defense Forces outside of Japan. The same is true for Germany. Germany could not readily deploy its forces outside the NATO area until the constitutional court ruling of 1994.

Traditional peacekeeping has also been relatively unproblematic. Since all four traditional peacekeeping operations occurred before 1990, neither Germany nor Japan participated in them. The number of personnel required in traditional peacekeeping has generally been modest. In Norway the legislature has given the executive authorization to assign up to a certain number of military personnel to UN traditional peacekeeping operations, though this authorization is limited to personnel who volunteer for such missions. In Canada and India, the executive branch of government routinely assigned personnel to traditional peacekeeping missions without raising the issue with their parliaments. The United States regularly provided transport and support services for traditional peacekeeping missions on the basis of executive decisions, and the president felt no need to request congressional authorization.

The other three types of uses of military forces, where the costs and potential risks are greater, have been more complicated. Because it is the extreme use of military forces, it is useful to start with enforcement operations. In at least some of the nine countries what has happened concerning enforcement has conditioned attitudes toward more modest uses of military forces.

We can start with the situation in the United States. President Truman felt that he had the authority to commit U.S. military forces in Korea.. USA, Senate, "Memorandum of July 3, 1950, prepared by the U.S. Department of State on the Authority of the President to Repel the Attack in Korea." in Military Situation in the Far East: Hearings Before the Senate Committee on Armed Services and the Committee on Foreign Relations, 82nd Congress, 1st session, Pt. 5 (Washington, D.C.: Government Printing Office, 1950) pp. 3373-81. Whether this case constituted a precedent for future authorizations to deploy U.S. military forces has been debated at length.

While Truman did consult with congressional leadership before ordering U.S. forces into combat, he acted without formal congressional authorization. Since the Korean War the authority of the executive to act without formal congressional authorization has become problematic. Congress insisted that it had to provide authorization for the use of U.S. military forces in the Gulf War. The British Parliament, the French *Assemblée N*ationale, and the Canadian Parliament all authorized their country's executive to deploy their national military forces to secure compliance with the Security Council resolution.

The involvement of the legislature in these four countries differed. In the United States, a republican president faced a congress controlled by democrats. The outcome of the vote was in question until the last minute. In the other three countries, the outcome of the vote was never in question. In all four of the countries, however, the involvement of the legislature was seen as a useful instrument in mobilizing popular support for the operation. Comparison of these two episodes suggests a trend toward increasing legislative involvement, but two cases do not provide a strong basis for generalizations.

In the case of the United States, however, the precedent established in the Kuwait case makes it likely that congressional authorization would be essential for the United States to participate in any enforcement action. This probably also applies to deploying U.S. military forces in peacekeeping plus state-building operations and using force to ensure compliance with international mandates. As the number of instances in which military forces were used under international institutions increased in the 1990s, both the executive and legislative branches took steps seeking to define the cases in which the United States would participate in such military actions. The executive branch's views were embodied in Presidential Decision Directive 25 (PDD-25), which was signed in May 1994.

According to PDD-25 the U.S. could vote for a UN resolution establishing a military operation only if there were a threat to international peace and security. PDD-25 further specified that the U.S. could vote for deploying military forces under Chapter VII of the UN Charter only if the threat to peace and security were significant. In addition, it specified that the U.S. could vote for deploying military forces under Chapter VI of the UN Charter only if a cease-fire were in place. PDD-25 also specified that for the U.S. to vote for a deployment of military forces there should be an identifiable end-point to the UN operation. PDD-25 directed that the United States should participate in a UN operation only if it advanced U.S. interests and if U.S. participation were essential for the success of the operation.

Congress has demanded that it be informed before the United States votes for the use of military forces under the auspices of the United Nations. The acts authorizing expenditures for the Departments of State and Defense for Fiscal Year 1998, which were adopted in 1997, require that the executive branch notify Congress fifteen days before the U.S. votes for a resolution authorizing the deployment of military forces under UN auspices.

In Operation Allied Force, the 1999 Kosovo air war, Congress refused to give the president broader authority "to use all necessary force and other means, in concert with United States allies, to accomplish United States and North Atlantic Treaty Organization objectives in the Federal Republic of Yugoslavia (Serbia and Montenegro)." The president acted on his own authority. Congress did, however, authorize the participation of U.S. forces in IFOR, SFOR, KFOR.

The U.S. position may be summarized as follows. First, the debate about Kosovo has not affected the authority of the president to deploy a limited number of military forces under his authority as commander in chief and under the authority vested in him under the UN Participation Act. There is an effective limit of about 1,000 forces under this authority. Second, there seems to be broad agreement among constitutional lawyers that deployment of substantial U.S. military forces would require specific congressional authorization, and the practice in the Kuwait crisis and with respect to IFOR, SFOR, and KFOR was in accord with this view. PDD-25 and the State and Defense Department Appropriations acts deal with traditional peacekeeping and peacekeeping plus state-building. There is a clear demand for legislative participation in decisions about such operations. Finally, the War Powers Act applies to the deployment of U.S. military forces in multilateral military operations although when and what is to be applied may remain unclear.

Although the debate in the United States has gone further than that in other countries, it has gone on in other countries as well. Five of the other eight countries in this study have parliamentary systems. Because of this, the debates and the legislative history in these countries have been less complex. Moreover, the parliamentary systems ensure that there will not be the partisan division between the executive and legislative bodies that frequently prevails in the United States.

In all of the countries in our study, there have been parliamentary discussions about the use of military forces under the auspices of international institutions. Often these discussion have ended with a resolution taking note of what the government was doing or planned to do. Such resolutions carry the implicit threat that in some future instance parliament could take a negative decision.

Even in Canada with its long history of participation in international peacekeeping, there was an attempt in 1995 to adopt legislation that would ensure that parliament would be involved before the Canadian military forces were committed to UN operations, but a proposed bill requiring this was defeated. In general, legislatures have become more concerned with UN military operations as the number of these operations has increased and as national military establishments have been reduced after the end of the Cold War and in response to budgetary pressures. There has been an increase in the demand for military forces to serve under international auspices and a decrease in the forces available for such service. This contradiction has heightened legislative concern.

In the decisions that Japan and Germany adopted in 1990s allowing them to participate in UN military operations, legislative approval is required in both cases for the deployment of troops. The German case is interesting because the constitutional court concluded that deployments outside the NATO area are permissible as long as they receive specific "constitutive approval" from the Bundestag for each deployment. This carefully crafted formula enabled all political parties in Germany to accept the overall concept of deployment of Germany forces outside of Germany by assuring them that they would always have a voice in the decision to deploy before any commitment to do so is made.

The practice that has been established in many countries in the Kuwait case and with respect to IFOR, SFOR, and KFOR and the legislation that has been adopted in many countries has in effect negated the automatic commitment to use military forces for collective action envisaged in the doctrine of collective security. In the legislative debates that occurred in the United States, the United Kingdom, France, Canada, and Norway the question of whether or not the UN had authorized the military operation was an important issue. In all cases, there were individuals and groups within the legislative bodies for whom UN authorization was an essential condition for giving legislative consent for the authorization to use the national military forces.

A second issue that has arisen concerns the conditions under which states will commit their military forces to an international operation. The Japanese peacekeeping law establishes the most stringent conditions. According to the law Japanese Self Defense Forces may only be deployed if a cease-fire has been established and if the host country gives its consent. In addition, the rules of engagement that Japanese Self Defense Forces must follow permit them to use deadly force only in response to direct attacks upon themselves. They may not use deadly force to defend the forces of another country. In effect, the Japanese peacekeeping law precludes the deployment of the Japanese Self Defense Forces in enforcement operations and operations that involve using force to ensure compliance with international mandates. India also insists on having host country consent. In addition, it will not allow its forces to be deployed in a conflict that involves a significant Muslim population. As mentioned above, through Presidential Decision Directive 25 and legislation the United States has also specified a variety of conditions for the involvement of U.S. forces.

The record indicates that under existing conditions democratic states are going to make independent decisions about the uses of their military forces under the auspices of international institutions. None of the nine countries whose practices we have reviewed has made an automatic commitment to engage its military forces except those six countries whose forces would be engaged were there an attack that called into play NATO's Article 5 commitment.

States have handled decisions about the uses of their military forces in operations conducted under the auspices of international institutions in ways that have been shaped by their national constitutions and traditions. Because of the separation of powers, the legislature has been more involved in the United States than in the other eight states, but legislatures have been involved in the others as well. Legislative approval when the governing party controls a parliamentary majority may be pro forma, but it is seen as an important instrument for gaining popular legitimacy. Traditionally executives have had considerable freedom to use military forces, particularly in parliamentary systems.

Do these national decisions to use military forces under the auspices of the UN and NATO meet standards of democratic accountability? Several things are clear. Five of the nine countries, France, India, the Russian Federation, the United Kingdom, and the United States, have used their military forces unilaterally in the period since the end of World War II. In terms of democratic accountability, their decisions to deploy their military forces unilaterally or collectively have been taken by roughly the same procedures.

Another point is that when large-scale and potentially dangerous military operations have been mounted; there have been many opportunities for enlightened public understanding. It was more than half a year between the time that Iraq invaded Kuwait and Operation Desert Storm began. An almost equal time elapsed between the time that the initial warnings were given to Serbia about its operations in Kosovo and Operation Allied Force began. The media provided vast amounts of information about the issues. There were public and legislative debates.

Karen Mingst points out the influences of political culture as well as political and societal relationships within democracies that work in tandem with the formal and legal constitutional set-ups to ensure accountability in decision making. She notes that democratic accountability is more complicated than constitutional structures and includes "indirect accountability through the political culture..." The question is whether these forms of political activity provide sufficient accountability for decisions to act taken at an international level. Or does the decision-making process at the international level have to accord with democratic principles independent of domestic political processes? If so, how would these international processes work? How do national debates affect the shaping of future international policy and law?

The implication of the fact that when serious risks are involved national governments will insist on deciding whether or not to deploy their military forces in an operation conducted under the auspices of an international institution is that such operations will never be automatic as the doctrine of collective security demanded, they will always be conducted by coalitions of the willing. In many cases, such coalitions are likely to be organized on a regional rather than a universal basis; that is, regional leadership will be necessary. Another implication is that probably only the United States can provide leadership for the most dangerous operations, enforcement actions. Only the United States has the military capacity to conduct such operations with a strong probability of success. At the same time, the U.S. has one of the most complicated structures for committing its armed forces.

CIVILIAN CONTROL, CIVILIAN RESPONSIBILITY, MILITARY RESPONSIBILITY

Although there has been less public discussion about issues of civilian control, civilian responsibility to the military and military responsibility to act in accord with basic norms, these are both areas deeply embedded in democratic practice with regard to military forces. The handling of issues that have arisen in these areas have provided preliminary guidance not only on national responsibility, but also on the need for new international standards and practices related to the conduct of military operations either for humanitarian purposes or other than war.

Civilian Control

In the UN's monitoring and observation, traditional peacekeeping, peacekeeping plus state-building operations lines of command have been established that ultimately involve military commanders reporting to the UN Secretary-General and Security Council. This has also been the case with respect to some of the UN's uses of force to ensure compliance with international mandates and the Korean enforcement action. IFOR, SFOR, and KFOR were different. In these cases the Security Council simply asked member states and indirectly NATO to supply military forces. The established NATO chain of command operated in these cases as it did in Operation Allied Force. Under the NATO chain of command, NATO commanders report to NATO's Secretary-General who in turn reports to the North Atlantic Council. The Gulf War was an exception in that neither the UN chain of command nor the NATO chain of command operated. The military forces involved operated under a broad authorization given by the Security Council as a coalition led by the United States, but reported to their own civilian authorities.

The situation, however, is even more complicated than this description. Although the nine states involved in this study have been willing to place their military forces under the operational control of an international institution, they have never given up command of their forces. This means among other things that in addition to reporting under an established international chain of command, commanders of national contingents in military forces operating under international institutions have maintained regular contact with their national authorities. It is highly unlikely that these commanders have ever followed an order given in the international chain of command to which their national authorities have not at least acquiesced if not given their approval. There are indications that military forces operating under international institutions have not conducted certain operations or modified planned operations because national contingents operating on the instructions of their national authorities would not participate.

Under Japan's peacekeeping law, Japanese Self Defense Forces are forbidden to follow an order of an international commander that would have them use deadly force other than for their own self defense.

Both international institutions and national institutions have taken steps to maintain civilian control. During the Korean war, it was President Truman who dismissed General MacArthur, not the UN Secretary-General or Security Council. The NATO operation against Serbia's actions in Kosovo, Operation Allied Force, demonstrated the North Atlantic Council's determination to maintain civilian control. Targets in the air war were chosen by consensus among the civilian authorities of the allies. A plan to interdict oil bound for Yugoslavia that the Supreme Allied Commander of NATO had advocated was put on hold because of allied concerns as to its legality. The dual reporting of national commanders has the potentiality for conflicts in the chain of command. Such a case occurred during Operation Allied Force in the dispute between NATO Supreme Allied Commander General Wesley Clark and the British commander in the field in Kosovo, General Michael Jackson, over the taking of Pristina airport before the Russians could in June 1999. General Jackson refused to obey General Clark's order to secure the airport. He consulted the British government, which supported his refusal to obey the order, and the U.S. government refused to support General Clark.

Civilian control has been maintained in military operations conducted under the auspices of international institutions, but the dual system that has prevailed could inhibit military effectiveness.

Civilian Responsibility

No mechanisms other than national ones exist for ensuring that the civilians who decide to deploy military personnel make their decisions so that these personnel are not subjected to unnecessary risks. No mechanisms exist for holding those who shape states' policies in the UN Security Council or the NATO Council accountable other than the normal bureaucratic and electoral processes that exist within national institutions. When UN forces were given the mandate to protect safe areas in the former Yugoslavia, but the UN Security Council and the Department of Peacekeeping Operations did not provide sufficient personnel and equipment to effectively carry out the mission, there were cries that someone should be accountable. Establishing responsibility in the way that it is established in democracies, however, proved impossible.

The UN Security Council as a responsible civilian authority is deficient in two respects. First, the Security Council does not always have reliable information about the military implications and consequences of their decisions. To the extent that it has information, it is provided by member states and may not be adequate or timely for informed decision making. Further, it can easily ignore military advice. A second problem is that Security Council proceedings are not fully transparent, and that those who will be implementing the decisions may not be part of the decision-making process and may not be able to address effectively the feasibility of a mandate. When military forces operating under the auspices of the UN are put in situations of high risk because they do not have adequate military equipment, a clear mandate, or some other problem, resolving operational issues and affixing responsibility becomes difficult if not impossible. National and international officials can easily engage in blame shifting. What role does the media and non-governmental organizations play in ensuring some measure of accountability? Can an international organization like the United Nations develop adequate information resources to assist decision making and to ensure that appropriate force is available to support UN operations?

MILITARY RESPONSIBILITY

In his chapter Robert Siekmann identified three bodies of law as bases for responsibility and accountability for military personnel:

- the local law of the area of operations, i.e., the national law of the receiving or host state;
- the law of the intergovernmental organization under the auspices of which the personnel operate. UN law is of particular relevance. There are two bodies of UN law—general and specific.

The best examples of general legislation are the UN Convention on the Safety of United Nations and Associated Personnel (1994) that makes attacks on UN personnel criminal offences which all states have a duty to punish, which was adopted in response to the killing of the Belgian soldiers in Rwanda, and the UN Model status-of-forces agreement for peacekeeping operations.

Specific law includes, rules and guidelines that are adopted for each operation concerning the mandate and the terms of reference and the rules of engagement.

- the law of the sending or participating state (troop-contributing nation) is relevant as the domestic, municipal law of the personnel.

National institutions have been important in ensuring that military personnel conduct themselves in accordance with established norms. Since states do not give up command of their forces, they are ultimately responsible for their conduct. There were major national inquiries into the conduct of the Dutch military forces in Srebrenica and the Canadian military forces in Somalia. Canadian military personnel were prosecuted under Canadian military law. Little exists, however, beyond these national controls.

Prior to 1999 to the extent that efforts were made to develop rules of conduct for military personnel operating under the United Nations, these were been based on the assumption that the missions were engaged in monitoring and observation or traditional peacekeeping. These assumed that the only legitimate use of force would be for self-defense. Thus they have not been applicable when force has been used to ensure compliance with international mandates. The situation with respect to the applicability of established international norms or warfare in enforcement actions is unclear. The NATO countries insisted that Operation Allied Force was not a war. Steps to change the situation with respect to forces under UN command were taken in 1999 when the Secretary-General of the United Nations declared that henceforth, military forces operating under UN commands would be bound by the Geneva Convention.

International tribunals, where they exist, could provide a measure of international accountability for decisions made and actions taken by individuals in military operations. The International Tribunals for the former Yugoslavia and Rwanda have jurisdiction over all military forces operating in the respective areas and the International Criminal Court's jurisdiction would include military forces operating under the auspices of international institutions. As of 2000, no international tribunal had indicted military personnel operating under a UN or NATO mandate.. Final Report to the Prosecutor by the Committee Established to Review the NATO Bombing Campaign Against the Federal Republic of Yugoslavia (July 2000).

The responsibility to ensure that military forces operating under the auspices of international institutions conduct themselves in accord with national and international legal requirements thus rests primarily with national authorities, though this may change.

9

Constructing a New Order for the Use of Military Forces

The challenge to constructing a new order for the use of military forces as the twentieth century closed stemmed from the multiple shifts that are taking place in established practices and assumptions in international relations.

- The locus of decision making shifted from the domestic to the international in matters regarding the use of military forces even though the principal institutions for ensuring democratic accountability were domestic – the legislature and public opinion.
- The focus for the use of force was being expanded to include humanitarian concerns in addition to maintaining territorial integrity.
- The role of the military changed as the Cold War ended and as countries sought to reduce their military expenditures. These factors led to a redefining of the role of the military in a world without a global enemy.
- The status of the individual has changed. Individuals can invoke the protection of the international community through international institutions for their rights. But the right also carried individual accountability to the international community for actions taken through institutions like international tribunals.

These shifts have taken place within a framework that is guided by principles of territorial integrity as the focus for the collective use of force and by democratic institutions that are still national rather than international in scope. It is the balancing of these changes through debate and political contest that now provides democracy a particularly important role in constructing the contemporary world order.

The international community has become considerably more sophisticated about using military forces under international institutions than it was when Woodrow Wilson and others first sought to give effect to the doctrine of collective security in the early years of the twentieth century. Practice has demonstrated that there is a range of ways in which military forces can be used under international institutions ranging from monitoring and observation through enforcement. The doctrine of collective self-defense was developed as a supplement to collective security. And in the closing years of the twentieth century, states began to struggle with the question of using military forces to ensure the safety of populations within states and the protection of their human rights. In some cases states have decided that military forces can be deployed to pacify intra-state as well as inter-state conflicts, thus overcoming the barrier of sovereignty.

In a more general sense, states have taken steps to expand the simple notions of democratic accountability that were involved in the stylized theory of collective security. Accountability was assumed to flow from acceptance of an international agreement that set out the conditions and circumstances for action and specified the possible actions. Acceptance of these obligations further assumed that all necessary domestic political considerations are adequately addressed. Questions within countries, however, will arise if a decision is made at the international level to take action outside the established and agreed upon framework.

Democracy provides the machinery that transforms public preference into policy. Further steps have to be taken before policy can take the form of law, but the testing and the debate all form part of the process of change. The more sophisticated and complicated forms of using military forces under international auspices that have developed now require the parallel development of domestic acceptance through democratic processes. This process in turn contributes to shaping both the practice and the scope for international action.

This process is not new. Such domestic debates have occurred throughout the development of a common international framework for using force. In the United States and the western European states, the failure of the League to be a successful guardian of the peace urged political leaders to seek actively through political consensus acceptance of the collective security obligations of the United Nations Charter and later of the North Atlantic Treaty. The subsequent debates that have occurred as international operations become more complex, more risky and more costly have taken place since the United Nations was called on to undertake these more interventionist operations that do not have the consent of the receiving state.

Debate therefore can be generated when there is a substantive change in how a country's military forces are being used and where the immediate national interest of such uses may not be very apparent. When action of a settled and established character takes place, little debate occurs. The debates sparked by the intervention in Kosovo that took place in the name of humanitarian concerns at the end of the twentieth century demonstrates the latest need for further development of the use of military forces under international auspices.

Many of the most important steps to amplify the structures and procedures for using military forces under international institutions were taken in the 1990s, the first decade after the end of the Cold War. Unlike the waves of innovation in international institutions that followed World Wars I and II these institutional steps were frequently taken quickly and in response to acute crises. In the waves of institution building that followed World Wars I and II national leaders drew on an immense store of specially prepared intellectual and political debate and capital as they considered the future of the international system and the shape of the system to come. Operation Allied Force triggered debate, but only after the operation was completed.

The democratic and capitalist states, whose goals had triumphed in the Cold War, did not have a clear vision about the international institutions that should constitute the new order. Even though four decades of economic and social change and technological development would seem to have warranted a reconsideration of the roles and purposes of international institutions including the system to ensure peace and security, this did not happen. It seemed reasonable to leaders and commentators alike to assume that the institutional vision put into place at the end of World War II to safeguard the territorial integrity and political independence of states could simply be reactivated. The Cold War was regarded by many states, including those in this study, as a temporary delay to putting into place fully the post World War II security system.

But this assumption was wrong because the character of issues that required international attention had changed during the fifty years since World War II. The absence of any concerted post-Cold War planning and setting of goals akin to the Inquiry conducted prior to the end of World War I or to the postwar planning undertaken from summer 1941 to prepare for the end of World War II, created a vacuum of direction, public awareness and interest in the institutions and tasks that will be required to deal with the world order problems of the twenty-first century.

The structure and procedures set up to use military forces under international institutions seem inadequate to respond to the problems that will be faced in the twenty-first century. In the cases of Korea and Kuwait, since the military forces acting under the auspices of international institutions turned back forces invading established boundaries, the system worked to respond, although the problems that may have initiated the cross border attacks may not have been solved. But the system was set up to control a particular use of force and to respond when a violation occurred. Many of the problems of the twenty-first century are likely to involve violent conflict within states and beyond the bounds of he existing legal framework. If action or an international decision exceeds commonly agreed on standards, debate may be generated after the action takes place and may affect the possibility of replicating this action in the future.

For democracies, we have assumed that accountability for decisions made and actions taken is ensured through domestic legal and political systems. Our study demonstrates that this has been the case and democracies have evolved to accommodate the uses of force that have emerged from the post World War II security system. However, as we observe the changes in expectations about how and where force will be used, we are beginning to see changes in expectations on how and where principles of democratic decision making and debate are needed.

The character of decision making in many international organizations seems to erode the legitimacy of their decisions particularly where they go beyond accepted practice and law. At the same time, international organizations are seeking to act in the name of human rights and self-determination — two cornerstones of democracy. So, while we have become more sophisticated at understanding the use of force, we need to develop greater sophistication about democracy and its relationship to international decision making and institutions. To answer Dahl's skepticism about making international activities democratically accountable will require innovations to allow for the transformation from preference to policy that democracy can provide. Up to this point, we see that debate can occur although it may take place after the fact. A full debate beforehand might be more desirable, but may be difficult to conduct in the abstract. Therefore, it seems that debates have always taken place after an action is proposed or taken.

The humanitarian concerns that have compelled the deployment of international operations within states with and without clear authorization by the UN Security Council have raised the most difficult questions. That the conflicts of today stem from intra-state rather than inter-state violence is an important difference and tests a key assumption of international law — that states are sovereign within their own territory. However, if the international law prohibiting genocide and providing for human rights protection appears to overcome, or even requires overcoming, the concerns of intervention in the internal affairs of states, new standards and procedures must be developed if international relations are not to revert to the unregulated unilateral great-power interventions of the nineteenth century.

Several habits have taken root in the course of the twentieth century that make a difference and may prevent a return to previous practices. One is the habit of multilateral consultation and seeking multilateral support and participation. Increasingly, even the most powerful states appear to be hesitant to use military forces without some form of international authorization, authorization that at a minimum involves some multilateral consensus. This protracted consensus building may not provide for speedy response, but provides for time to consider a measured response in cases other than the clear ones of an invasion across borders. It provides for appropriate parliamentary consultation and public debate where necessary. It provides a measure of protection against abuse by a single powerful military power.

Until clear systems for determining the legitimate grounds for intervention and procedures for taking decisions about this are set up, the problem will remain one of avoiding "ad hoc opportunism" by strong military powers or inaction. International law is essential because it shapes the question of whether force can and should be used by making clear what present law permits. How the answers involving international law and its application will be tailored will inevitably grow out of experience and the political process including democratic debate nationally and in some form, internationally.

In a presidential address to the 1917 Annual Meeting of the American Society of International Law, Elihu Root stressed the importance of respect for democracy and democratic procedures and values in bringing about orderly change and establishing lasting institutional structures. He first noted the problem:

As we consider how it may be possible to reestablish the law of nations upon a durable basis, we must realize that past experience indicates that no system of law which depends upon the physical partition of the earth dictated by the expediency of the time, no law which must be broken to order that living wrongs shall be redressed, or in order that the new ideas of the future may find room for growth, can be permanent.

Revisions to the law — international and domestic — will be made, but will be adjusted by the outcomes of history and politics. Root anticipated this in his speech:

Democratic government cannot be carried on except by a people who acquire the habit of seeking true information about facts, of discussing questions of right and wrong, of interest, and of possible consequences, who have kindly consideration for opposing opinions, and a tolerant attitude towards those who differ. The longer a democracy preserves itself through the exercise of these qualities, the better adapted it is to apply the same methods in the conduct of its international business, and the result is a continually increasing certainty that international law will be observed in a community of democratic nations.

Root's words are as valid for the twenty-first century as they were for the twentieth. For the immediate future, democratic accountability for using military forces under international institutions will have to be assured primarily by actions at the national level. This is because firmly established democratic procedures exist only at that level, the international community has not yet conceived what democratic institutions and processes at the global level would look like, and of existing international institutions with security functions, only NATO is a collection of democracies, the United Nations includes all states whether or not they are democratic. But as Root prophesied, democracy at the national level is an essential condition for efforts to apply democratic tenets in relations among states.

THE PROSCRIPTION OF THE USE OF FORCE

There are two aspects of international law dealing with the law of force: *jus ad bellum*, or the rules relating the use of force, and *jus in bello*, or the rules regulating the conduct of hostilities. This paper primarily addresses the *jus ad bellum*, or the legality of the attack on Iraq, and the consequences of that, as well as aspects of *jus in bello,* in particular the obligations of belligerent occupants of attacked territories.

Following World War I, sixty-three nations renounced war as an instrument of foreign policy in the Kellogg-Briand Pact of 1928. The United States, Australia, Great Britain, Italy and Japan were among the countries that signed that treaty, which provided that the Parties "solemnly declare in the names of their respective peoples that they condemn recourse to war for the solution of international controversies, and renounce it, as an instrument of national policy in their relations with one another." That Pact failed to prevent World War II, but in condemning recourse to war and renouncing war as an instrument of national policy it formed the basis for 'crimes against peace', which were described in the Charter of the Nuremberg tribunal as those crimes aimed at the planning, preparation, initiation or waging of a war of aggression or a war in violation of international treaties. The Nuremberg Tribunal observed that "[w]ar is essentially an evil thing. Its consequences are not confined to the belligerent states alone, but affect the whole world. To initiate a war of aggression, therefore, is not only an international crime; it is the supreme international crime differing only from other war crimes in that it contains within itself the accumulated evil of the whole."

The crime against peace under international common law was recognised by the Nuremberg Tribunal following World War II, noting that the Pact was evidence of a sufficient crystallization of world opinion to authorise a judicial finding in favour of the existence of a 'crime against peace'. The International Criminal Court does potentially have jurisdiction over crimes of aggression, and the Court can exercise jurisdiction over the crime of aggression once a provision is adopted defining the crime and setting out the conditions under which the Court shall exercise jurisdiction. The legal position as stated by the Nuremberg Tribunal is that those who perpetrate crimes of aggression commit not only a crime under international law but commit the supreme international crime. The inability of the ICC to take jurisdiction at this stage does not negate the nature of the crime but merely the ICC's ability to hold perpetrators accountable.

The United Nations Charter was concluded "to save succeeding generations from the scourge of war, which twice in our lifetime has brought untold sorrow to mankind" and the United Nations was established with the purposes:

1. *To maintain international peace and security, and to that end: to take effective collective measures for the prevention and removal of threats to the peace, and for the suppression of acts of aggression or other breaches of the peace, and to bring about by peaceful means, and in conformity with the principles of justice and*

international law, adjustment or settlement of international disputes or situations which might lead to a breach of the peace;

2. *To develop friendly relations among nations based on respect for the principle of equal rights and self-determination of peoples, and to take other appropriate measures to strengthen universal peace;*

Article 2(3) requires that all members shall settle their international disputes by peaceful means in such a manner that international peace and security, and justice, are not endangered and Article 2(4) requires that all members shall refrain in their international relations from the threat or use of force against the territorial integrity or political independence of any state, or in any other manner inconsistent with the purposes of the United Nations.

The ICJ in the *Nicaragua* case was in no doubt as to the status of the prohibition on the use of force:

"The Court finds that both Parties take the view that the principles as to the use of force incorporated in the United Nations Charter correspond, in essentials, to those found in customary international law.... They therefore accept a treaty-law obligation to refrain in their international relations from the threat or use of force against the territorial integrity or political independence of any State, or in any other manner inconsistent with the purposes of the United Nations...

The general rule prohibiting force established in customary law allows for certain exceptions... [Resolution 2625 (XXV)] demonstrates that the States represented in the General Assembly regard the exception to the prohibition of the use of force constituted by the right of individual or collective self-defence as already a matter of customary international law.

The only stated exceptions in the Charter lie in article 51, which preserves the "inherent right of individual or collective self-defense if an armed attack occurs against a Member of the United Nations, until the Security Council has taken measures necessary to maintain international peace and security," and collective actions under Chapter VII, and in particular article 42.

The often cited legal test for necessity and proportionality in self-defence relates to a dispute between Britain and the United States. In the winter of 1837, British and Canadian forces believed that an American flagged ship, the *Caroline,* was ferrying arms, recruits, and supplies from the American side of the border to anti-British rebels on the Canadian side of the border during an anti-British insurrection. While most of the crew slept, British and Canadian troops boarded the ship, attacked the crew and passengers, set her on fire, and towed her into the river toward Niagara Falls, killing two. In a formulation which has been widely cited as the standard test for necessity in self defence, American Secretary of State Daniel Webster responded to a British claim of self defence by saying that "[i]t will be for that [British] Government to show a necessity of self-defence, instant, overwhelming, leaving no choice of means, and no moment for deliberation. While the Caroline case concerned a case of anticipatory self-defence, it pre-dated the Kellogg-Briand Pact and the United Nations Charter prohibitions on the use of force and does not necessarily stand as a contemporary justification for pre-emptive force or anticipatory self-defence. It is to be noted that even anticipatory self defence as a doubtful justification for the use of force. Christine Gray notes that the actual invocation of the right to anticipatory self-defence is rare and that states prefer to take a wide view of armed attack rather than openly claim anticipatory self-defence: "It is only where no conceivable case can be made for this that they resort to anticipatory self-defence. This reluctance expressly to invoke anticipatory self-defence is in itself a clear indication of the doubtful status of this justification for the use of force." This may be another reason the United States and United Kingdom sought to justify their use of force against Iraq by reference to resolutions 678 (1990) and 687 (1991) rather than attempt to justify them on a basis of anticipatory self-defence of the Bush doctrine of preventive war.

THE BUSH DOCTRINE OF 'PREVENTIVE WAR'

President Bush declared in an introduction to the "National Security Strategy of the United States," published in September 2002, that the United States will act against "emerging threats before they are fully formed." The document states that: For centuries, international law recognized that nations need not suffer an attack before they can lawfully take action to defend themselves against forces that present an imminent danger of attack. Legal scholars and international jurists often conditioned the legitimacy of pre-emption on the existence of an imminent threat—most often a visible mobilization of armies, navies, and air forces preparing to attack.

We must adapt the concept of imminent threat to the capabilities and objectives of today's adversaries. Rogue states and terrorists do not seek to attack us using conventional means. They know such attacks would fail. Instead, they rely on acts of terror and, potentially, the use of weapons of mass destruction—weapons that can be easily concealed, delivered covertly, and used without warning.

Thus the statement implied that the United States in this new posture is willing to act beyond the constraints of international law and even beyond limits it has observed in the past. The distinction between 'preventive war' and pre-emption in the new Bush doctrine was described in a Brookings Institute report as follows: "The concept is not limited to the traditional definition of pre-emption—striking an enemy as it prepares an attack—but also includes prevention—striking an enemy even in the absence of specific evidence of a coming attack. The idea principally appears to be directed at terrorist groups as well as extremist or "rogue" nation states; the two are linked, according to the strategy, by a combination of "radicalism and technology."

The Australian government, however, accepted that this doctrine would require an amendment of the Charter. Australian Prime Minister John Howard said that "[w]hen the United Nations Charter was written, the idea of attack was defined by the history that had gone before and that is the idea of an army rolling across the border of a neighbouring country, or in the case of the Japanese in Pearl Harbour, bombing a base. Now that's different now, you don't get that now. What you're getting is this non-state terrorism which is just as devastating and potentially even more so and all I'm saying, I think many people are saying, is that maybe the body of international law has to catch up with that new reality." Australian Defence Minister Robert Hill similarly called for amendment of Article 51 of the Charter.

It may be that the United States and United Kingdom governments were frustrated by an inability to obtain the necessary Security Council resolutions. The call by the Australian government for a change in international law to address terrorism may also be seen to be a product of frustration. However if change is to be effected, it must be carried out in way that promotes international peace and security through multilateral action and the rule of law. This may be time consuming and frustrating, but the alternative danger is a weakening or even abandonment of the rule of law and undermining the prohibition on the use of force which has been the product of not only the international consensus to avoid war following two world wars but decades of consensus. The danger of setting a precedent for the use of force by other states is self evident. As one scholar recently observed in a different context, "[i]f the principle of reciprocity ensures that any state claiming a right under general customary international law accords that same right to every other state, states will only claim rights which they are prepared to see generalized. This is because a generalized right subjects the state to corresponding obligations *vis-à-vis* all other states."

In this context, Mr Howard's citation of the attack on Pearl Harbour was of interest since a claimed motivation for Japan's attack on Pearl Harbour was to prevent a feared military buildup by the United States. In the following decade, in 1950, following a debate on a pre-emptive strike on the Soviet Union, the United States President Truman said that, "you don't 'prevent' anything by war...except peace." Already following the attack on Iraq, Indian officials have suggested there is a strong case for military action against Pakistan and United States officials and leaders have used threatening rhetoric against Syria and Iran. If a 'preventive war' by the United States against North Korea is perceived to be avoided due to the possession by North Korea of nuclear weapons, then that would be a powerful incentive for non-nuclear states to seek to acquire nuclear weapons to protect themselves against attack and would thus be a stimulus for nuclear proliferation rather than the rule of law.

The Bush doctrine is on the face of it far removed from 'pre-emptive' war, which is narrowly defined on the basis of self defence against an actual imminent attack. That the United States did not base its claimed justification for its attack on Iraq on a claim of 'preventive war' but rather on a spurious reliance on the Security Council resolutions which were passed following the invasion of Kuwait, demonstrates that even the United States does not have confidence on its own doctrine. And this is not surprising. The doctrine departs from the development of international law prohibiting the use of force from the Kellogg-Briand pact, the establishment of the Nuremberg Charter, the conclusion of the United Nations Charter and the establishment of the International Criminal Court and marks a return to a readiness to use force in international relations.

State Responsibility and The Use of Military Force Against Iraq

A number of international lawyers have written opinions stating that it would be a violation of international law if the United States, United Kingdom and other States were to use military force against Iraq without specific, new Security Council authorization. These arguments will not be repeated here and reference should be made to those opinions. Notable are the opinions by Rabinder Singh and Charlotte Kilroy of Matrix Chambers.

The International Commission of Jurists denounced the attack as an illegal invasion of Iraq which amounts to a war of aggression. Sixteen senior teachers of international law from the United Kingdom and France wrote a statement stating that "[o]n the basis of the information publicly available, there is no justification under international law for the use of military force against Iraq.... Before military action can lawfully be undertaken against Iraq, the security council must have indicated its clearly expressed assent. It has not yet done so. A decision to undertake military action in Iraq without proper security council authorisation will seriously undermine the international rule of law." 31 Canadian law professors said that US attack "would be a fundamental breach of international law and would seriously threaten the integrity of the international legal order that has been in place since the end of the Second World War," and 43 Australian legal experts said that the initiation of a war against Iraq by the self-styled 'coalition of the willing' would be a fundamental violation of international law and said that the United States doctrine or pre-emptive self defence contradicts the cardinal principle of the modern international legal order and the primary rationale for the founding of the UN after World War II-the prohibition of the unilateral use of force to settle disputes. On March 11, United Nations Secretary-General Kofi Annan said that "[i]f the U.S. and others were to go outside the Council and take military action it would not be in conformity with the Charter."

Briefly stated, it is clear from Article 2(4), Article 42 and Article 51 of the UN Charter that Member States are to refrain from the threat or use of force against the territorial integrity or political independence of any State. Force may only be used if specifically approved by the Security Council or proportionate force may be used in self defence when a threat is imminent. In the latter case, in the words of the Nuremberg Tribunal, "preventive action in foreign territory is justified only in case of 'an instant and overwhelming necessity for self-defense, leaving no choice of means, and no moment of deliberation'."

On Thursday 14 March, White House Press Spokesman Ari Fleischer read a formal statement setting out the administration's formal legal position:

MR. FLEISCHER: The United Nations Security Council Resolution 678 authorized use of all necessary means to uphold United Nations Security Council Resolution 660, and subsequent resolutions and to restore international peace and security in the area. That was the basis for the use of force against Iraq during the Gulf War. Thereafter, United Nations Security Council Resolution 687 declared a cease-fire, but imposed several conditions, including extensive WMD related conditions. Those conditions provided the conditions essential to the restoration of peace and security in the area. A material breach of those conditions removes the basis for the cease-fire and provides a legal grounds [sic] for the use of force. The United States administration thus relies on resolution 687 (1991), and before that resolution 678 (1990), to provide legal grounds for the use of force.

The second operative paragraph of the earlier resolution 678 (1990) states that the Security Council: Authorizes Member States co-operating with the Government of Kuwait, unless Iraq on or before 15 January 1991 fully implements, as set forth in paragraph 1 above, the foregoing resolutions, to use all necessary means to uphold and implement resolution 660 (1990) and all subsequent relevant resolutions and to restore international peace and security in the area.

The Final Operative Paragraph of Resolution

Decides to remain seized of the matter and to take such further steps as may be required for the implementation of the present resolution and to secure peace and security in the area.

Even if Iraq had committed a material breach of the cease-fire resolution 687, it does not follow that a Member State such as the United States or United Kingdom was authorised to use force. The authorisation to use all necessary means was made in resolution 678 (1990), not 687 (1991). As has been noted by Professor Vaughan Lowe, when resolution 687 was passed on 3 April 1991, the force that the Security Council had earlier authorised in resolution 678 in 1990 to restore the borders of Kuwait had effectively expired as the matter was back into the hands of the Council.

It is clear from resolution 687 (1991) that it is the Security Council, and not individual Member States, that were to take further steps as may be required. This is entirely consistent with the prohibition on the use of force under Article 2(4) of the UN Charter, and the provision that enforcement action is to be taken 'by the Security Council' under Article 42 of the Charter.

Of course, some eleven years later, resolution 1441(2002) was passed by the Security Council to address the issue of weapons of mass destruction, which was the principal justification for the invasion. The passage of that resolution and the fact that the United States sought and failed to gain

Security Council authorization for the use of force in Iraq following resolution 1441 (2002) in fact imply that the United States implicitly accepted that further authorization of the Security Council was required for the use of force.

Resolution 1441 (2002) specifically decided (in operative paragraph 1) that Iraq was in material breach of its obligations under resolution 687 (1991), granted Iraq a final opportunity to comply and set up the enhanced inspection regime (in operative paragraph 2). It did not authorise the use of force by individual Member States. That is why the United States and United Kingdom sought a further resolution.

It is significant that the United States administration in its formal position statement did not refer to resolution 1441 (2002). In that resolution, the Security Council decided to remain seized of the matter and to take such further steps as may be required for the implementation of resolution 1441 (2002) and to secure peace and security in the area. The United States cannot ignore that resolution and return to the earlier resolutions 687, 678 and 660 to justify its own use of force against Iraq.

Nowhere in the existing Security Council resolutions on Iraq is there an authorization of the use of force by Member States relating to weapons of mass destruction, or, for that matter, relating to regime change. The argument used by the United States administration does not stand and the attack on Iraq constituted an unlawful use of force under international law.

Members of the 'coalition of the willing' which aided or assisted in the invasion of Iraq could also be held responsible under international law. Article 16 of the International Law Commission's Articles on State Responsibility recognise that a state which aids or assist another State in the commission of an internationally wrongful act is internationally responsible for doing so if it does so with knowledge of the circumstances of the internationally wrongful act and the act would be internationally wrongful if committed by that State. The obligation not to use force may be breached by permitting another state to use its territory to carry out an armed attack against a third State such as Iraq.

Additionally, States aiding or assisting the United States and United Kingdom after the invasion may still be held responsible for their illegal acts in that the assisting State may be found to have adopted the acts of the invading States.

Obligations Accompanying the Occupation of Iraq

States may send personnel to Iraq following the invasion and occupation following Security Council resolution 1483 (2003). Currently the United States and United Kingdom are the occupying powers and accordingly have obligations under international law. Penal laws must remain in force, with the exception that they may be repealed or suspended by the Occupying Power in cases where they constitute a threat to its security or an obstacle to the application of the Fourth Geneva Convention. Similarly, subject to the latter consideration and to the necessity for ensuring the effective administration of justice, the tribunals of the occupied territory shall continue to function in respect of all offences covered by the said laws.

The resolution expressly recognizes the status of the two occupying powers in its preamble where it in states that

Noting the letter of 8 May 2003 from the Permanent Representatives of the United States of America and the United Kingdom of Great Britain and Northern Ireland to the President of the Security Council (S/2003/538) and recognizing the specific authorities, responsibilities, and obligations under applicable international law of these states as occupying powers under unified command (the "Authority"),

Noting further that other States that are not occupying powers are working now or in the future may work under the Authority,

Welcoming further the willingness of Member States to contribute to stability and security in Iraq by contributing personnel, equipment, and other resources under the Authority.

In operative paragraph 5 the Security Council

It must be understood that the 'Authority' is not the United Nations but is the United States and United Kingdom as occupying powers. Thus the resolution provides that states which go to Iraq expressly work under the United States and

United Kingdom, not under the United Nations. Funds in the Development Fund for Iraq are disbursed at the direction of the Authority (paragraph 13), in consultation with the Iraqi interim administration. The Development Fund shall enjoy privileges and immunities equivalent to those enjoyed by the United Nations (paragraph 22) and petroleum, petroleum products and natural gas enjoy immunities, but this gives no protection to Member States or their officials from liability under the Geneva Conventions, Hague Regulations or other provisions of international or national law including the Rome Statute of the International Criminal Court and the NPT.

Looting, Maintenance of Order and Cultural Property

In failing to prevent the looting that has occurred of the Baghdad museum, the occupying powers breached the Hague Convention for the Protection of Cultural Property in the Event of Armed Conflict, which requires that the Parties undertake to prohibit, prevent and, if necessary, put a stop to any form of theft, pillage or misappropriation of, and any acts of vandalism directed against, cultural property." The Hague Regulations provide that the occupying power shall take all the measures in its power to restore, and ensure, as far as possible, public order and safety, while respecting, unless absolutely prevented, the laws in force in the country. In contrast, the United States forces did protect the oil ministry and oil fields.

Ensuring Food and Medical Supplies

Article 55 of the Fourth Geneva Convention provides that "[t]o the fullest extent of the means available to it the Occupying Power has the duty of ensuring the food and medical supplies of the population; it should, in particular, bring in the necessary foodstuffs, medical stores and other articles if the resources of the occupied territory are inadequate." Article 56 requires that "to the fullest extent of the means available to it, the Occupying Power has the duty of ensuring and maintaining, with the cooperation of national and local authorities, the medical and hospital establishments and services, public health and hygiene in the occupied territory, with particular reference to the adoption and application of the prophylactic and preventive measures necessary to combat the spread of contagious diseases and epidemics. Medical personnel of all categories shall be allowed to carry out their duties."

Protocol I, many of the provisions of which represent customary international law, supplements the duties specified in Article 55 of the Fourth Convention concerning food and medical supplies. The Occupying Powers are required, to the fullest extent of the means available to them and without any adverse distinction, to also ensure the provision of clothing, bedding, means of shelter, other supplies essential to the survival of the civilian population of the occupied territory and objects necessary for religious worship.

There are indications that the applicable obligations are not being met.

- The President of the International Committee of the Red Cross (ICRC), Jakob Kellenberger, said recently that the United States as occupying power has very clear rights and duties under international law, and called on the United States to fulfil its duty to ensure security.
- It has been reported that in urban centers throughout southern and central Iraq, millions of civilians are facing disease, including cholera, and possible death due to inadequate access to water as a result of the US-British invasion.
- The President of Medicins Sans Frontieres, Morten Rostrup, said that the coalition has failed to meet its responsibility under international humanitarian law to ensure that the health and well being of the Iraqi people is being provided for."
- Amnesty International called on the US/UK coalition forces to urgently address the situation of refugees, asylum-seekers and third country nationals in Iraq, saying that "As the occupying powers the US and UK are responsible under international humanitarian law to protect all civilians from human rights abuses, and particular attention must be paid to the situation of vulnerable groups such as refugees and other foreign nationals."

- A number of NGOs made a joint statement on 2 May calling on the United Nations to have a central role, saying the situation is critical, saying that "Already under severe strain and under-resourced before the war began, hospitals, water plants and sewage systems have been crippled by the conflict and looting. Hospitals are overwhelmed, diarrhoea is endemic and the death toll is mounting. Medical and water staff are working for free, but cannot continue for long. Rubbish including medical waste is piling up. Clean water is scarce and diseases like typhoid are being reported in southern Iraq."

RESPONSIBILITY FOR DAMAGES AND OIL REVENUES

The occupying powers are bound by the Hague Regulations with respect to dealing with Iraq's oil resources. Article 55 of the Hague Regulations requires that the occupying State shall be regarded only as administrator and usufructuary of public buildings, real estate, forests, and agricultural estates belonging to the hostile State, and situated in the occupied country. It must safeguard the capital of these properties, and administer them in accordance with the rules of usufruct. In other words, it must safeguard the capital of the oil wells, and may only use the revenue for the purposes of the occupation. Private contracts must be respected by the occupying forces and occupation may give rise to a claim for all damages to those rights.

Of course these provisions must be read in light of the United Nations sanctions and oil-for-food programme as well as the overriding claims for an illegal war and occupation and thus cannot be read in isolation. Following the Iraqi invasion of Kuwait, the Security Council passed resolution 660 (1990) on August 2, 1990 calling for the withdrawal of Iraqi troops. This was followed on August 6 by Resolution 661 (1990), which authorised economic sanctions against Iraq (and occupied Kuwait), declaring a trade blockade, and blocking Iraq and Kuwaiti assets, in the latter case to protect the assets. Resolution 687 (1991), provided that the sanctions will be lifted "upon Council agreement." Under the Oil for Food programme, which expires on 3 June 2003, some oil may be exported under strict conditions to fund compensation claims, weapons inspection and humanitarian needs in Iraq. These resolutions would thus override any rights the belligerent occupants would have to sell oil.

If held responsible for illegally invading Iraq, the United States, United Kingdom, Australia and other belligerent parties would be liable as Iraq was for its unlawful invasion and occupation of Kuwait.

Responsibility and Liability of Coalition and Officials

Since the United States has not declared the war over, reportedly because the United States did not wish to trigger the release of Iraqi prisoners of war and prevent U.S. forces from trying to kill Saddam Hussein if he is still alive, states sending personnel to Iraq under current circumstances do so as occupying powers and have obligations under international law, including the Geneva Conventions and Hague Regulations. They may also share responsibility for acts committed by the coalition forces.

Although the United States is not a Party to the Statute of Rome, and in fact 'unsigned' it, many members of the 'coalition of the willing' are. If acts are carried out by a coalition involving the United States which may constitute war crimes, even if other forces are not primarily involved, coalition officials could be liable under the provisions of Article 25 of the Rome Statute of the ICC, which provides for liability for a person who solicits or induces the commission of a crime, including if the crime is attempted, and for persons who aid, abet, or assist. Liability is also attached for any person who in any other way contributes to the commission or attempted commission of such a crime by a group of persons acting with a common purpose.

A number of incidents have been reported to have been initiated by the coalition forces involving civilian casualties, including the bombing of a Syrian bus, use of cluster bombs, destruction of electricity supplies leading to disruption of civilian water supplies, attacks on Iraqi television stations, on Al-Jazeera and on the Palestine hotel, on markets at Al-Shaab and Shula, on civilians at Nasiriya and Hilla, on a van at Najaf, shooting at ambulances, and shooting of protesters. In addition, there have been reports of a failure to restore water, electricity and other humanitarian needs and encouragement, toleration and failure to avoid looting, including of nuclear installations. State responsibility and individual criminal liability for these and other actions has yet to be determined. Any responsibility or liability assistance after the fact of other States or individuals or the adoption of these acts by other States, or the actions of States as belligerent occupants in Iraq, could be determined by the International Criminal Court, the International Court of Justice or an *ad hoc* or arbitral tribunal.

INTERNATIONAL LAW AFTER THE INVASION OF IRAQ

The framework of international law is currently under threat by the determination of the United States to redraw international law to allow its strategic imperatives. The unilateralist 'unsigning' by the United States of the Rome Statute of the International Criminal Court, its withdrawal from the Antiballistic Missile (ABM) Treaty, its failure to ratify the Comprehensive Test Ban Treaty thus ensuring that it will not enter into force, and its decision not to ratify the Kyoto Protocol all represent significant departures from multilateralism and the rule of law. The United States role in the NPT is of particular concern in the current context. There are two issues of particular note.

(1) Article VI of the NPT requires each of the Parties to undertake to pursue negotiations in good faith on effective measures relating to cessation of the nuclear arms race at an early date and to nuclear disarmament, and on a treaty on general and complete disarmament under strict and effective international control. This is an ongoing obligation that was further described at the 2000 NPT Review Conference as 'an unequivocal undertaking by the nuclear-weapons States to accomplish the total elimination of their nuclear arsenals leading to nuclear disarmament'.

(2) Anxious to achieve the indefinite extension of the NPT, the United States agreed to conclude the CTBT by the end of 1996 and the extension was linked with a fissile

> material cutoff at an unspecified later date and on "[t]he determined pursuit by the nuclear-weapon States of systematic and progressive efforts to reduce nuclear weapons globally, with the ultimate goals of eliminating those weapons, and by all States of general and complete disarmament under strict and effective international control." The failure of the United States to ratify the CTBT or enter into substantive disarmament negotiations as it has agreed, the acknowledgement by North Korea that it possesses nuclear weapons, the declaration by the United States of its willingness to enter into 'preventive war' and the subsequent decision by the United States supported by the 'coalition of the willing' to use military force against Iraq are all ominous developments for nonproliferation, the NPT and the rule of law.

The NPT has also become relevant in Iraq after the looting of Tuwaitha and the reported refusal of the occupying powers to grant the IAEA access. All States have undertaken to co-operate in facilitating the application of International Atomic Energy Agency safeguards on peaceful nuclear activities, and the IAEA safeguards apply on all source or special fissionable material in all peaceful nuclear activities carried out under the control of a non-nuclear-weapon State Party to the Treaty anywhere. Additionally the failure of the occupying powers to prevent looting and to safeguard the site, with the result of reported radiation sickness, could give rise to responsibility under the Hague Regulations and Geneva Conventions.

Conclusion

The international community finds itself in at a critical juncture. The guarantees of international peace and security and the determination to avoid the scourge of war put in place following World War II have been undermined and even imperiled by the use of military force under the doctrine of 'preventive war' and the invasion of Iraq. It is critical that member States following the attack on Iraq re-acknowledge their commitment to avoiding war and to the principles and purposes of the United Nations Charter, in order that the role of the rule of law in avoiding future wars may prevail.

In its National Security Strategy, the United States described the utility of 'coalitions of the willing' as standing outside the current institutions, saying that "[t]he United States is committed to lasting institutions like the United Nations, the World Trade Organization, the Organization of American States, and NATO as well as other long-standing alliances. Coalitions of the willing can augment these permanent institutions." Thus the United States has put itself and, by extension, the 'coalition of the willing', apart from the permanent institutions and international law, and is setting its own law and policy unilaterally.

States in the 'coalition of the willing' have aligned themselves with the policy of 'preventive war' and with the legal position of the United States in the Iraqi war, a war described by the UN Secretary-General as not in conformity with the Charter, and a war which still continues. This position also aligns States with a strategy which espouses a unilateralist approach to international problems and thus threatens a rift with other institutions which underpin the international system. Nations have a stark choice: they can choose multilateralism, the rule of law, and respect for international law, treaties and institutions; or, they can choose a unilateralist approach in which States pursue their own interests, irrespective of the will of the world community, and accept the rule of economic and military power.

10

International Law and Relationships between the States

International law (*ius gentium, droit des gens, Völkerrecht*) is usually defined as the totality of norms regulating the relationships between states. Here is a typical definition: "International law is the totality of norms defining the rights and duties of states in their mutual relations with one another". We find the same definition in the Germans Hareis, Holtsendorf, Bulmering, Liszt and Ulman; in the Belgian Rivie; in the Englishmen Westlake and Oppenheim; in the American Lawrence etc.

But absent from this formal, technical definition, of course, is any indication of the historical, i.e. the class character of international law. It is extremely clear that bourgeois jurisprudence consciously or unconsciously strives to conceal this element of class. The historical examples adduced in any textbook of international law loudly proclaim that *modern international law is the legal form of the struggle of the capitalist states among themselves for domination over the rest of the world.* However, bourgeois jurists try, as much as possible, to silence this basic fact of intensified competitive struggle, and to affirm that the task of international law is "to make possible for each state what none could do in isolation, by means of co-operation between many states".

Nor did the theorists of the Second International move far from these bourgeois jurists. Abandoning the class conception of the state, they were naturally compelled to discover in international law an instrument, standing outside and above classes, for the co-ordination of the interests of individual states and for the achievement of peace.

It was from this perspective that the well-known Bernstein, and the equally-famous Renner, approached international law. With great assiduity, both of these gentlemen stressed the "peaceful functions of international law", but in so doing they forgot that the better part of its norms refer to naval and land warfare, i.e. that it directly assumes a condition of open and armed struggle. But even the remaining part contains a significant share of norms and institutions which, although they refer to a condition of peace, in fact regulate the same struggle, albeit in another concealed form. Every struggle, including the struggle between imperialist states, must include an exchange as one of its components. And if exchanges are concluded then forms must also exist for their conclusion.

But the presence of these forms does not of course alter the real historical content hidden behind them. At a given stage of social development this content remains the struggle of capitalist states among themselves. Under the conditions of this struggle, every exchange is the continuation of one armed conflict and the prelude to the next. Here lies the basic trait of imperialism.

Capitalists [wrote Lenin] divide the world, not out of any particular malice, but because the degree of concentration which has been reached forces them to adopt this method in order to receive profit. And they divide it "in proportion to capital", "in proportion to strength", because there cannot be any other method of division under commodity production and capitalism. But strength varies with the level of economic and political development. In order to know what is taking place, it is necessary to know what questions are decided by the changes in strength. The question of whether these changes are "purely" economic or extra-economic (military, for example) is secondary... To substitute the question of the content of the struggle and agreements (today peaceful, tomorrow warlike, the next day peaceful again), is to descend to sophistry.

When Renner depicts the development of international law as the growth of institutions which ensure the general interest of all states, and when he tries to show that this development has been retarded by the larcenous and selfish policy of only one of the states, Great Britain, then he too descends to sophistry. He must, moreover, be in the service of Austro-German imperialism.

Conversely, we can see that even those agreements between capitalist states which appear to be directed to the general interest are, in fact, for each of the participants a means for jealously protecting their particular interests, preventing the expansion of their rivals' influence, thwarting unilateral conquest, i.e. in another form continuing the same struggle which will exist for as long as capitalist competition exists. One may instantiate any international organization, even the international commissions for the supervision of navigation on the erstwhile "treaty rivers" (the Rhine, the Danube, and after Versailles, the Elbe and the Oder).

Let us begin with the fact that the very composition of these commissions perfectly reflects specific relations of forces, and is usually the result of war. After the World War, therefore, Germany and Russia were ousted from the European Commission on the Danube. At the same time the Commission on the Rhine was transferred to Strasbourg and fell into French hands. Under the Treaty of Versailles, the very transformation of German rivers into treaty rivers, which were controlled by international commissions, was an act which divided the spoils among the victors.

The International Administration of Tangiers, a port in Morocco where the interests of France, England and Spain intersect, is the same type of organization for joint exploitation and supervision. A final and typical example is the International Organization for the Extortion of Reparations from Germany (q.v.): the reparation commission and all types of supervisory agencies envisioned by the expert's plan. As soon as some power feels strong enough to take the plunder into its exclusive possession, it starts to combat internationalization (q.v.). Thus, at the 1883 London Conference, Tsarist Russia succeeded in placing the Kiliisky branch of the Danube outside the control of the European Commission provided for by the international treaty of 1889. The Commission for the Supervision of the

Neutralization of the Suez Canal could not be constituted at all: it was eliminated by a separate agreement between England and France, whereby the first bought itself freedom of action in Egypt in exchange for the latter's taking of Morocco (English-French Convention of April 8th, 1904). The struggle among imperialist states for domination of the rest of the world is thus a basic factor in defining the nature and fate of the corresponding international organizations.

There remain the comparatively few and narrowly-specialized interstate agreements. These have a technical character and correspond to purposeful combines or so-called international administrative unions, for example the International Postal Union. These organizations do not serve primarily as an arena for the struggle between administrative groupings, but they occupy a secondary and subordinate position. The origin of most of these organizations was in the 1870s and 1880s, i.e. in the period when capitalism (q.v.) had still not fully developed its monopoly and imperialist traits. The intensified struggle for the division of the world has moved forward to such an extent since that time, that the actual ability of capitalist states to serve general economic and cultural needs has diminished rather than expanded. In this respect a very clear regression was marked by the World War in that it caused the downfall of a whole series of cultural (in particular) and, for example, scientific links.

The bourgeois jurists are not entirely mistaken, however, in considering international law as a function of some ideal cultural community which mutually connects individual states. But they do not see, or do not want to see, that this community reflects (conditionally and relatively, of course) the common interests of the commanding and ruling classes of different states which have identical class structures. The spread and development of international law occurred on the basis of the spread and development of the capitalist mode of production. However, in the feudal period the knights of every European country had their codes of military honour and, accordingly, their class law, which they applied in wars with one another; but they did not apply them in inter-class wars, for example in the suppression of burghers and the peasantry. The victory of the bourgeoisie, in all the European countries, had to lead to the establishment of new rules and new institutions of international law which protected the general and basic interests of the bourgeoisie, i.e. bourgeois property. Here is the key to the modern law of war.

While in feudal Europe the class structure was reflected in the religious notion of a community of all Christians, the capitalist world created its concept of "civilization" for the same purposes. The division of states into civilized and "semi-civilized", integrated and "semi-integrated" to the international community, explicitly reveals the second peculiarity of modern international law as the class law of the bourgeoisie. It appears to us as the totality of forms which the capitalist, bourgeois states apply in their relations with each other, while the remainder of the, world is considered as a simple object of their completed transactions. Liszt, for example, teaches that "the struggle with states and peoples who are outside the international community must not be judged according to the law of war, but according to the bases of the love for mankind and Christianity". To assess the piquancy of this assertion recall that, at the time of the colonial wars, the representatives of these lofty principles, e.g. the French in Madagascar and the Germans in Southwest Africa, liquidated the local population without regard for age and sex.

The real historical content of international law, therefore, is the struggle between capitalist states. International law owes its existence to the fact that the bourgeoisie exercises its domination over the proletariat and over the colonial countries. The latter are organized into a number of separate state-political trusts in competition with one another. With the emergence of Soviet states in the historical arena, international law assumes a different significance. It becomes the form of a temporary compromise between two antagonistic class systems. This compromise is effected for that period when one system (the bourgeois) is *already* unable to ensure its exclusive domination, and the other (proletarian and socialist) has *not yet* won it. It is in this sense that it seems possible, to us, to speak of international law in the transitional period. The significance of this transitional period consists in the fact that open struggle for destruction (intervention, blockade, non-recognition) is replaced by struggle within the limits of normal diplomatic relations and contractual exchange. International law becomes *inter-class* law, and its adaptation to this new function inevitably occurs in the form of a series of conflicts and crises. The concept of international law during the transitional period was first put forth, in Soviet literature, by E. Korovin.

Finally, international law assumes an entirely different meaning as the inter-state law of the Soviet states. It now ceases to be a form of temporary compromise behind which an intensified struggle for existence is hidden. Because of this the very opposition between international law and the state, so characteristic of the preceding period, disappears. The proletarian states, not having merged formally into one federation or union, must present in their mutual relationships an image of such a close economic, political and military unity, that the measure of "modern" international law becomes inapplicable to them.

Turning now to consider the legal form of international law, we will first note that orthodox theory considers the subject of international legal relations to be the state as a whole, and only the state. "Only states are subjects of international law, the bearers of international legal obligations and powers." The real historical premise for this viewpoint is the formation of a system of independent states which have, within their boundaries, a sufficiently strong central power to enable each of them to act as a single whole. "The sovereignty of the state, i.e. its independence from any authority standing above it-this is the basis of international law."

These premises were historically realized in Europe only at the end of the Middle Ages, in the period of the formation of absolute monarchies which consolidated their independence, with respect to Papal authority, and which severed internal resistance by the feudal lords. The economic basis of this was the development of mercantile capital. The emergence of standing armies, the prohibition of private wars, the instigation of state enterprises, customs and colonial policy – these are the real facts which lie at the heart of the theory of the state as the sole subject of the international legal community. The Catholic Church, which had claimed the position of supreme leader of all the Christian states, was delivered a decisive blow by the Reformation. The Treaty of Westphalia, which in 1648 proclaimed the basis of equality between the Catholic and the "heretical" (Protestant) states, is considered the basic fact in the historical development of modern (i.e. bourgeois) international law.

The revolutions of the seventeenth and eighteenth centuries made further strides along the same road. They completed the process of separating state rule from private rule, and transformed political power into a special force and the state into a special subject. The legal relations of the state flowed independently, and they were not to be confused with those persons who at any given moment were the bearers of state authority.

Having subordinated itself to the state machine, the bourgeoisie brought the principle of the public nature of authority to its clearest expression. It may be said that the state only fully becomes the subject of international law as the bourgeois state. The victory of the bourgeois perspective over the feudal-patrimonial perspective was expressed, among other things, in the denial of the binding force of dynastic treaties for the state. Thus, in 1790 the National Assembly of France rejected the obligations which flowed from the family treaty of the house of Bourbon (1761), on the grounds that Louis XV had acted as a representative of the dynasty and not as a representative of France.

It is typical that at the same time as French authors (Bonfils, for example) consider this rejection to be proper, German monarcho-reactionary professors (Heffken) find that the National Assembly violated international law in this action.

The Roman Papacy is a curious vestige of the Middle Ages. After the Church entered the constituency of Italy in 1870, the Pope continued extra territorially to enjoy the right to send and receive ambassadors, i.e. he had certain essential attributes of sovereign authority. When bourgeois Jurists are forced to explain a phenomenon which contradicts their doctrine, they usually argue that the Papal throne occupies a quasi international status and that it is not in the strict sense a subject of international law.

In fact, of course, the influence of the leader of the Catholic Church is no less in international affairs than that of the League of Nations (q.v.). All authors classify the latter as an exception to the independent subjects of international law along with individual states. As a separate force which set itself off from society, the state only finally emerged in the modern bourgeois capitalist period.

But it by no means follows from this that the contemporary forms of international legal intercourse, and the individual institutions of international law, only arose in the most recent times. On the contrary, they trace their history to the most ancient periods of class and even pre-class society. To the extent that exchange was not initially made between individuals, but among tribes and communities, it may be affirmed that the institutions of international law are the most ancient of legal institutions in general.

Collisions between tribes, territorial disputes, disputes over borders – and agreements as one of the elements in these disputes – are found in the very earliest stages of human history. The tribal pre-state life of the Iroquois, and of the ancient Germans, saw the conclusion of alliances between tribes. The development of class society and the appearance of state authority make contracts and agreements among authorities possible.

The treaty between Pharaoh Rameses II and the King of the Hittites is one of the oldest surviving documents of this type. Other forms of relationships are equally universal: the inviolability of ambassadors; the custom of exchanging hostages; one might also point to the ransoming of prisoners, the neutrality of certain areas, and the right to asylum. All these practices were known and used by the peoples of the distant past. Ancient Rome observed various forms for the declaration of war (*ius fetiale*), concluded treaties, received and sent ambassadors. The ambassadors of foreign countries enjoyed inviolability etc. A special college of herald-priests dealt with these rules in Rome, and the majority of legal rules were protected by the gods at that time. The sanction of religion did not, however, prevent the fact that they were sometimes violated in the grossest manner.

On the other hand, a series of rules were formed which related to international intercourse. These were necessary both for regulating conflicts among tribes and peoples, and also for ensuring commercial exchange between individuals who belonged to different clans and tribes. Later, these rules were extended to include state organizations. In this way so-called private international law developed.

For example, during the period when Athens was flourishing, there were no less than 45,000 foreign inhabitants. They enjoyed all civil rights and were protected by a representative elected from their midst (embryos of consular representation). The protection of foreigners thus applied to merchants who were temporary residents. We see the same phenomenon in ancient Rome where the special office of *praetor peregrinus* was instituted for the hearing of foreigners' judicial cases. Moreover, the so-called *actiones fictitiae* aided in overcoming those strict requirements of Roman procedure which gave the foreigner no possibility of defending his rights.

In the understanding of the Roman jurists, the law of nations (*ius gentium*) embraced equally that which is now termed public international law, and also that which is inaccurately termed private international law. Thus, for example, we read in the Digests: "By this law of nations (*ius gentium*), wars are waged, nations are divided, kingdoms are founded, property is distributed, fields are enclosed, buildings are erected, trade, purchases, sales, loans and obligations are established – with the exception of certain transactions that are conducted in civil law." From this list it seems that the essential characteristic of international law was deemed to be not merely that it regulated relations (borders, war, peace etc.) among states but, and in contrast to the ius civile, that it established the basis of a legal community devoid of local peculiarities and free from tribal and national colouration. These universal rules could be nothing other than a reflection of the general conditions of exchange transactions, i.e. they were reduced to the bases of the equal rights of owners, the inviolability of ownership and the consequent compensations for damages and freedom of contract. The bond between the *ius gentium* – in the sense of laws inherent in all nations – and norms regulating the mutual relations of states, was consciously strengthened by the first theorist of international law, Hugo Grotius (1583-1684). His whole system depends on the fact that he considers relations between states to be relations between the owners of private property; he declares that the necessary conditions for the execution of exchange, i.e. equivalent exchange between private owners, are the conditions for legal interaction between states. Sovereign states co-exist and are counterposed to one another in exactly the same way as are individual property owners with equal rights. Each state may "freely" dispose of its own property, but it can gain access to another state's property only by means of a contract on the basis of compensation: *do ut des*.

The feudal-patrimonial structure greatly aided the theory of territorial rule in acquiring a clearly civilist hue. Suzerains or "Landesherren" considered themselves as the owners of those holdings over which their authority extended; the holdings were thought of as their private right, a subject of alienation by the owner. Entering into relations with one another, they disposed of their holdings as owners dispose of their objects, and alienated them according to the system of private (Roman) law. From the very beginning, therefore, many of the institutions of international law had a private law foundation – including the theory of *modi aecuirendi dominii* in international relations. Other methods were also recognized: inheritance, dowry, gift, purchase and sale, exchange, occupation, prescription.

On the basis of natural law doctrine, Grotius's ideas continued to be developed by subsequent theorists: Puffendorf (1632-1694), Tomasius (1655-1728), Wolff (1679-1754), Vattel (1714-1767) and Burlamaki (1694-1748). These theorists laid the foundation for an abstract or philosphical theory of law. In contrast to this school, which had given preference to abstract, concepts, there began the collection and systematization of actual international customs and treaties and the study of international practice. The forefather of this positive, historico-pragmatic school is considered to be Zouch (1590-1669), an Oxford professor and Admiralty judge; the Dutchman

Binkerskuch (1673-1743), and Martens (1756-1821) were later representatives. The doctrine of natural law ceased to enjoy the recognition of most jurists in the second half of the nineteenth century. However, even in our day Grotius's formulae continue to exist in international law textbooks, under the guise of so-called "basic or absolute rights" of the state. For example, Hareis in Institutionen des Volkerrechts (1888), lists four such "basic rights": the right to self-preservation; the right to independence; the right to international exchange; and the right to respect.

We read exactly the same in Liszt: "From this basic idea (international legal intercourse] directly follows a whole series of legal norms, by which are defined the mutual rights and obligations of states and do not require any special treaty recognition in order to have obligatory force.

They comprise a firm (!) basis for all the unwritten legal rules of international law, and are its oldest, most important and holiest content." It is most obvious that we are dealing here with ideas drawn from the sphere of civil law relationships with a basis in equality between the parties.

To a certain degree the analogy may be extended. Bourgeois private law assumes that subjects are formally equal yet simultaneously permits real inequality in property, while bourgeois international law in principle recognizes that states have equal rights yet in reality they are unequal in their significance and their power. For instance, each state is formally free to select the means which it deems necessary to apply in the case of infringements of its right: "however, when a major state lets it be known that it will meet injury with the threat of, or the direct use of force, a small state merely offers passive resistance or is compelled to concede." These dubious benefits of formal equality are not enjoyed at all by those nations which have not developed capitalist civilization and which engage in international intercourse not as subjects, but as objects of the imperialist states' colonial policy.

In civil law transactions, however, the relationships between the parties assume legal form not only because they derive from the logic of objects (from the logic of the exchange act, more accurately), but also because this form finds real support and defence in the apparatus of judicial and state authority. Legal existence is materialized in a special sphere, partitioned off from the intrusion of naked fact. In his language the lawyer expresses this by asserting that every subjective right depends upon an objective norm, and that private legal relationships arose because of the public legal order.

Moreover, in international law the subjects of legal relationships are the states themselves as the bearers of sovereign authority. A series of logical contradictions follows from this. For the existence of international law it is necessary that states be sovereign (for sovereignty in any given case is equated with legal capacity). If there are no sovereign states then there are no subjects of the international law relationship, and there is no international law. But, on the other hand, if there are sovereign states, then does this mean that the norms of international law are not legal norms?

For in the opposite case, they must possess an external power which constrains the state, i.e. limits its sovereignty. Conclusion: for international law to exist it is necessary that states not be sovereign. Bourgeois jurisprudence has devoted a great amount of fruitless effort in solving this contradiction. For instance, Pruess – the author of the present German (Weimar) Constitution tended to the position of sacrificing the concept of sovereignty for the sake of international law. Conversely, writers such as Zorn and, most recently, Wendel, are more ready to abandon supra-state international law. However, these dogmatic arguments change nothing in reality. No matter how eloquently the existence of international law is proved, the fact of the absence of an organizational force, which could coerce a state with the same ease as a state coerces an individual person, remains a fact.

The only real guarantee that the relationships between bourgeois states (and in the transitional period with states of another class type) will remain on the basis of equivalent exchange, i.e. on a legal basis (on the basis of the mutual recognition of subjects), is the real balance of forces. Within the limits set by a given balance of forces, separate questions may be decided by compromises and by exchange, i.e. on the basis of law. Even then there is the qualification that each government calls upon law when its interests demand it, and in every way will try to avoid fulfilling some norm if it is profitable for it. In critical periods, when the balance of forces has fluctuated seriously, when "vital interests" or even the very existence of a state are on the agenda, the fate of the norms of international law becomes extremely problematic.

This particularly relates to the imperialist period, with its unprecedented intensification of the competitive struggle which derives from the monopolisitic tendencies of finance capital, and from the fact that after the whole globe has already been divided then further expansion can only occur at the expense of robbing one's neighbour.

The best illustration of this is afforded by the last war, of 1914-1918, during which both sides continuously violated international law. With international law in such a lamentable condition, bourgeois jurists can be consoled only with the hope that, however deeply the balance was disturbed, it will nevertheless be reestablished: the most violent of wars must sometime be ended with peace, the political passions raised by it must gradually be reconciled, the governments will return to objectivity and compromise, and the norms of international law will once again find their force. However, in addition to this hope the fact is adduced, as an argument in favour of the positive nature of international law, that every state in violating international law also tries to depict the matter as if there had been no violation whatsoever. We find in Ulman, for example, this curious reference to state hypocrisy as proof of the positive nature of international law. Another group of jurists simply deny the very existence of international law. Among them is the founder of the English school of positivist jurisprudence, Austin. Defining "law in the proper sense", as an order emanating from a definite authority and strengthened by a threat in the case of disobedience, he finds that international law is *contradictio in adjecto*. "To the extent that it is law, it is not international; to the extent that it is truly international, it is not law." Gumplowicz holds the same opinion: "In a definite sense international law is not law inasmuch as state law also is not law." Lasson says: "The norms of international law are but rules of state wisdom which the state follows having in mind its own welfare, and from which it can deviate as soon as its vital interests so demand."

But the perspective of Austin, Lasson, Gumplowicz and others is not shared by the majority of bourgeois jurists. The open denial of international law is politically unprofitable for the bourgeoisie since it exposes them to the masses and thus hinders preparations for new wars. It is much more profitable for the imperialists to act in the guise of pacifism and as the champions of international law.

Therefore, for example, the English writer Walker censures the terminological cavils of Austin, who did not want to define international law as law in the proper sense, and who exclaims "it is better to permit peace and passivity to reign without correct terminology, than to permit accuracy of language to exist with the spirit of lawlessness!" jurists who preach the cult of force in international relations are both useless to the bourgeoisie (it needs not preaching, but real force), and also dangerous because they conceal the irreconcilability of the contradictions of capitalist society, and because they compromise peace and tranquility needed even by a thief when he has had his fill and is digesting his spoils.

From the Marxist perspective this nihilist criticism of international law is in error since, while exposing fetishism in one area, it does so at the cost of consolidating it in others. The precarious, unstable and relative nature of international law is illustrated in comparison with the largely firm, steady and absolute nature of other types of law. In fact, we have here a difference in degree. For only in the imagination of jurists are all the legal relationships within a state dominated one hundred per cent by a single state "will". In fact, a major portion of civil law relationships are exercised under influence of pressures limited to the activities of subjects themselves. Furthermore, only by taking the viewpoint of legal fetishism is it possible to think that the legal form of a relationship changes or destroys its real and material essence. This essence, on the contrary, is always decisive. The formalization of our relationship with bourgeois states, by way of treaties, is part of our foreign policy, and is its continuation in a special form. A treaty obligation is nothing other than a special form of the concretization of economic and political relationships. But once the appropriate degree of concretization is reached, it may then be taken into consideration and, within certain limits, studied as a special subject. The reality of this object is no less than the reality of any constitution – both may be overturned by the intrusion of a revolutionary squall.

It is commonplace to distinguish a general and a special component in relation to the systematization of international law. The first contains the theory of the state as the subject of international law. Here lies the theory of sovereignty, the various forms of limiting sovereignty, the theory of international law and legal capacity etc. Starting from the traditional division of the state into three elements – authority, territory and population – most treatises include within this general component the regulation of territorial questions (borders, territorial waters, methods of territorial acquisition etc.), and population questions (citizenship, preference, etc.). The special component considers the organization and forms of international legal relationships – here he diplomatic and consular representation, international courts and other international organizations, the theory of international treaties etc. Further conceptual areas are usually delineated as regulatory international legal agreements (transportation, commerce, navigation, post and telegraphy, the battle with epidemics, the protection of property etc.). Finally comes the part dedicated to the law of war. This is usually prefaced with a consideration of the peaceful means of settling conflicts (arbitration decisions). The law of war may be divided into the law of military war, the law of naval warfare and the theory of the rights and obligations of neutral states.

Bibliography

Bassiouni, M. Cherif: *International Criminal Law*. New York: Oxford University Press, 2008

Bhaskara Rao: *Military Conversion : Impact on Science and Technology*, Discovery, Delhi, 2003.

Bouchet-Saulnier, Francoise, Laura Brav: *The Practical Guide to Humanitarian Law,* Lanham, MD: Rowman & Littlefield Publishers, Inc., 2007.

Cassese, Antonio: *The Attack on the World Trade Center: Legal Responses. European Journal of International Law,* Discussion Forum, 2002.

Chadwick, Elizabeth: *Self-determination, Terrorism, and the International Humanitarian Law of Armed Conflict*. The Hague, Boston Mass.: Martinus Nijhoff, 1996.

Chesterman, Simon: *Just War or Just Peace: Humanitarian Intervention and International Law*. New York: Oxford University Press, 2003.

Credi, A.: *Molecular Devices and Machines: a Journey into the Nano World*, Weinheim, Wiley-VCH, 2003.

Daniels, Ronald J., Patrick Macklem, and Kent Roach: *The Security of Freedom: Essays on Canada's Anti-Terrorism Bill*. Toronto: University of Toronto Press, 2001.

Duffy, Helen: *The 'War on Terror' and the Framework of International Law*. Cambridge, UK: Cambridge University Press, 2005.

Erickson, Richard: *Legitimate Use Of Force Against State Sponsored Terrorism*. US Air War College, 1989.

Galtung, Johan: *Pax Pacifica: Terrorism, the Pacific Hemisphere, Globalisation and Peace Studies*. London: Pluto Press, 2005.

Gray, Christine: *International Law and the Use of Force*. Second edition. New York: Oxford University Press, 2004.

Gupta, Asha: *Military Rule and Democratization : Changing Perspectives*, Deep & Deep, Delhi, 2003.

Juvale, R.P. : *Military Strategy and Diplomacy*, Cyber Tech Publications, Delhi, 2010.

K.C. Anil: *Military Wars and Rescue Techniques*, Sumit Enterprises, Delhi, 2009.

Kumar, Raj : *Weapons and Military Technology*, Sumit Enterprises, Delhi, 2009.

Lele, Ajey: *Strategic Technologies for the Military : Breaking New Frontiers*, Sage, Delhi, 2009.

M.S. Jaswal: *Study and Practice of Military Law*, Deep and Deep, Delhi, 2006.

Macedo, Stephen: *Universal Jurisdiction: National Courts and the Prosecution of Serious Crimes Under International Law.* Philadelphia: University of Pennsylvania Press, 2006.

Mary, W.: *Military Space Force: the Cultural Dimensions of Authority*, Cambridge, Belknap Press, 1985.

P. Huntington: *The Soldier and the State : The Theory and Politics of Civil-Military Relations*, Natraj Pub, Delhi, 2005.

P. Panda: *China's Path to Power : Party, Military and the Politics of State Transition*, Pentagon, Delhi, 2010.

Prabla, Dixit: *Communalism: A Struggle for Power*, New Delhi, Orient Longman, 1981.

Reydams, Luc: *Universal Jurisdiction: International and Municipal Legal Perspectives*. New York: Oxford University Press, 2005.

Rudolph, Heimanson: *Dictionary of Military*, N.Y.: Oceana Publications, 1967.

Schabas, William A.: *An Introduction to the International Criminal Court*. Cambridge: Cambridge University Press, 2007.

Suresh Goel: *International Encyclopaedia of Military, Security and Intelligence Agencies*, MD Publications, Delhi, 2009.

Walker, Clive: *The Prevention of Terrorism in British Law*. New York: Manchester University Press & St. Martin's Press, 1992.

Index